Turbo C++
Step by Step

An easy to follow, step by step guide to learning the Turbo C++ programming language

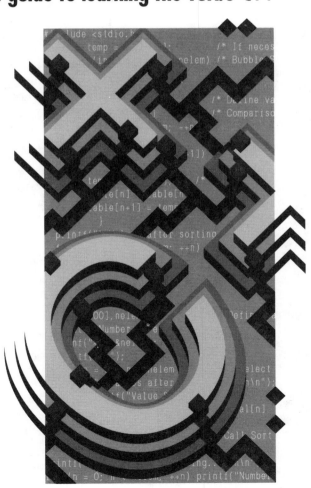

+ Fundamentals of C and C++

+ Using the IDE

+ Simplifying complex programming techniques

+ Demystifying the debugger

+ Using the C++ Libraries

by W. Deiss

Abacus
A Data Becker Book

Library of Congress Cataloging-in-Publication Data

Deiss, Wolfgang, 1963-
    Turbo C++ step-by-step/ Wolfgang Deiss.
       p.   cm.
    Includes index.
    ISBN 1-55755-156-1 : $34.95
    1.   C++ (Computer program language)   2.   Turbo C++
(Computer program) I. Title.
    QA76.73.C15D439 1992   92-25038
    005.26'2--dc20   CIP

10 9 8 7 6 5 4 3 2 1

Table of Contents

Preface..vii

1.   Installation 1
1.1   Borland Turbo C++.......................................3
1.2   The Companion Diskette 8
1.2.1 Installing the files.......................................9
1.2.2 Configuring the IDE for use with the companion diskette....9

2.   Programming Environment.............................11
2.1   Turbo C++ Menus.......................................13
2.2   The Turbo C++ Editor..................................16
2.3   "Hello": Your First C Program........................20
2.4   Compiling and Editing..................................24
2.5   Error Messages...26

3.   Variables 31
3.1   Defining and Initializing Variables...................33
3.2   Input/Output of Variables..............................36
3.3   Operations with Variables and Constants.............42

4.   Conditional Statements And Loops 49
4.1   The IF Statement and Structure by Blocks...........51
4.2   While, Do-While and For Loops.......................58
4.3   Switch and Break Statements..........................64
4.4   Operators and Logical Variables 68

5.   Arithmetic Expressions 73
5.1   Types and Definition Fields...........................75
5.2   Variable Types and Precedence........................79

6.   Arrays, Pointers, And Structures 85
6.1   Arrays and Strings.......................................87
6.2   Pointers...92
6.3   Pointer Arithmetic......................................97
6.4   Structures..102
6.5   Combination of Types and Typedef..................106

7.   Functions And Structure Of Programs 113
7.1   Functions...115
7.2   Parameters and Return Values 120
7.3   The main() Function....................................126
7.4   Initializing Global Variables..........................129
7.5   Recursion...134

8.   Modular Structure **139**
8.1   Programs and Modules 141
8.2   Declarations and Header Files 145
8.3   Standard Library Header Files............................151
8.4   Range and Duration of a Variable, Storage Classes..........155
8.5   Turbo C++ Preprocessor Directives...............159

9.   C++ Function Libraries **163**
9.1   Access to the Files 165
9.2   Keyboard and Screen Management 171
9.3   Mathematical Functions...................................174
9.4   Manipulating Strings..178
9.5   Memory Models..183

10.   Turbo C++: Better Than C **189**
10.1 The Concept of Class..191
10.2 Object Oriented Programming............................194
10.3 Data Abstraction...205

11.   Utilities...**211**
11.1 The Integrated Debugger...................................213
11.2 Turbo Profiler...216

Appendices **223**
Appendix A: Primary Keywords Of C++ 225
Appendix B: List Of Operators......................................227
Appendix C: Hierarchy Of The Operations 228
Appendix D: Answers For The Exercises 229
Appendix E: Glossary 252
Appendix F: ASCII Table..269
Appendix G: Introduction To Number Systems 271
Appendix H: The Companion Diskette.................................274

Index..**285**

Preface

Today, the C language is no longer reserved for professional programmers. The appearance of new C compilers has caused C to gain favor with a growing number of independent programmers. It has many strong points possessing the advantages of a high level language which is both very structured and very close to machine language. The speed of its compiled programs is comparable to equivalent programs written in assembly language. Furthermore, C is portable. This means that programs written in it can easily be transferred to other systems. Many factors have helped make this language into a true standard which is destined to continue growing more and more popular.

This book is a training manual for beginners who have only a few general ideas about programming. We'll discuss all the essential characteristics of C++ step by step and then apply them to examples. After each chapter is a summary and after each subject several exercises are included for you to try.

Although this book discusses Borland Turbo C++ V 3.x for IBM PC's and compatible computers, you'll find the information may be applied to any of the C++ compilers available today.

We'll start with a brief discussion on how to install Borland's Turbo C++ for DOS. This is followed by an introduction to the programming environment and the process of compiling. Chapter 8 explains how to carry out a C program which consists of several modules.

Chapter 10 uses several examples to describe one of the innovative concepts of C++: Object Oriented Programming.

The companion diskette contains the programs presented in this book, including the examples and exercises. In most cases, the source code, as well as executable programs, is included. You will also find some utilities which can be used as parts of your future C++ applications.

Appendix D has the complete list of the programs furnished.

Wolfgang Deiss

✔ Explanation of the icons

This icon introduces a paragraph that explains basic theory. Study these paragraphs carefully. They contain important information.

This icon is used to draw your attention to a particular danger. If you don't pay attention to the advice given here, you could lose data, crash your system, or even damage your hardware (although hardware damage is quite unlikely through any programming errors.

The letter *sigma* marks a summary of the lesson.

The keyboard symbol introduces practical exercises that you should try on your computer. Even though the source code is included on the companion diskette, we recommend that you type in each line from the listings, examining each line as you enter it.

This icon draws your attention to more complete exercises aimed at solving every day practical problems.

Chapter 1

Installation

Borland Turbo C++

The Companion Diskette

Installing The Files

Configuring the IDE for use with the companion diskette

1. Installation

Before you can start programming, you must install your compiler.

This chapter briefly describes the standard installation procedure for Borland's Turbo C++ for DOS. The procedure for other versions of C++ is quite similar. Refer to the documentation for your version of C++ for specific information.

Before installing any program, you should make backup copies of the original diskettes. Use only these copies during the installation process, never the originals.

One little error could destroy the originals forever.

1.1 Borland Turbo C++

The Borland Turbo C++ compiler can only be installed on a hard drive. Use the INSTALL.EXE program from the first diskette to carry out this installation. You'll need about 10.5 Mbytes of free disk space for a complete installation as discussed in this chapter.

❶   As the installation program starts up, the following screen appears:

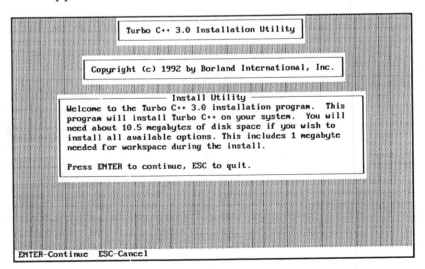

Starting the Turbo C++ installation process

Press (Enter) to display the following screen and select the drive containing the installation master diskette.

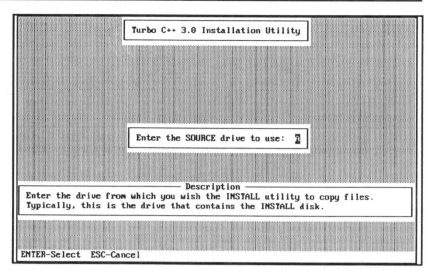

The Source directory for Turbo C++

❷   Next, select the drive and directory for installing Turbo
    C++. The default directory is C:\TC as the following shows.

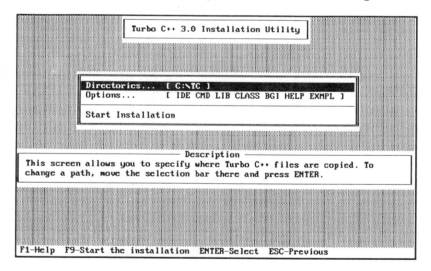

The Turbo C++ Directory

❸   Pressing (Enter) permits changing the drive or directory.

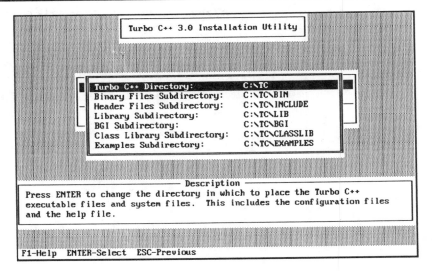

Selecting a new directory

❹   Changing all directories is easy.

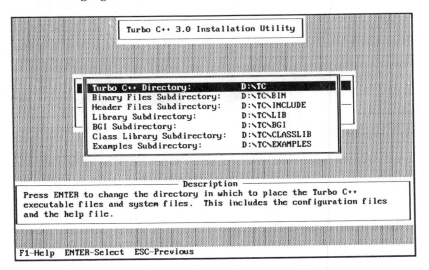

Changing Turbo C++ directories

❺   After the path has been set, other options may be specified.
     We recommend accepting the default settings.

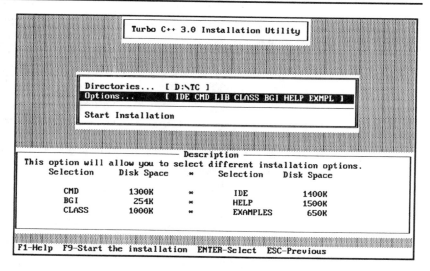

The options screen

❻   Press F9 to begin the installation process. Then, follow the
      prompts to insert a new master diskette as necessary.

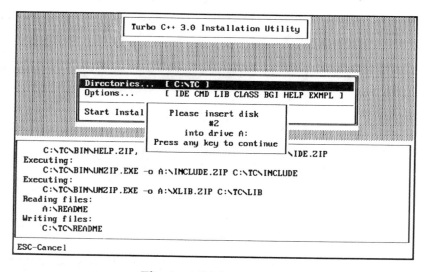

The installation process

You will be informed when Turbo C++ has been installed
successfully. Remember to change your CONFIG.SYS and
AUTOEXEC.BAT files as indicated by the installation program.

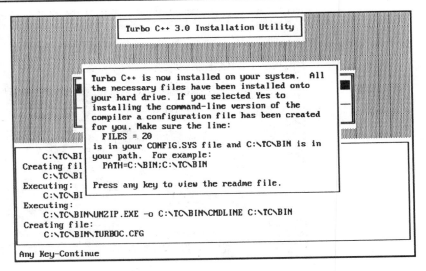

Turbo C++ is installed

The README file contains information about your version of Turbo C++. Make sure to take time to read it.

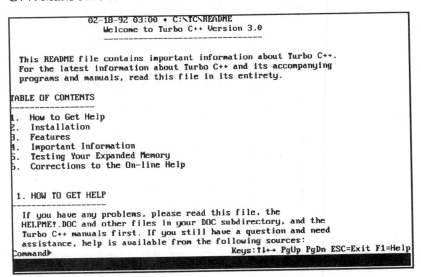

The README file

To run Turbo C++, change to the C:\TC\BIN directory and type:

TC [Enter]

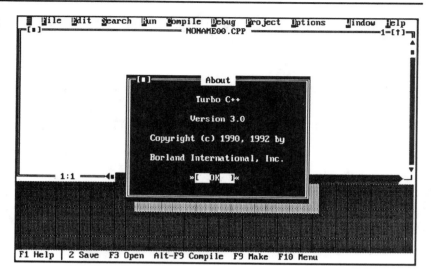

The IDE (Integrated Development Environment)

To simplify using this book, it's essential that we all use the same menu commands. (Borland C++ provides a means of changing the menus to suit your preferences.)

Run Turbo C++ as previously described and open the *Options* menu either with the mouse or by pressing (Alt)(O). Next, select the *Environment* menu item. Another menu will open listing environmental selections. Choose *Preferences*. The *Preferences* dialog box will then be displayed. Activate the *Command Set* window either by pressing (Tab) or with the mouse. Use the mouse or the cursor keys and spacebar to select *Alternate* to activate the alternate menus.

These menus are similar to those used by other Borland products such as Turbo Pascal, and will provide a common reference point for the discussions which follow.

1.2   The Companion Diskette

The companion diskette included with this book is intended to simplify the learning process. It can be quite frustrating to type in a program from a listing, then get errors when trying to compile the program. Make sure you have at least 1.5 Mbytes of free space on your hard drive before running the installation program.

Often these errors are caused by typos. An omitted semi-colon or set of brackets can be very hard to spot. The Borland IDE helps find many problems. To eliminate one level of frustration, we have included the examples and solutions to some of the exercises on the diskette.

We do recommend that you begin by typing in the examples and at least attempt to solve the exercises without loading the source code into the IDE. Later, you can load the source code and modify it for experimentation.

1.2.1 Installing the files

The installation process for the companion diskette is very simple. From the DOS command line, change volumes to the drive containing your companion diskette. For example, make the A: drive your current drive.

```
A:>
```

Then enter the following command:

```
A:>INSTALL
```

The installation program will ask you to identify the drive which contains the companion diskette. Pressing (Enter) accepts the default configuration of drive A: for the source drive. Enter the designation appropriate for your computer system.

Next, you will be asked which drive should be used for installing the sample files. Pressing (Enter) accepts the default drive, C:. You may choose a different drive by entering the appropriate drive designation.

From this point, the installation is completely automatic. The files will be extracted and installed on your hard drive into a directory named TCPP, which contains sub-directories named ANSWER, EXAMPLE, PROGRAMS, and UTIL.

When the installation is complete, you will return to the DOS command line. Start Turbo C++.

1.2.2 Configuring the IDE for use with the companion diskette

To simplify the instructions in this book, set up the Turbo C IDE as follows.

Open the *Options* menu and select the *Directories* menu item.

Change the Output Directory and the Source Directories in the Directories dialog box to show the paths as installed on your system. The dialog box should appear similar to the following illustration.

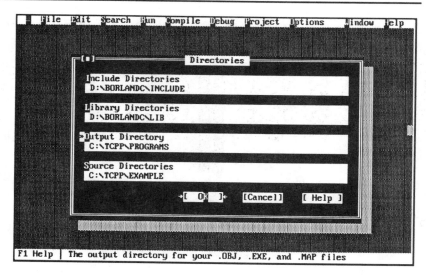

The IDE should be configured to work with the files from the companion diskette

After the appropriate changes have been made, select OK and return to the IDE. You are now ready to use the IDE to work with the example programs in this book.

Chapter 2

Programming Environment

Turbo C++ Menus

The Turbo C++ Editor

"Hello": Your First C Program

Compiling and Editing

Error Messages

2. Programming Environment

2.1 Turbo C++ Menus

Your first step in learning Turbo C++ is to learn how to use the menus of the IDE (Integrated Development Environment). The IDE offers many options. We'll only discuss the most important aspects.

  If you have a mouse, you can click on any menu using the left mouse button. In a text window, the cursor will follow the movements of the mouse.

LESSON

When Turbo C++ is booted, the IDE displays the main menu on the upper part of the screen. This menu consists of a list of keywords that group the possible actions of the compiler into several headings with a common theme. Access the main menu by pressing the (F10) key.

You can use the cursor keys ((↑), (←), (→) and (↓)) to move from one menu option to another:

Right or left arrow   Select an option in the main menu.
Up or down arrow   Select an option in a sub-menu.

To activate an option you've selected, press the (Enter) key. If you press (Enter) by mistake, you can get out of this undesirable situation by pressing the (Esc) key. This will take you back one step in the menu.

Instead of using the cursor keys, you can also select menu options by using letter keys. Simply press the letter key corresponding to the letter highlighted in the menu item.

Some frequently used options can be activated using specially designated function keys or other keyboard combinations. The combination of keys to use are indicated after the options concerned. These keys are often referred to as "Hotkeys".

In Turbo C++, a corresponding explanation is displayed at the bottom of the screen.

Turbo C++ has the distinctive feature of displaying "dialog boxes". They appear when you select certain options that require supplementary information or parameters before they can be executed. Inside these dialog boxes you can move from one selection field to another by using the (Tab) key (to move to the following field) or (Shift) (Tab) (to return to the preceding field). You can also move directly to a selection area by using the key combination:

(Alt)+<Letter highlighted>

Each selection area has a highlighted letter corresponding to the key to be pressed in conjunction with the (Alt) key.

Selection areas with brackets [] are check boxes and can be activated or deactivated by pressing (Spacebar) or with the mouse.

At the bottom of the dialog boxes, buttons sometimes appear displaying actions that can be executed by pressing (Enter). The default active button is displayed by a double border. The (Enter) key always activates the double bordered button. You can select another button by pressing the (Tab) key.

The (F1) function key is especially useful. It activates the Help function.

Let's look at how Turbo C++ loads and saves source files. Use DOS to copy the file LOADSAVE.TXT taken from the EXAMPLE\ directory of the companion diskette into your work directory. After starting Turbo C++, open the *File* menu by pressing:

(Alt)+(F)

Choose the *Open* menu item to load the file. A file selector dialog box will be displayed, which allows you to choose the filename to load. You can either type in LOADSAVE.TXT or choose from the displayed list.

You may need to change the displayed file type in the *Name* field. This is the default active field when the file selector dialog box is opened. The easiest way to change the file type filter is to simply type in the file type. For example, type *.TXT in the *Name* field. All files of the selected type in the active directory are displayed and you can choose the file you want. You may move into the directory area by pressing (Tab).

After pressing (Enter), the selected file is displayed in the text window and is ready to be edited. The LOADSAVE.TXT file is a table briefly describing the main commands of the *File* menu:

```
/********************************************************
**                    LOADSAVE.TXT                    **
**                                                    **
**       Copyright (c) 1990 Micro-Application         **
**       Copyright (c) 1992 Abacus Software           **
********************************************************/
```

Main Options of the File menu for reading or saving
programs:

	Menu	Function Key
Read File	Open	F3
Save File	Save	F2
Save with new name	Save As	

The *Save* menu item lets you save the file that you have just
edited either on a diskette or on the hard drive. The *Save As* menu
item lets you save the file under another name.

Lesson Summary

- Main menu selection in Turbo C++.
- Selecting menus by using the cursor keys or by typing the
  highlighted letter.
- Turbo C++ dialog box: Choose the selection area using [Tab] and
  [Shift]+[Tab] or [Alt]+ <Highlighted letter>.
- Activation/Deactivation of checkmark items using [Spacebar] or
  the mouse.
- File menu: reads and saves files:
  -use the mouse
  -dialog boxes sometimes appear so you can choose
    supplementary options.

➡

Exercises:

❶   What is the next to last option of the *File* menu? What is it
     used for?

❷   Open the *Help* menu by pressing [F1]. Look for information
     about the editor commands.

     (If you need help, press the [F1] key a second time.)

❸   Load any .CPP file from the EXAMPLE directory on the
     companion diskette. Then temporarily exit Turbo C++ to go
     to DOS and print this file. Finally, come back to your
     software in the same environment and print the file again,
     using the *Print* menu item from the *File* menu.

❶   Load any C file from the EXAMPLE directory of the
      companion diskette. Then save this file, renaming it
      TRIAL.CPP on your work diskette or hard drive.

2.2   The Turbo C++ Editor

Turbo C++ places both the compiler and editor at your disposal.
Using the editor (IDE) may remind you of the Wordstar word
processor. The Turbo C++ editor is almost identical to the Turbo
Pascal editor. If you've already worked with Turbo Pascal and are
just now tackling Turbo C++, you can skip the following
paragraphs.

LESSON

Turbo C++ text editing is done in the Edit window. Turbo C++ has
two command sets: the Common User Interface (CUI) and the
Alternate command set popularized by previous Borland Products.
For simplicity, our discussion will cover the Alternate command
set. If you have not already done so, select *Option | Preferences*
from the menu and select the *Alternate* command set.

In order to give you a better overview of the entire process, let's
divide the main edit commands into groups.

✓   **Cursor movements, delete commands, insert
      mode**

You can move the cursor using the numeric keypad. Other keys
activate the following actions:

Key	Alternate Key	Action
↑	Ctrl+E	The cursor moves one line up.
↓	Ctrl+X	The cursor moves one line down.
→	Ctrl+D	The cursor moves one character right.
←	Ctrl+S	The cursor moves one character left.
Backspace	Ctrl+H	The cursor moves to the left and deletes the character at that location.
Home	Ctrl+Q+S	The cursor goes to the beginning of the line.
End	Ctrl+Q+D	The cursor goes to the end of the line.
PgUp	Ctrl+R	The screen goes back one page.
PgDn	Ctrl+C	The screen advances one page.
Del	Ctrl+G	The character at the cursor is deleted.
Ctrl+Y		The line where the cursor is located is deleted.
Ins	Ctrl+V	The insert mode is activated or deactivated.

When the insert mode is activated, any characters typed push the rest of the line to the right. If the insert mode is deactivated (i.e., Overwrite mode is active), any characters typed will replace the character under the cursor. To determine whether the insert mode is activated, look at the cursor:

Underline bar   Insert mode activated
Square   Overwrite mode activated

✓ Block commands

Turbo C++ lets you work with blocks of text which can be moved, copied, etc., by using a "Clipboard" to receive the selected text. To select a block, first place the cursor on the first line and using (Shift) and a cursor key move to the end of the block. All movement keys are valid. Text may be copied into the clipboard two ways:

(Ctrl)+(Ins)   Copies without removing the block of text.
(Ctrl)+(Del)   Copies by removing the block of text.

Pressing (Shift)+(Ins) allows you to copy text from the clipboard to the current cursor position. These commands may also be found in the *Edit* menu.

✓ Search commands

It's possible to look for strings of characters in a file. Activate the *Find* menu item from the *Search* menu by using this combination of keys:

(Alt)+(S) (F)

Enter the search string in the dialog box which appears and specify any special options. If you don't want to specify any options, press (Enter). The file is searched beginning at the cursor position. As soon as the specified string is found, the search procedure is interrupted and the cursor appears on the string. You can continue searching by pressing:

(Ctrl)+(L)

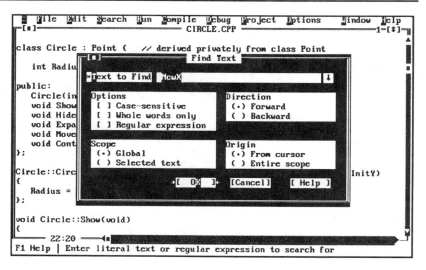

The Find Text Dialog Box

The *Replace* menu item is activated by:

Alt + S R

You must indicate the string you're looking for and the one to replace it.

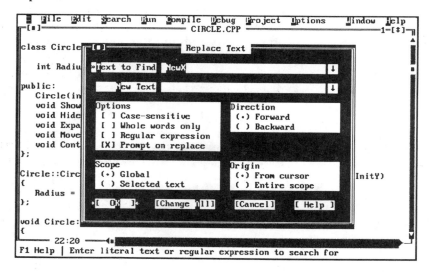

The "Replace Text" dialog box

Only the primary edit commands are described here. For more details, refer to the user's manual for your version of C++. You'll find the complete list of commands and options in Appendix A of the Borland Turbo C++ Users Guide. You may also get additional information from the on-line Help files.

Example

To familiarize ourselves with the commands previously noted, let's create a file with some text: (file FAUST.TXT).

Select *New* from the *File* menu, then enter the following lines of text.

```
I studied philosophy,
law and medicine,
and even, alas, theology!
I studied everything
with zeal and passion
and that's where I stand,
poor fool that I am,
knowing no more about them now
than I did before.

Goethe (Faust)
```

Save the file as "FAUST.TXT" by selecting *Save As* from the *File* menu.

Note: Goethe wasn't talking about C programmers.

While entering this text you'll probably use most of the cursor keys. Maybe you'll even notice that the editor automatically indents lines. For instance, if you type one of the shorter lines and accidentally indent the line, pressing (Enter) aligns the new line under the preceding one. You can return to the beginning of a line by pressing the (Home) key.

Let's try moving a block.

Position the cursor on the third line and press (Shift)+(↓) twice. Copy the block selected into the Clipboard by pressing (Shift)+(Del). Notice that the defined text block disappears.

Now position the cursor at the beginning of the seventh line and press (Shift)+(Ins); the block reappears at the position of the cursor.

To test the search command, first move the cursor to the beginning of the file. Then press (Alt)+(S) (F). Next, indicate the string of characters you're looking for. For example, choose the word "and" (don't enter the quotation marks). After pressing (Enter) the cursor moves to the first occurrence of "and" in the text. When you press (Ctrl)+(L), the cursor advances to the second one and after another (Ctrl)+(L), it goes to the third, and so on.

Σ

> **Lesson summary**
>
> - Cursor movements: Use the commands on the numeric keypad.
>
> - Block commands:
>
> | | |
> |---|---|
> | Shift + ↑, ←, → or ↓ | Select the block. |
> | Shift + Del | Copy the block into the Clipboard and remove it from the text. |
> | Ctrl + Ins | Copy the block into the Clipboard. |
> | Shift + Ins | Insert the contents of the Clipboard into the text. |
>
> - Search commands:
>
> | | |
> |---|---|
> | Alt + S F | Search for a character string. |
> | Alt + S R | Search for a string and replace it with another. |
> | Ctrl + L | Continue the search. |

➡

Exercises:

❶   Save the text that you've just entered in your work directory.

❷   Search the text for words beginning with the letter "p".

❸   Insert the contents of any C file from the companion diskette into your text file.

     Hint: Open a second file first.

❹   Finally, here's an exercise. Edit the ORDER.TXT file in the EXAMPLE\ directory of the companion diskette. You'll find the first words of a nursery rhyme all mixed up. Use the block copy and move commands to reconstruct the text in the proper order.

2.3   "Hello": Your First C Program

Now that we've covered the basics, let's write our first C program. We'll begin by stating some basic rules for programming in C: how to define the main program, what form to give to statements, and how to mark the beginning and end of a program.

LESSON

A computer program is generally made up of a part that is executed first when the program is booted and several sub-programs, also called functions. In the C language, the main program is also considered to be a function. But unlike other functions whose names may be defined, the main program must be called *main()*. The syntax looks like this:

```
main()
{
<Statements>
}
```

The main function is made up of the header *main()* followed by a "body" that contains the set of statements surrounded by a pair of brackets. C++ expects every function to return a value. Often return values are unnecessary, or even undesirable. To simplify things, the following definition may be used to specify that no value is returned:

```
void main()
```

How you arrange the elements of the language is practically up to you as long as you respect the syntax. This is how the *main()* function is correctly written. This method won't cause any problems when you compile it:

```
void main(){}
```

Don't abuse this freedom or you'll make the program difficult to read. A well written program should look good. The way it is arranged should indicate how it works. This explains the way the brackets are set up. You can easily see that lines of code are related when they start in the same column.

The first statement that we're going to examine is *printf()*. It is used to display the text on the screen. Here is its syntax:

```
printf(<Text>);
```

```
for example:
```

```
printf("abc");
```

<Text> represents anything included within quotation marks. Notice the semicolon. It's at the end of each statement and is used to separate one from another. Comments are written in the following way:

You can place comments anywhere in a program. But you shouldn't have nested comments. In other words, don't insert one comment inside another. In Turbo C++, comments on one line can be marked as:

```
//1 comment line
```

Comments which extend to more than one line can be entered as:

```
/* 1st comment line
    2nd comment line
    . . .
    last comment line */
```

Example

Let's call our first C++ program HELLO.CPP. By standard convention, source code files created for C++ are given the filename extension .CPP. Files created for compiling with a standard C compiler are generally given the filename extension .C. Source files created in this book are all named with the .CPP extension, as our intended subject is C++.

We recommend that you type in the lines for the various examples in this book, but the source code may be found in the EXAMPLE directory created when you installed the companion diskette. This program simply displays the word "Hello".

```
/*************************************************************
**    HELLO.CPP                                           **
**           Copyright (c) 1990 Micro Application         **
**           Copyright (c) 1992 Abacus Software, Inc.     **
*************************************************************/

#include <stdio.h>

void main()

{
printf("Hello\n");                    /* Display text */
}
```

Here the *printf()* function appears as an statement in brackets. Even though this statement is the only one in the body of the *main()* function, and isn't followed by any other, it still ends with a semicolon. In fact, the separator ";" absolutely must end each and every statement . The text displayed by the *printf()* function is the string of characters:

```
"Hello\n"
```

The character sequence "\n" might be confusing to you at first. It represents a control character, in this case, a "linefeed" character. When the program is executed, this character does the same thing as pressing the (Enter) key in the editor. After the word "Hello" is displayed, the cursor moves to the beginning of the next line. The following is a list of other common control characters:

Control character	Meaning
\t	Tab (Horizontal)
\a	Sound Beep
\b	Cursor moves backward

To compile and execute the program, we must load it in the edit window and then select compile either from the menu or by pressing (Alt)(F 9).

Σ

Lesson Summary

- main() function:

```
main()
{
<Statements>
}
```

- The main() function is the first one to be executed when the program is run.

- printf() function:

```
printf(<Text>);
```

- Comments:

```
/* <Comment> */
or // <Comment>
```

➠

Exercises:

❶   How can you display several lines of text using only the *printf()* function?

❷   Modify HELLO.CPP so that after "Hello" is displayed, you hear a sound.

❸   Modify HELLO.CPP without using any space in the *printf()* function so that "Hello" is displayed near the center of the screen.

❶   Write a *main()* function that displays your last name, first
     name and address. The program should also display your
     city and zip code. Finally, make a sound at the beginning
     and end of the display.

2.4   Compiling and Editing

A C program text file, called source code, must be translated into
machine language so the computer can understand and execute it.
This translation is done in several steps. You should have a basic
understanding of this process. This area of knowledge was once a
major stumbling block for many potential C programmers.
Fortunately, Borland has minimized this problem with the IDE.
It's now a matter of only minor curiosity.

   LESSON

The language "translator" is made up of two parts: the compiler
and the link editor (or "linker").

The compiler performs the first translation of the source by taking,
as input, the .CPP file concerned. It furnishes, as output, a file of
the same name but with the extension .OBJ (= Object code).
However, this translation is still incomplete because it lacks
instructions on how to execute the functions.

The link editor ("linker") takes, as input, the .OBJ file and a
library containing all the functions used. It links the application
program to all necessary external library programs and generates
an executable program with the filename extension .EXE. You can
run this last version of the file from the DOS command line.

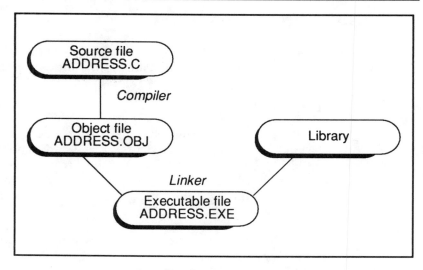

Translation of a C program

Σ

Lesson Summary

•   The two steps in translating machine language:

Compile = Translating C files without external functions.
Link = Joining OBJ files and incorporating external functions.

•   The compiling and linking process is automatic with the Turbo
C++ IDE.

Compile: Alt + F9
Make: F9

•   A program written in C++ must use the filename extension
.CPP.

⇒   **Exercises**

❶   Activate the executable program from DOS.

❷   Put an intentional error in the program by deleting the first
bracket. Then start compiling and watch what happens.
How do you return to the edit window?

❸   Other than the source program, which files are created
during linking in Turbo C++?

2.5   Error Messages

It's a fact of life. Programmers spend most of their time correcting errors. Turbo C++, with its IDE, simplifies this process.

LESSON

When the C compiler analyzes a source program, it detects two kinds of errors: fatal errors ("Errors") and minor errors that give you a warning ("Warnings"). Fatal errors immediately stop the compiler. Warnings call the programmer's attention to mistakes which, although abnormal, don't really break the rules of the language.

The Turbo C++ compiler indicates errors by displaying special messages.

In case of an error, compiling is stopped and a window is opened displaying information about the error.

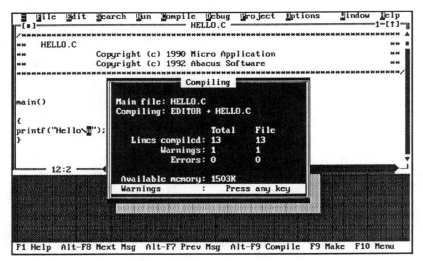

Turbo C++ displays warning for less serious problems

After you've pressed a key, a window displays a list of all the errors committed with an indication of their seriousness: "Error" or "Warning". One of the lines is in inverse video. You can move this marking bar by using the vertical arrow keys. Press the (Enter) key and the editing window appears and the cursor automatically jumps to the place where the error is.

```
 ▓  File  Edit  Search  Run  Compile  Debug  Project  Options    Window  Help
┌─────────────────────────────── HELLO.C ──────────────────────────1─┐
│/***************************************************************************│
│** HELLO.C                                                              **│
│**              Copyright (c) 1990 Micro Application                    **│
│**              Copyright (c) 1992 Abacus Software                      **│
│***************************************************************************/│
│                                                                        │
│                                                                        │
│main()                                                                  │
│                                                                        │
│{                                                                       │
│printf("Hello\n");                  /* Display text */                  │
│}                                                                       │
│                                                                        │
│                                                                        │
│└─ 12:2                                                                  │
┌─[■]─────────────────────────── Message ──────────────────────2─[↑]─┐
│  Compiling HELLO.C:                                                    ▲│
│•Warning HELLO.C 12: Function should return a value                    o│
│                                                                        ■│
│                                                                        ▼│
│└◄■──────────────────────────────────────────────────────────────────►│
 F1 Help  Space View source  ◄┘ Edit source  F10 Menu
```

A window displays additional information about the error condition

If additional errors exist, press [Alt]+[F8] to move to the next error. The corresponding error message is displayed. Pressing [Alt]+[F7] allows you to return to the preceding error. You can use the [F6] key to move from the editing window to the message window and vice versa.

Example

The file ERROR.CPP contains two errors that your compiler will definitely detect. Compiling this program will also generate a warning:

```
/***************************************************************
**    ERROR.CPP                                             **
**            Copyright (c) 1990 Micro Application          **
**            Copyright (c) 1992 Abacus Software, Inc.      **
**                                                          **
**      Note: This program contains deliberate errors.      **
***************************************************************/

#include <stdio.h>

main()
{
printf(t); /* Error 1: Undefined symbol 't'   */
printf("Hello!\nThis is C++\n");
            /* Error 2: Function call missing */
}           /* Warning 1 : Function should return a value */
```

The first error is that the letter "t" is an unknown object for the compiler. It doesn't know what it should do with it. Next, there is one parenthesis missing in the second *printf()* function. Finally, C++ expects a function to return a value, so a warning is generated.

If you try to compile this source file the compiler displays three error messages:

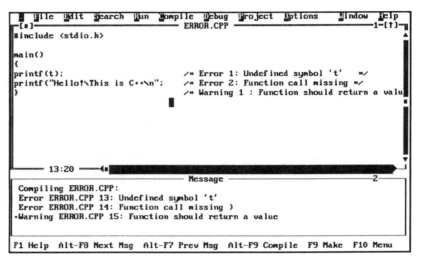

Compiling ERROR.CPP generates two error messages and one warning

The errors are noted in the message window. Highlight the second error and press (Enter). The edit window becomes active and the cursor moves to the place where the error is. A message explaining the error is displayed. By pressing (Alt)+(F7) or (Alt)+(F8), you can move through the list of errors without having to return to the message window.

Σ

Lesson Summary

- Error messages: Divided into Errors and Warnings.

- Look for errors:

    Use (Alt)+(F7) or (Alt)+(F8) to move from one error to another. Pressing (F6) lets you move from the message window to the edit window and vice versa.

➠

Exercises:

❶   Compile the program HITHERE.CPP. Locate and correct the errors.

❷   All the error messages from the compiler are documented in your Borland Turbo C++ User's Guide. What does the following message mean?

```
Error writing output file
```

❸   Why don't errors that are simple warnings (Warnings) interrupt the compiler?

❹   According to what you know so far, what would be the smallest program you could write in C? What is the size of the EXE file that's produced?

❺   Create a C program with only one *printf()* function which, when executed, produces the following display. Be careful, since the two characters \ and " are used by C language itself, you must type them twice. Call this program INITIAL.CPP.

```
Initials: _ _
Code ?: _ _


Birth: _ _/_ _/_ _
     Lucky number: _ _\_ _
Text : "_ _ _ _"
```

Chapter 3

Variables

Defining and Initializing Variables

Input/Output of Variables

Operations with Variables and Constants

3. Variables

3.1 Defining and Initializing Variables

Memory is used for storing a number of things: numbers, characters, etc. When a program has to work with variables, you must reserve a section of memory for the data in question.

The compiler automatically reserves space, but it needs to know the number and type of variables. Therefore, at the beginning of the program, you must provide a complete list of the variables used by mentioning their type. This operation is called declaring variables, or simply declaration.

LESSON

Let's look at three predefined types of variables in C:

Type in C	Meaning
int	whole numbers
float	numbers with a floating decimal point
char	isolated letters or characters

In order to use a variable in your program, you must place it in one of these categories. For instance, if you want to store a year, you must define an *int* variable (i.e., one of the int type). Mathematical operations generally require a *float* type. Here is how you should define a variable:

```
<Type> <Name of the variable>;
```

for example:

```
int year;
```

This statement defines an integer (whole number) called "year". If you want to define several variables of the same type, they can appear on the same statement line separated by commas:

```
<Type> <Var1>, <Var2>, ... , <VarN>;
```

for example:

```
int year, month, day;
```

You can choose the names of the variables arbitrarily. However, there are two restrictions:

☞   Special characters cannot be used (except '_').

☞   The first character in the name must be a letter or an underline ("_").

Here are several acceptable names: counter, Name1, HELP, total4_5.

On the other hand, the following names are *not* permitted: 7th, Careful!, Dupont&Co.

Notice that C language distinguishes between upper and lowercase letters. That means you can designate two different variables using the names "form" and "FORM". To the compiler these two variables are completely separate.

Now we know what a variable definition looks like. But we haven't told you where in the program to put it. The answer is simple: at the very beginning of the program immediately following the left bracket.

The text of the program to be executed can only begin after the variables are completely defined. The following example illustrates the file structure.

The variables are defined in the first part of DEFVAR.CPP:

```
/****************************************************
**    DEFVAR.CPP                                  **
**          Copyright (c) 1990 Micro Application   **
**          Copyright (c) 1992 Abacus Software, Inc.  **
****************************************************/

/* This is NOT an executable program. */

#include <stdio.h>

int main()

{                   /* Declaration of variables */
int number;         /* Definition of a variable consisting
                       of a whole number      */
int sum, difference, factor; /* Variables of the
                                same type */
char letter, Letter, symbol; /* Variables containing one
                                character each. */
float pi, Exponant1, n23;    /* Variables with a floating
                                decimal point */
```

```
/* Executable portion follows......      */
     .
     .
     .
 }
```

The part of the source code reserved for defining variables begins right after the left bracket. First, define an integer. The next line in the source code shows that it's possible to define several variables of the same type simultaneously. Just separate their names with commas.

Next, define three *char* variables. Even though the first two names have the same spelling, the compiler has no problem in distinguishing between them because one of the names begins with a small letter and the other with a capital letter.

Finally, three variables with a floating decimal point are defined. Two of the names contain numbers, which is allowed since the numbers are not at the beginning of the name. But if we had written "1st" for name of one of the variables, the compiler would have refused to do the job.

The part of the program to be executed follows the definitions. For the moment, we won't say any more about the structure of the program. But the way we've showed you for arranging it is absolutely necessary. If you don't follow the rules, the compiler will stop with an error message.

Σ

Lesson Summary

- Types of standard variables in C:
  - int   whole numbers
  - float   numbers with a floating decimal
  - char   isolated letters or characters

- Syntax: <Type> <Var1>, <Var2>, <Var3>, ...,<VarN>;

- Definition of the variables is always at the beginning of the program.

- Give any names to the variables but:
  - no special characters except '_'
  - must begin with a letter or an underline (_)

- The compiler distinguishes between upper and lowercase characters.

Exercises:

❶   Which variables in the following list are valid?

number	Auto	Dollar$	Line4
17:20	RAIN_BOW	reD7	green/yellow
"Fish"	Percent	description of interface1
n	ZoRRo	tree()	Light!

❷   Indicate the correct definitions:

```
int Radius, Area, Volume;
char silent, noisy light, dark;
float Old, new, old;
char counter_0, counter_1, counter_3;
float tele-copier;
```

❸   Write the definition of the variables for the following program:

```
main()
{
    /* Definition of the variables */
    .
    .   ?
    .
    /* Executable part */
    pi=3.14;        /* Several assignments */
    Year_of_birth= 1963;
    Month=10;
    Day=10;
    letter='b';
}
```

3.2   Input/Output of Variables

If we want to transfer various parameters from the keyboard to a program there must be a function that processes the data entered at the keyboard. Input is always stored in the variables. The program can then process these variables and their contents.

The function opposite of entering data is displaying on the screen. It is only when they are displayed that the results become a visible reality to the user. The functions of input and output link the program to the outside world. You already know one output function: *Printf()*.

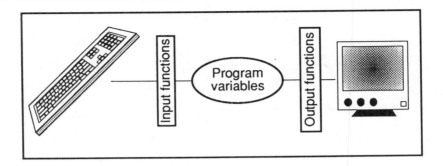

   LESSON

First let's deal with data output. You've probably already guessed that we'll use the *printf()* function. We saw it in the preceding chapter, presented like this:

```
printf(<Text>);
```

for example:

```
printf("Hello\n");
```

However, we now have a question of displaying text and variable parameters. We must use a longer form of *printf()*:

```
printf(<Format string>,
 <Variables or constants>);
```

for example:

```
printf("Year %d \n",year);
```

<Format string> can be ordinary text enclosed by quotation marks. To display a variable parameter, the format string must include a format specification. In our example, this format specification is %*d*. This specifies the kind of parameter displayed and the way it is to be represented.

When the following line is executed, the text within the quotation marks is displayed.

```
Printf("Year %d \n",year);
```

The symbol %*d* is replaced by the contents of the year variable. For example, if the year is 1990, the screen shows *Year 1990*.

The text within the quotation marks is always displayed. In the following example, C replaces each occurrence of %*d* with the contents of the corresponding variable.

Format Specification	Type	Representation
%d	int	decimal
%d	char	decimal (ASCII code)
%g	float	decimal/exponential
%c	char	letter/character
%f	float	floating decimal
%s	char	string of characters

With the char type, you can use two format specifications: %c to represent the memorized character and %d to display its ASCII code.

A single *printf()* can simultaneously display several variables and constants:

```
printf(<Format string>, <Param1>, <Param2>, ...);
```

for example:

```
printf("Year %d, Month %d, Day %d \n",yy,mm,10);
```

Here, *yy* and *mm* are int type variables while 10 is a constant. The format string must always contain as many format specifications as there are parameters.

Data input functions in a similar way. It is taken care of by a function called *scanf()* that has the following syntax:

```
scanf(<Format string>, &<Var1>, &<Var2>, ...);
```

for example:

```
scanf("%d/%d/%d", &day, &month, &year);
```

The format string has the same format specifications as in the case of the *printf()* function. However, when the program is executed, you enter all of the characters in the exact order as they are to appear. In our example, the three numbers representing the day, month and year must be separated by slashes.

Only characters, such as '\n' or '\t' or a blank space don't follow this rule. If one of these characters is a part of the format string, you can select as many blank characters as you wish, or none at all, at the place where it is located in the string.

Only variables are authorized to appear as parameters in the *scanf()* function. Constants cannot be used. The name of each variable must have the symbol & before it. We'll explain the meaning of this symbol later.

One additional thing, you'll notice another new function added to this program, *fflush(stdin)*. This function is used immediately before *scanf()* to clear the input buffer. This ensures that data we want is stored in the variables.

Example

The program INOUT.CPP lets you use the keyboard to select several *int* or *char* type variables and then display them on the screen.

```
/**********************************************************
**      INOUT.CPP                                      **
**              Copyright (c) 1990 Micro Application   **
**              Copyright (c) 1992 Abacus Software, Inc. **
**********************************************************/
#include <stdio.h>

int main()
{
  int year, month, day     /* Definition of the variables
*/
  char name1, name2;

  printf("Enter the first letter of your first name: ");
                                    /* Text to display
                                       as a prompt */
  fflush(stdin);
  scanf(" %c", &name1);             /* Input */
  printf("Enter the first letter of your last name: ");
  fflush(stdin);
  scanf(" %c", &name2);

  printf("Enter your birth date (mm/dd/yy): ");
                                    /* Prompt for birth
                                       date */
  fflush(stdin);
  scanf(" %d/%d/%d", &month,&day,&year);
                                    /* Get date */

  printf("\nYour initials are %c.%c.\n", name1, name2);
                                    /* Output */
  printf("You were born on %d/%d/%d\n", month, day, year);

  printf("\nCODE ASCII: %c=%d, %c=%d\n", name1, name1,
name2, name2);
  return(0);
}
```

After defining the variables, the program displays a string of characters that request the operator to type a letter. Notice that this string does not end with a '\n' because the letter asked for should be typed on the same line.

The *scanf()* function then reads the letter typed. The parameter of the function is a *char* type variable (preceded by the symbol *&)* and the format specification is written as %*c*. Furthermore, the first character of the format string is a blank character. So before typing the letter requested you can press the `Spacebar` or the `Tab` key as many times as you wish. The input is accepted only if you type a "real" letter followed by `Enter`.

The program also asks you to enter your birthday. This date is broken down into the month, day, and year which make up three *int* variables and require as many %*d* format specifications. Between the specifications, insert slashes.

The display that makes up the rest of the program functions in the same way. The format specifications are identical. On the first line is a *printf()* function that uses the two possible display modes for a character: %*c* lets you represent the character as it is, while %*d* causes the character to be displayed as an ASCII code. Here's how the program output looks:

```
Enter the first letter of your first name: A
Enter the first letter of your last name : D
Enter your birth date (mm/dd/yy):5/8/47

Your initials are A.D.
Your were born on 5/8/47
ASCII CODE: A=65, D=68
```

Σ

Lesson Summary

- Syntax for printf():

  ```
  printf(<Format string>, <Par1>, <Par2>, ...);
  ```
  Par1 and Par2 refer to variables (month, year, ...) or constants (10, "Walked", ...). You must have as many specifications (%) as parameters.

- Syntax of scanf():

  ```
  scanf(<Format string>, &<Var1>, &<Var2>, ...);
  ```
  Var1 and Var2 refer exclusively to variables. They are preceded by the symbol &. You must have as many specifications (%) as parameters.

- Format specifications for printf() and scanf():

%d	int	decimal
%d	char	decimal (ASCII Code)
%c	char	characters/letters
%f	float	floating decimal
%g	float	decimal/exponential
%s	char	string of characters

➡ **Exercises:**

❶   Describe the differences between *printf()* and *scanf()*:

  - role of the function
  - syntax
  - meaning of the format string

❷   What format specifications are needed to get the following display on the screen?

Variable	Representation
int address;	decimal
char initial;	character
char letter;	decimal
float const;	decimal/exponential
int age;	decimal

❸   Give an example of how to use each variation of the scanf() function.

Specify the type of each variable used.

❹   Create a program requesting the user to enter 3 letters. The program should give you the ASCII codes for the 3 letters chosen. Remember the following points:

- The user has to validate the selection of each letter by pressing Enter.
- An example of execution would be as follows:

```
C:\TCPP\EXAMPLE>letter
Enter three letters:abc
The corresponding ASCII values of the three letters are:
a--->97
b--->98
c--->99
C:\TCPP\EXAMPLE>
```

Sample output from your program

3.3   Operations with Variables and Constants

The contents of a variable is a definite value (a number, for example), while the variable itself plays the role of a function, managing a location in memory. It is possible to write statements like a mathematical formula without having to indicate the exact values of the input parameters.

Different operations are available to process information contained in the variables. The most important ones are assignments and arithmetic operations.

LESSON

We've already learned how to recognize three different types of variables: int, float, and char. The simplest operation with variables of this kind is assignment. In C we use the equal sign to assign values:

```
<Var> = <Expression>
```

for example:

```
number=34;   or   letter='C';
```

<Expression> represents any value, including the result of a calculation, which is assigned to the variable <Var>. The first assignment may be done when the variable is defined:

```
<Type> <Name of the variable> = <Expression>, ...;
```

for example:

```
int count = 25;
```

We also say that the variable is "initialized". In this case <Expression> must be a constant expression.

We can also use the four basic operations of arithmetic (addition, subtraction, multiplication and division) with variables and constants. Their symbols are +,-,*,/. Multiplication and division usually have priority over addition and subtraction. Furthermore, the *char* type variables can be linked by these four math operations. The operations focus on the ASCII codes of the variables concerned.

There is an operator which, unlike the previous ones, only joins two whole numbers. This is the "modulus" operator and gives the remainder of whole division. This symbol is the same as the one for percent %. Here is an example of a calculation:

```
r=23 % 8;
```

The result of this operation assigns *r* the value of 7, since 23 divided by 8 has a quotient of 2 and a remainder of 7.

C has one interesting distinctive feature: assignment can be combined with certain operators, creating compound operators: +=, -=, *=, /= and %=. You can also replace an assignment like this:

```
<Var> = <Var> <Operator> <Expression>
```

for example:

```
number=number+1;
```

by the equivalent shortened assignment:

```
<Var> <Compoundoperator> <Expression>
```

for example:

```
number+=1;
```

In the second form it's unnecessary to repeat the name of the variable. You'll welcome this abbreviated form when the name of the variable is long.

In our example you can shorten the statement further by using increment and decrement operators. To increase or decrease a variable by one unit, you could use the following notation:

++<Var>;	corresponds to:	<Var>+=1;
--<Var>;	corresponds to:	<Var>-=1;

The statement :

```
++number;
```

increments the number variable. If you write:

```
--number;
```

you decrement the variable.

Example

We now know enough to be able to write some short math problems. The program SPHERE.CPP calculates the surface and the volume of a sphere:

```
/****************************************************
**    SPHERE.CPP                                 **
**          Copyright (c) 1990 Micro Application  **
**          Copyright (c) 1992 Abacus Software Inc. **
**              Area = 4*PI*Radius*Radius          **
**              Volume = 4/3*PI*Radius*Radius*Radius **
****************************************************/

#include <stdio.h>

void main()
{
  float R, S, V, pi;          /* Define variable */
  pi = 3.14;

  printf("Enter the radius of the sphere (in inches): ");
                              /* Get the radius */
  fflush(stdin);
  scanf(" %g", &R);

  S = 4. * pi * R * R;      /* Calculate      */
  V = 4. / 3. * pi * R * R * R;

  printf("Area: %g inches    Volume: %g inches\n", S, V);
                              /* Display results*/
}
```

Warning

For this program to function correctly, if you have no co-processor, the "Emulation" option for the calculation must be activated. This is the default setting for Turbo C++.

After defining the variables, initialize the variable *pi* and get the radius of the sphere. The following lines carry out the calculations for the area, *S*, and the volume, *V*, and display the result.

Perhaps you noticed that the constants in the calculations contained a decimal point. The decimal point makes these constants the *float* type, which is necessary since the calculation is done in exponential mode.

Of course, you must remember that the type of a variable specifies the data category that this variable is able to accept. The constants used in the program also constitute data. So they must have a type which is specified by the way they are written:

Type	Characteristic	Example
int	only contains numbers	5296
float	contains a decimal point	293.16
float	exponential representation	2.24e-12
char	characters in quotes	'X'

Float type constants may be written either with a floating decimal or exponentially.

Let's clear up once and for all the difference between these two ways of representing the constants:

Floating decimal	----->	%f
Exponential	----->	%g

When you execute the preceding program, you might get this result:

Radius of the sphere:	400
Surface:	2.0096e+06
Volume:	2.674947e+08

Return to the source and change %g to %f. You'll get this result:

Radius of the sphere:	400
Surface:	2009600.125000
Volume:	267946672.000000

In the following example, CHARA.CPP, we've used compound operators as well as the increment operator. The relationship between the *char* and *int* types is particularly evident in this example:

```
/*********************************************************
**    CHARA.CPP                                        **
**          Copyright (c) 1990 Micro Application       **
**          Copyright (c) 1992 Abacus Software, Inc.   **
*********************************************************/

#include <Stdio.h>

void main()
{
  char chara = 'a';         /* Definition */
  printf("Lower Case: %c  ASCII Code: %d \n",chara,chara);
                            /* Display    */
  chara -= 32;              /* same as chara = chara - 32
                               and means Subtract 32    */
  printf("Upper Case: %c  ASCII Code: %d \n",chara,chara);
  ++chara;                  /* same as chara = chara + 1
                               and means add 1 */
  printf("Following Letter: %c   ASCII Code: %d
\n",chara,chara);
  chara /= 2;                   /* Divide by 2   */
  printf("Letter / 2: %c  ASCII Code: %d \n",chara,chara);
}
```

Just as in the program INOUT.C, the *printf()* functions use two different specifications for the same output parameter. With the format specification *%c* you display the character and *%d* displays the ASCII code. The first compound assignment is -=. You could have written it in its equivalent form:

```
chara = chara - 32;
```

A little farther on the increment operator is used and it increases by 1 the value of the ASCII code of chara. Towards the end of the program the /= operator appears. In our example it could be replaced by:

```
chara = chara / 2;
```

All these operations deal with the ASCII code. The output of the program looks like this:

```
Lowercase:          a  ASCII code: 97
Uppercase:          A  ASCII code: 65
Following letter: B  ASCII code: 66
Letter      / 2: !  ASCII code: 33
```

The similarity between the *int* and *char* variables goes a long way. You could have even written the initialization at the beginning of the program as:

```
int chara = 97;
```

The only difference lies in the range of their values. The range for *char* variables is between -128 and +127. This interval is just enough for all the letters and special characters. The biggest advantage of *char* variables is the small amount of space they occupy in the memory. Each *char* variable only takes up one byte. This becomes valuable when you want to load large quantities of data. Of course, this data must be complete and located within the indicated field of definition.

Σ

Lesson Summary

- Assignment operator: =

- Initializing   variables:
  <Type> <Name of variable> = <Expression>;

- Arithmetic operators: +,-,*,/,%

- Compound assignment operators: +=, -=, *=, /=, %=

- Increment and decrement operators: ++, --

- char variables can also be considered as whole numbers with a value between -128 and +127.

- Constants of the type:
  int   Only numbers
  float   Decimal or exponential
  char   Between apostrophes

Exercises:

❶   Rewrite the following statements by using compound assignment operators:

```
memory=memory+1;
move=move-nbyte;
word=word*8;
coin=coin-1;
A=A%B;
part=part/nber_persons;
```

In the statements that allow it, replace the compound operators by increment or decrement operators.

❷   Write a program that calculates the area of a circle.

❸   Write a program that converts a decimal number less than 64
       into a two digit octal number using the following method:

```
First digit of the octal number = remainder(decimal
number/8)
Second digit = whole part (decimal number/8)
```

In case you need help, the result of two *int* numbers is always
a whole number.

❹   Write a program that moves the ASCII code of a character
       forward by 32 units. The result should still be in ASCII code.

Chapter 4

Conditional Statements and Loops

The IF Statement and Structure by Blocks

While, Do-While and For Loops

Switch and Break Statements

Operators and Logical Variables

4. Conditional Statements And Loops

4.1 The IF Statement and Structure by Blocks

Among the most powerful programming tools available are conditional jumps. Some statements or program portions are only executed if a defined condition has been met.

The computer is capable of redirecting the progress of the program according to specific input parameters.

The block structure of programs written in C facilitates the way this works. Sequences of statements can be represented as closed blocks.

LESSON

Conditional jumps are programmed using the *if* statement. The syntax for the *if* statement is:

```
if ( <Expression> ) <Statement>;
```

for example:

```
if (A>B) printf("A is greater than B\n");
```

If the <Expression> is met, then the <Statement> is carried out.

In the previous case, if A is greater than B, the text "A is greater than B" is displayed.

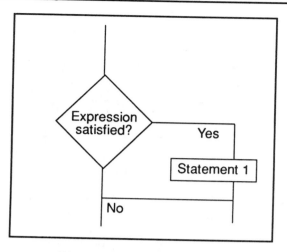

Diagram of the if statement

If the expression is not met, the program jumps over the
<Statement> and moves to the following line. The *if* statement can
also use *else*:

```
if (<Expression>) <Statement 1>; else
<Statement 2>;
```

for example:

```
if (A>B) C=A-B; else C=B-A;
```

<Statement 1> is called up if the <Expression> is met. However,
if <Expression> is not met, then <Statement 2> is carried out.

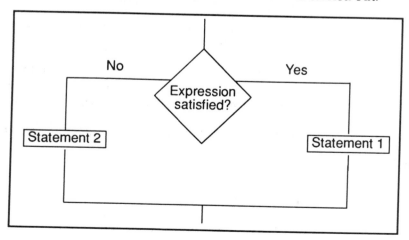

Diagram of the if ... else statement

The <Expression> used in the *if* statement must be a logical expression. You usually will use comparison operators. One of these is the operator ">" that we used in our example. But there are several others, as shown in the following chart.

Operator	Meaning	Example of its use
==	equal to	if (A==B) ...;
!=	not equal to	if (A!=B) ...;
>	greater than	if (A>B) ...;
<	less than	if (A<B) ...;
>=	greater than or equal to	if (A>=B) ...;
<=	less than or equal to	if (A<=B) ...;

The operator that tests equality is formed by two "=" signs side by side, which distinguishes it from the assignment operator. If you use *if* statements with the form we've previously described, a logical jump is only done towards an isolated statement.

However, it's often necessary to connect an entire program sequence. To solve this problem, C defines the block.

A block can be defined as a series of statements included between two brackets:

```
{
        <Statement 1>
        <Statement 2>
}
```

for example:

```
{
        printf("Hello\n");
        printf("What do you think of my IBM PC ?\n");
}
```

The block follows the same syntax as that of the program introduced by *main()*. You can think of it as a kind of program inside a program, which can be called in its entirety.

An *if* statement can activate execution of an entire block:

```
if (<Expression>)
<Block>
```

for example:

```
if (A<B)
{
        printf("A is less than B\n");
        C=B-A;
}
```

The same rules apply to the *else* statement, which can also apply to an entire block of statements. To better identify the block, generally you will indent the lines which make up the block.

This indentation is very useful in programs that are bulky and complicated. The way the program is presented visually gives you an idea of the way it progresses logically.

Example:

The following example, DIVI13.CPP tests to see whether a number is divisible by 13.

```
/***********************************************************
**       DIVI13.CPP                                    **
**             Copyright (c) 1990 Micro Application     **
**             Copyright (c) 1992 Abacus Software, Inc.  **
***********************************************************/

#include <stdio.h>

void main()
{
  int counter, remainder;    /* Definition of variables  */
  printf("Enter a number : ");       /* Get input */
  fflush(stdin);
  scanf("%d", &counter);
  if (counter < 0) counter = -counter;
                       /* Make sure number is positive. */
  remainder = counter % 13;
                       /* Calculate the remainder */
  if (remainder == 0)
                       /* Display is determined by the
  {                              result. */
    printf("This number is evenly divisible by 13.\n");
    printf("The result of dividing  %d / 13 is %d\n",
            counter, counter / 13);
  }
  else
  {
    printf("This number is not evenly divisible by
            13.\n");
    printf("Dividing %d by 13 results in %d with a
            remainder of %d.\n", counter,
            counter / 13, remainder);
  }
}
```

The first *if* statement appears after the number has been entered from the keyboard and tests whether the number typed is negative. If the number is negative, its sign is changed.

Next, the % (modulo) operators used to calculate the remainder when the number entered is divided by 13.

If there is no remainder, then the number is divisible by 13 and the result is displayed. The *else* statement deals with just the opposite case. The result of dividing the number by 13 and the remainder are displayed.

You've undoubtedly noticed that the *printf()* function uses a math expression as a parameter. For example:

```
printf("The result of dividing %d / 13 is %d\n",counter,
counter/13);
```

Actually, the parameters of *printf()* do not have to be variables or constants, but can be made up of complete expressions. The following example shows that *if* statements can be nested. The program EQUALIN.CPP solves linear equation of the following form:

```
a11*x1 + a12*x2 = c1
a21*x1 + a22*x2 = c2
```

The technique for solving this is based on the calculation of determinants. For non mathematicians, here's how the process of solving it works:

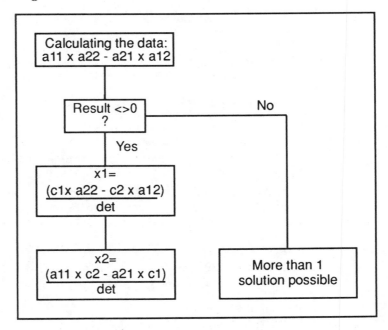

```
/***************************************************************
**         EQUALIN.CPP                                       **
**            Copyright (c) 1990 Micro Application           **
**            Copyright (c) 1992 Abacus Software, Inc.       **
***************************************************************/
```

```
#include <stdio.h>

void main()
{
  float      a11, a12, a21, a22, c1, c2;
                          /* Definition of Variables */
  float      det, det1, det2, x1, x2;
  printf("Values used in the equation:\n");
                          /* Get input */
  printf("a11, a12, c1  = ");
  scanf("%g, %g, %g", &a11, &a12, &c1);
  printf("a21, a22, c2  = ");
  scanf("%g, %g, %g", &a21, &a22, &c2);
  det = a11 * a22 - a21 * a12;
                          /* Calculate the determinant */
  if (det != 0)           /* Is there a solution ? */
  {
    det1 = c1 * a22 - c2 * a12;
                          /* Calculate the codeterminants */
    det2 = a11 * c2 - a21 * c1;
    x1 = det1 / det;      /* Here are the solutions */
    x2 = det2 / det;
    if (x1 == x2) printf("The solutions are equal: ");
                          /* Display */
    printf("x1 = %g, x2 = %g\n", x1, x2);
  }
  else
    printf("There is more than one solution.\n");
}
```

 You should enter coefficients line by line, separated by commas.
Here's an example of how to make a selection:

```
Coefficients of the system of equations:
a11,a12,c1 = 2.3,5.1,-0.5
a21,a22,c2 = -2.4,1.0,-5.8
```

The *if* statement tests the value of the main determinant. If it's not
zero, solutions x1 and x2 are calculated and displayed. If it's equal
to zero, the system has more than one solution and the appropriate
message warns the operator. We won't go into any further details
about this solution.

In the first case, a supplementary *if* statement verifies whether
the two solutions are equal. If necessary, a special message has
been prepared. Using the preceding data, here is the solution:

```
x1 = 2, x2 = -1
```

Now let's get back to the problem of nesting. If the "internal" *if*
statement had jumped the execution not to an isolated statement
but to a block of statements, the latter would have in turn been
indented. You can usually recognize the depth of nesting of a
structured program by the depth of the indentations.

Σ

Lesson Summary

- Syntax of if:

```
    if (<Expression>)        or        if (<Expression>)
    <Block>                            <Statement>;
```

- Syntax of if - else:

```
    if (<Expression>)        or        if (<Expression>)
    <Block>                            <Statement>;
    else                     else
    <Block>                            <Statement>;
```

- Comparison operators: ==, !=, <, >, <=, >=
- Structure by blocks
- The parameters of printf() can also be statements.

Exercises:

❶   Explain the arrangement of the semicolons in the *if* and *if-else* statements. In the following statements, tell which ones are correct:

```
*   if (number<1) ++number;
*   if (x<limit) x*=2 else x/=2;
*   if (supply>demand)
        price*=0.95;
    else
        price*=1.07;
*   if (cara>='a');
    {
    printf("Lower case\n");
    cara-=32;
    }
*   if (frequency==red)
    {
    frequency=green;
    printf("green\n");
    }
```

❷   Write a program that determines whether the character that you type is a lowercase letter (ASCII code between 97 and 122) or an uppercase letter (ASCII code between 65 and 90). Use only the statements you've learned up to this point.

❸   Write a program that determines the smallest of three numbers entered by the user.

4.2   While, Do-While and For Loops

The computer has the advantage of being able to react rapidly and repeat things without ever getting tired. This is important in resolving many data processing problems.

C has statements which repeat execution of a block as long as a specified expression is satisfied. These statements are the *while*, *do-while* and *for*.

LESSON

First, let's look at the syntax of the *while* statement. Its structure is identical to that of the *if* statement:

```
while (<Expression>)
          <Block>
```

for example:

```
while (n<20)
{
  printf("Iteration %d\n",n);
  ++n;
}
```

You can use a single statement as you did with *if* instead of <Block>. This is a general rule. From now on, we'll simply use the term <Block> to suggest both possibilities at the same time.

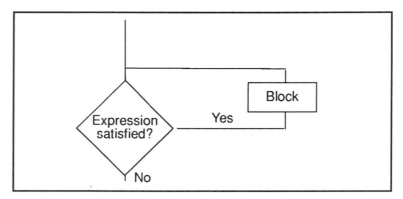

Diagram of the while loop

The <Expression> represents the execution condition of the loop. This means that the <Block> is executed as long as the <Expression> is satisfied.

In our example, the variable is displayed and incremented only until it reaches the value of 20.

At that moment the <Expression> is no longer satisfied, the loop is interrupted and the program continues with the statement following the loop. The program displays:

```
Iteration 0
Iteration 1
        .
        .
        .
Iteration 19
```

The *do-while* statement is similar and looks like this:

```
do
        <Block>
     while (<Expression>);
```

for example:

```
do
{
  printf("Iteration %d\n",n);
  n++;
}
while (n<20);
```

The *while* statement is different in this regard: The execution condition is tested only at the conclusion of the first execution of the <Block>. The <Block> is always executed at least once.

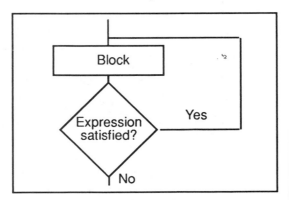

Diagram of the do-while loop

If you want to initialize a variable at the start of the loop, you can use the *for* statement like this:

```
for (<Init-exp>; <test-exp>; <Increment-exp>;)
          <Block>
```

for example:

```
for (n=0; n<20; ++n)
  printf("Iteration %d\n",n);
```

The first time through, the <Init-exp> expression is executed. Then the <Block> and <Increment-exp> expressions cover the loop as long as the <Expression> is satisfied.

In our example, the screen would display:

```
Iteration 0
Iteration 1
...
Iteration 19
```

You should note that inside the loop, the <Block> is executed first, followed by <Increment-exp>. The variable used in the *for* statement (n) is also called the "index variable".

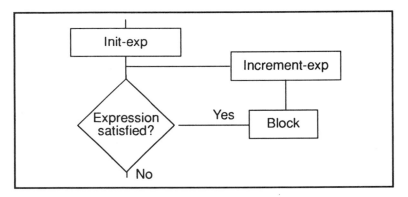

Diagram of the for loop

We've shown you an example of a standard *for* loop. In theory, you can put any statement you wish in the place of <Init-exp> or <Increment-exp>.

Example

The program SUM.CPP uses a *while* loop to calculate the sum of the whole numbers included between 1 and some specified limit:

```
/*************************************************************
**      SUM.C                                               **
**              Copyright (c) 1990 Micro Application        **
**              Copyright (c) 1992 Abacus Software, Inc.    **
*************************************************************/

#include <stdio.h>
```

```
void main()
{
  int sum = 0, number = 0, limit;    * Define variables  */
  printf("Generate the sum of the numbers from 1 to :");
/* Enter upper limit */
  fflush(stdin);
  scanf("%d", &limit);
  while (number <= limit)                /* Loop */
  {
      sum += number;
      ++number;
  }
  printf("Result: %d", sum);           /* display results */
}
```

Before the loop begins, its condition of execution is tested. After all, it would be entirely possible for you to have typed a negative number as an input parameter, in which case the program jumps over the *while* block and the loop is never executed.

As long as the expression is satisfied, the number variable is added to the sum variable and *number* is increased by one unit. At the end of the loop the *printf()* function displays the result of the calculation.

You can see how a *do-while* loop functions in the following program called ADDITION.CPP, which adds up all the floating point numbers you enter:

```
/***********************************************************
**       ADDITION.CPP                                     **
**             Copyright (c) 1990 Micro Application        **
**             Copyright (c) 1992 Abacus Software, Inc.    **
***********************************************************/

#include <stdio.h>

void main()
{
  float addit, cumul = 0;          /* Define variables */
  printf("\nCalculate the sum of these numbers (Enter a 0 to end):\n\n");
  do                               /* Input loop */
  {
      printf("Add : ");
      fflush(stdin);
      scanf("%g", &addit);
      cumul += addit;              /* Do addition */
  }
  while (addit != 0);
  printf("------------------\n");  /* Display results */
  printf("Sum = %g\n", cumul);
}
```

After the *scanf()* function, the number that's entered is added to the sum of the preceding entries. The loop is executed as long as the number typed is not zero.

You should be aware that the test for a zero is only done at the end of the loop.

Here's an example of the *for* loop. POWER2.CPP displays a list of numbers, which when raised to the second power, are less than the number given.

```
/*************************************************************
**      POWER2.CPP                                       **
**              Copyright (c) 1990 Micro Application     **
**              Copyright (c) 1992 Abacus Software, Inc. **
*************************************************************/

#include <stdio.h>

void main()
{
    int result, limit, exponent = 0;   /* Define variables */
    printf("List of the powers of 2 less than:  ");
                                        /* Get input      */
    fflush) stdin);
    scanf("%d", &limit);
    for (result = 1; result <= limit; result *= 2)
                                        /* Loop */
    {
        printf("2 to the %d power = %d\n", exponent, result);
        ++exponent;
    }
}
```

At the beginning of the program, the exponent variable is initialized at 0. The <Init-exp> expression of the loop is:

```
result=1;
```

The first time the <Block> is executed, the screen displays:

```
2 to the 0 power = 1
```

It is only at the end of the block that the <Increment-exp> is carried out. The result variable is multiplied by 2.

The test of the condition of execution is always done before entry into the loop. If you enter a value of 0, the program jumps over the <Block> of the loop and nothing is displayed on the screen.

$$\Sigma$$

Lesson Summary

- Syntax of while:

```
while (<Expression>)
    <Block>
```

- Syntax of do-while:

```
do
    <Block>
while (<Expression>);
```

In the do-while loop, the block is executed at least once.

- Syntax of for:

```
for (<Init-exp>; <Test-exp>; <Increment-exp>)
        <Block>
{
statement1;
statement2;
 .
 .
 .
}
```

Exercises:

❶   Explain what the following loops do:

```
*  int n = 1;
   while(n<40)
   {printf(value %d\n",n);
   n*=2
   }
```

```
*  int count = 0
    do
   {printf("%d ",count);
   ++count;
   }
   while(count%8!=0);
```

```
* while (n==0);
```

```
* for (x=0; x<1000; ++x) printf("%d ",x);
```

```
* for (money=100; money<10000; money*=1.5)
      printf("Fortune= %g\n",money);
```

❷   What is the value of the variable after execution of each of
     the following loops?

```
* for (number=0;  number<1000; ++number);

* for (number=1;  number<1000; number*=2);

* for (number=24; number>6;   number/=3);
```

❸   Write a program to find all numbers whose value squared is
        less than 500.

❹   Write a program that displays the multiplication table of a
        number the user enters. The user shouldn't be able to enter a
        number greater than or equal to 10.

4.3   Switch and Break Statements

The *if* statement is very practical for distinguishing between two
cases. Either the <Expression> is satisfied or it is not. But you will
need to do a test that determines more than that. That's when
you'll use the *switch* statement.

LESSON

The syntax of the *switch* statement is fairly complex:

```
switch (<Expression>)
   {
     case <ValA>: <StmtA1>;
       <StmtA2>;
       ...
       <StmtAN>;
     case <ValB): <StmtB1>;
       <StmtB2>;
       ...
       <StmtBN>;
     case ...
   }
```

for example:

```
switch (number)
  {
    case 1: printf("Case 1\n");
      --number;
    case 2: printf("Case 2\n");
      --number;
    case 3: printf("Case 3\n");
      --number;
  }
```

The <Expression> may consist of an expression having an *int* or
char type result. Subsequently, the comparisons with *case* focuses
on its value. If the expression possesses the value <Val#>, all the

statements <Stmt#> from the corresponding case onwards are executed, including those which are below them.

Here is how our example is displayed:

<expression>	number=1	number=2	number=3
Display	Case 1 Case 2 Case 3	Case 2 Case3	Case 3

It may seem a little strange that all the cases below the "correct" one are executed as well. In practice, you need an allocater to process only one case at a time.

The *break* statement actually lets you eliminate this problem. It causes the block under switch to be left alone. Now we can correct our example like this:

```
switch(number)
{
    case 1: printf("Case 1\n");
      --number;
      break;
    case 2: printf("Case 2\n");
      --number;
      break;
    case 3: printf("Case 3\n");
      --number;
      break;
    default: printf("Other cases\n");
      break;
}
```

The fourth clause is peculiar to the *switch* statement. It takes care of all the cases that aren't dealt with by a preceding case.

In conclusion, we should mention that you also use *break* in other circumstances. You can use it to interrupt execution of a *while, do-while,* or *for* loop. The program continues with the statement following the loop.

Example

The program OPERAT.CPP lets us carry out one of the four basic math operations on any two numbers:

```
/*****************************************************************
**      OPERAT.CPP                                             **
**              Copyright (c) 1990 Micro Application           **
**              Copyright (c) 1992 Abacus Software, Inc.       **
*****************************************************************/

#include <stdio.h>
```

```
void main()
{
  float number_1, number_2, result;
     /* Define variables */
  char operation;
  printf("Enter numbers and operation (Number 1 operation
          Number 2) :");
  fflush(stdin);
  scanf(" %g %c %g", &number_1, &operation, &number_2);

  switch (operation)                      /* switch block */
  {
    case '+' : result = number_1 + number_2;
      break;
    case '-' : result = number_1 - number_2;
      break;
    case '*' : result = number_1 * number_2;
     break;
    case '/' : result = number_1 / number_2;
     break;
    default  : result = 0.;
  }
     /* Next, display results */
  printf("Result : %g %c %g = %g\n", number_1, operation,
          number_2, result);
}
```

After defining the variables the program selects the desired operation. The *scanf()* function uses the following format for input:

<Number> <Operator> <Number>

for example:

23.5 + 253

The operation variable contains the operator that is identified by a switch block. The corresponding operation is then carried out in a case. Then the block is abandoned and you move on to the display of the result.

If you typed an invalid symbol instead of the operator, the resulting variable has 0 as its value. A default statement takes care of this. You could eliminate the last break since no other case follows it. An *if-else* statement could be added to handle any error resulting from faulty input.

Σ

Lesson Summary

- Syntax for the switch statement:

```
switch (<Expression>)
        {
case <ValA>): ...
case <ValB>): ...
          .
          .
          .
default: ...
        }
```

- break: Interrupts the loop in progress or the block below the switch.

Exercises:

❶ Replace the following *if* statement with an equivalent *switch* statement:

```
if (x==0)
        printf("Error\n" );
      else
        printf("100/%d=%f\n",x,100./x);
```

Create a little program to verify this transformation. Remember that x is an *int* or *char* type.

❷ Write a program that converts dollars into marks, Yen, pounds sterling, Swiss francs, and Canadian dollars. Use the current exchange rate. To select it use the following:

```
scanf(" %g %c",&amount,&currency);
```

where "amount" means the sum of money to be converted into the foreign "currency".

Note: We used the following monetary exchange rates*. You might want to check for the current exchange rates and use them instead.

German Mark	1.6035
Swiss Franc	1.47
Yen	127.35
British Pound	1.8185
Canadian Dollar	.8328

*Rates from June 4, 1992 Wall Street Journal

❸   Explain how the following loop works:

```
scanf("%d",&limit);
 for (n=0;n<20;++n)
  {
    if (n>=limit) break;
    printf("Iteration n%d\n",n);
  }
```

4.4   Operators and Logical Variables

So far, we've learned how to manage loops, often by controlling an expression. This expression was of the *(n>limit)* or *(value!=0)* type. However, the results from this conditional testing is a *YES* or *NO* answer.

The <Expression> parameter discussed in this section is capable of taking either of two values: "true" or "false". It's possible to consider the <Expression> as the result of a calculation that would furnish one of these two values.

The resulting values can in turn be combined by logical operators or assigned to variables. It also appears that we must introduce a new type of data.

LESSON

For the time being we won't give you the name of the new type of data. Let's suppose that it's called BOOLEAN. If this kind of data exists, you can state it like all the others in the following way:

```
BOOLEAN expression1, expression2;
```

You can assign BOOLEAN type values whose contents are "true" or "false" to these variables. For example, you can write:

```
expression1= (a>b);
```

There are ways to combine data of this type by using logical operators. In C, they are represented by the following symbols:

Symbol	Operator	Example
& &	AND	C=A&&B;
||	OR	C=A||B;
!	NOT	C=!C;

The symbol "|" is the ASCII code 124. If it isn't on your keyboard, hold the (Alt) key while pressing the 1, 2 and 4 keys on the numeric keypad.

In conditional jumps we can use, as <Expression>, a combination of logical expressions. For example:

```
if ( (A==B) || (B==C) ) printf("Expression met\n");
```

You can describe the <Expression> represented in the *if* statement like this:

```
If A is equal to B, or if B is equal to C, activate the
display
```

By using Boolean variables you can write this in an equivalent way:

```
exp1= (A==B);
exp2= (B==C);
if ( exp1 || exp2 ) printf("Expression met\n");
```

Now we'll let you in on what's going on. The name BOOLEAN does not exist in C. In fact, we invented it.

Here's the solution: In C, instead of BOOLEAN, you simply use the *int* type. The values 0 or 1 of a simple whole number variable correspond to the "true" or "false" contents of our BOOLEAN type variable. The examples previously given are entirely correct if you replace BOOLEAN with *int*.

Example

The TANDF.CPP program calculates and displays the truth table for the *AND* logical operator.

```
/*****************************************************************
**      TANDF.CPP                                             **
**          Copyright (c) 1990 Micro Application             **
**          Copyright (c) 1992 Abacus Software, Inc.         **
*****************************************************************/

#include <stdio.h>

void main()
{
  int a, b, c;        /* Definition of variables */

  printf("   A      |   B      |  A AND B\n");
                      /* Truth Table */
  printf("---------+---------+-----------\n");
  for (a = 0; a < 2; ++a)
     for (b = 0; b < 2; ++b)
        {
         c = (a && b);   /* AND Operator */
         if (a) printf("  true   | "); else printf("  false
| ");
```

```
        if (b) printf(" true    | "); else printf(" false
| ");
        if (c) printf(" true \n"); else printf(" false
\n");
    }
}
```

The three variables *a*, *b* and *c* are first defined as being of a whole type (i.e., as logical).

The two overlapping loops assign *a* and *b* with all possible combinations of the values 0 and 1. Upon execution you see the order in which these combinations take place. Next, apply the AND operator to the variables using the following:

```
c=(a&&b);
```

In conclusion, three *if* statements display the "true" and "false" values in the table.

As you see, the <Expression> is simply composed of the logical variable concerned. If its value is 1, it is considered as met. If not, you apply an *else* statement.

Here is the display:

A	B	A AND B
false	false	false
false	true	false
true	false	false
true	true	true

Lesson Summary

- You can also use *int* type variables as logical variables.

- The logical operators are &&, | | and !.

- <Expression> = 0   =>   false
  <Expression> # 0   =>   true

Exercises:

❶   Write a program similar to TANDF.CPP and display the truth table for the OR operator.

❷   Interpret the following:

```
a=a&&1;
```

and:

```
a=a&&(x!=y);
```

Note: If you're having any problems, refer to Section 3.3.

❸   Explain the danger of the following loop:

```
while(1) printf("you continue...\n);
```

Chapter 5

Arithmetic Expressions

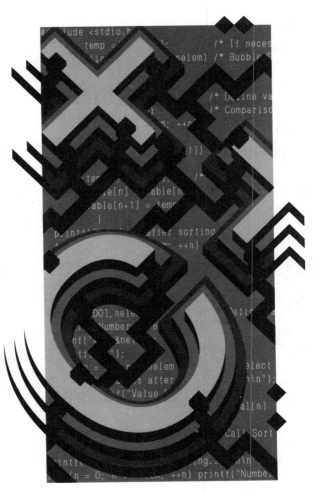

Types and Definition Fields

Variable Types and Precedence

5.   Arithmetic Expressions

5.1   Types and Definition Fields

In mathematics, variables can take on any value. But in computer languages, a variable type defines a certain range of possible values. Up to this point we've ignored this rule. If we haven't made any errors in calculation, it's because we haven't exceeded any of the ranges for the different variables yet.

However, when you start to combine different types of variables using mathematical operators, you may have to perform conversions to move a given number from one type to another.

LESSON

The following table shows valid ranges for some of the different types in C language:

Type	Min	Max
char	-128	+127
unsigned char	0	+255
int	-32768	+32767
unsigned int	0	+65535
short	-32768	+32767
unsigned short	0	+65535
long	-2147483648	+2147483647
unsigned long	0	+4294967295
....	....	....
float	3.4E-38	3.4E+38
double	1.7E-308	1.7E+308

In this table you'll notice several new types. Notice the valid ranges of the variable types. The range for *long* and *double* type variables is definitely more extensive than for *int* and *float* variables. You should understand the meaning of *unsigned* from reading the table: the valid range is simply shifted forward so that its lower limit is zero.

The range for *short* is identical to that of *int*. This type of variable has been created because C language is used on different systems. You should note that the ranges of *int, float* and *double* may also depend on the type of computer used. The values given where taken from the Turbo C++ manuals.

What happens if you exceed these ranges? As a matter of fact, Two things can happen:

❶   With *double* and *float* the program being executed is interrupted by an Overflow Error message.

❷   With *int* types only a specific number of bits are considered:

Type	Number of bits considered
char	8
int, short	16
long	32

For example, if you define the result variable as:

```
unsigned char result;
```

the statement:

```
result=255+1;
```

assigns a value of 0 to the result because only the first 8 bits are considered.

Binary System	Decimal System
11111111	255
+00000001	+ 1
---------	----
(1)00000000	256 -> 0

The variety of the valid ranges has significant consequences when combining numbers or variables of different types when it is absolutely necessary to do conversions. Of course, the compiler automatically takes care of these conversions. But you still have to know about them so you can control any resulting errors. You shouldn't be surprised to see the value 2.36E+13 disappear once you've assigned it to a *char* type variable.

Without going into detail about conversion errors (which are covered in depth in your Borland C++ User's Guide), there are two important rules you should know:

❶   When making an assignment, the result of the expression to the right of the equal sign is converted to reduce any loss of data.

❷   If you combine two values of different types, the value of the "weaker" type is converted into a value of the "stronger" type. The "strength" of the types increases from top to bottom in the table previously shown.

In cases where it's necessary to control the conversion, use parentheses like this:

```
(<Type>) <value>
```

For example:

```
(int)132.45       changes to 132
```

Example

In the program TYPES.CPP, you carry out several operations on variables and constants by mixing the types:

```
/*******************************************************
**      TYPES.CPP                                     **
**              Copyright (c) 1990 Micro Application  **
**              Copyright (c) 1992 Abacus Software, Inc. **
********************************************************/

#include <stdio.h>

void main()
{
    double result1, result2;  /* Define the variables */
    long result3;
    unsigned int     result4;

    result1 = 4. / 3;
            /* Result of division : double -> double */
    result2 = 4 / 3;
            /* Result of division : int -> double  */
    result3 = result1;
            /* double -> long */
    result4 = -result1;
            /* double -> unsigned int */
    printf("double:        4. / 3  = %lf\n", result1);
            /* Display */
    printf("double:        4  / 3  = %lf\n", result2);
    printf("long:          4. / 3  = %ld\n", result3);
    printf("unsigned int: -(4. / 3) = %u\n", result4);
}
```

After defining the variables, the program carries out two operations that are almost identical. The only difference lies in the decimal point after the number 4. This decimal point indicates that the constant has a floating decimal value and is, therefore, a *double* type. (In Section 3.3 we cheated a bit so this problem wouldn't appear sooner than we wanted. Constants with a floating decimal are not *float* type but *double* type.) The 3 is an *int* type and is, therefore, "weaker", so it is converted to *double* type. It's only at this point that the operation is activated and its result is assigned to the result1 variable (result1=1.333333).

The second operation works differently. The two constants 4 and 3 are not *int* types and have the same "strength". Any division to be carried out is, therefore, whole division and the result of that division is shortened to a whole value. The fact that the result is then assigned to a *double* value changes nothing in its value since the result remains whole (result2 = 1).

In the next line you pick up the correct result left in result1 and assign it to a long variable. This conversion makes all the digits after the decimal point disappear.

After this, things get a bit complicated. The result from the first operation is changed to a negative and this value (in this case -1.33333) is assigned to an unsigned int type variable. You should expect result4 to contain a value having no connection with the initial result. In fact, the program displays the following data:

```
double:               4. / 3  = 1.333333
double:               4  / 3  = 1.000000
long:                 4. / 3  = 1
unsigned int:       -(4. / 3) = 65535
```

Once again, note this little characteristic of the *printf()* function. The format specifications are %*ld* for the *long* type and %*u* for the *unsigned int* type. The *double* variables also give rise to a special format. You can see that the new types of variables require new format specifications. The Lesson Summary contains a table of these new formats.

Σ

Lesson Summary

- Types and format specifications

char	%c,%d	unsigned char	%c, %u
int	%d	unsigned int	%u
short	%hd	unsigned short	%hu
long	%ld	unsigned long	%lu
float	%g	double	%lg

- In assignments that need a type conversion, the compiler tries to minimize the loss of data.
- When you combine different types, the "stronger" prescribes the conversion.
- To force a conversion to take place: (<Type>) <Value>

Exercises:

❶   Give the results of the following calculations and specify the type:

```
3.5*6=?              (int)85.35*2=?
243*-83=?            'w'-2024= ?
(int)(20.35*24)=?    23/9=?
```

❷   What should the variable type be so that, when the following are assigned, there will not be any rounding error:

```
var=12+'g';          var+=2.5
var=(1<3);           var=255+1;
var=13-274.3;        var=2/7.;
```

5.2   Variable Types and Precedence

Higher mathematics teach us that multiplication and division are carried out before addition and subtraction. But these rules only apply to basic operations. What about the new operations that we've introduced? What are their relative priorities?

By studying this theme we'll discover an important characteristic of C. The assignment can play the role of an operator by supplying a result that you can use later.

LESSON

If the assignment produces a result, you should be able to assign that result to a variable:

```
B=(A=4)
```

First let's examine the expression in parentheses. The variable A gets the value of 4. Then you assign the result of the operation to the variable B. What is its value?

This statement is, in fact, equivalent to the sequence:

```
A=4;
B=A;
```

The parentheses have the effect of transmitting to B the value that's assigned to A.

This procedure is also valid for compound operators. The case of decrementation or incrementation is particularly interesting. To this point we have placed the signs -- or ++ before the variable affected. But you can also place them after the variable:

```
<Var>--     or       <Var>++
```

for example:

```
number--    or       number++
```

Let's try to understand the difference between ++*number* and *number*++ :

Given the instructions:

```
number = 10;
result = ++number;
```

number is initialized at 10. Then it is incremented by 1 and the total value of 11 is assigned to *result*, which is displayed.

```
number = 11
result = 11
```

Now let's take:

```
number = 10;
result = number++;
```

number is initialized at 10. This value is first assigned to *result*, then *number* is incremented by 1, which changes the output to:

```
number = 11
result = 10
```

So you see that the variable using ++ is identical in both cases but assigning alters the output.

If ++ is placed before the variable <VAR>, incrementation precedes the assignment. If ++ is after the variable, incrementation follows assigning.

<VAR2> = ++<VAR1>;<==> { VAR1= VAR1 + 1;
                         VAR2 = VAR1;

<VAR2> = <VAR1>++;<==> { VAR2 = VAR1;
                         VAR1= VAR1 + 1;

Now let's study the order of the operations in any arithmetic expression. You can resolve this question by referring to the priorities table:

Operator	Priority
()	high
++ -- (<Type>) !	
* / %	
+ -	
< > >= <=	
== !=	
& &	
||	
= += -= *= ...	low

The higher the position in the table, the more priority an operator has. As you might expect, since the parentheses are right at the top, they always receive top priority.

Example

The program ARITH.CPP uses three long arithmetic expressions:

```
/*****************************************************
**        ARITH.CPP                                **
**           Copyright (c) 1990 Micro Application   **
**           Copyright (c) 1992 Abacus Software, Inc. **
*****************************************************/

#include <stdio.h>

void main()
{
  int m = 24, n = 2;                    /* Define variables */
  int result1, result2, result3, boolean;

  result1 = result2 = 3 + n++ * 24 - (m -= 25);
             /* Arithmetic Expressions */
  result3 = result1--;
  boolean = result1 > result3 && 1 || n < (m *= 12);
  printf("result1 = %d\n", result1);  /* Display */
  printf("result2 = %d\n", result2);
  printf("result3 = %d\n", result3);
  printf("boolean = ");
  if (boolean) printf("True\n"); else printf("False\n");
}
```

If you've understood the different priorities, try to find the correct answers. In the first expression, the parentheses immediately draw our attention. Since they have the highest priority, the assignment $m-=25$ is executed first. Up to this point m had a value of 24. After being assigned, it has a value of -1.

In descending order of priority, next we have the ++ operator. Since it is placed after the incremented variable, the value used in the calculations is 2. n takes the value of 3 after assignment. The rest of the expression is evaluated according to the general principle: "Multiplication and division is carried out before addition and subtraction". This principle is also applicable to your priorities table. So *result2* and *result1* take the value of 52.

Contrary to our first example, the double assignment does not use parentheses. They are not necessary because assignments systematically take place from right to left. Here, the program first calculates the expression on the right and stores the result in *result2*. Then it executes the assignment to *result1*.

In the second expression, *result1* is decremented, but only after its initial value has been transferred into *result3*.

You can describe the third expression like this:

```
Expression      result1 > result3 && 1 || n < (m *= 12)
Stage 1         result1 > result3 && 1 || n <   -12
Stage 2         result1 > result3 && 1 || 0
Stage 3         0  && 1 || 0
Stage 4         0  && 1
Stage 5         0
```

Finally the program displays:

```
result1 = 51
result2 = 52
result3 = 52
Boolean = false
```

Σ

Lesson Summary

- Value of an assignment: Contents of the variable after executing the assignment.

- Increment / decrement operator
    result = number++;<==>{result=number;
                                       {number=number+1;
    result = ++number;<==> {number=number+1;
                                       {result=number;

- Hierarchy of the operators (see table).

Exercises:

❶   What is the value of the following expressions:

```
3*(4+2)        1&&0||1
3*(4>4)+2.5    3+(n>n-1)
(4==[.1)/2+1   !1&&0||!0
```

❷   Give the contents of the *int x* variable after each statement of the following program sequence:

```
x=2;
x=3+(3>x);
x+=x-=2;
x=(++x-6)*3;
x*=(5>x)*(3+23);
```

❸   In the following statements, locate the useless parentheses:

```
a=(x*w)+3;       m=k>(b||1);
f*=15-(3+f);     h=(n+=12);
g=(g++ +g)*3;    b*=(20+3);
```

Chapter 6

Arrays, Pointers and Structures

Arrays and Strings

Pointers

Pointer Arithmetic

Structures

Combination of Types and Typedef

6. Arrays, Pointers, And Structures

6.1 Arrays and Strings

An array is a set of data that can receive a specified number of the same kind of values. It is comparable to a list of indexed variables. This means it is possible to store large quantities of data in the computer while keeping open the option of individually accessing each element.

LESSON

An array is a type of variable. It is defined as any other variable:

```
<Type> <Name of the variable> [<Nmax>],...;
```

for example:

```
int number[20];
```

Remember: You can type square brackets [] using the numeric keypad by typing ⒜+⑨+① and ⒜+⑨+③.

The syntax is similar to ordinary variables. First, indicate the type for each element, then the name of the variable. You also must give a number in square brackets: [*Nmax*] . This number is a whole number that indicates the maximum number of elements in the array.

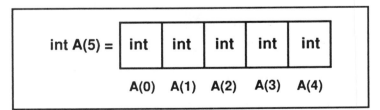

Array of int type variables with 5 elements

Our new variable is now ready for use. You access different elements by using an index included between 0 and [*Nmax*]-1. For example, for *int Number[20]*:

```
first=number[0];   or   number[0]=first
last=number[19];   or   number[19]=last;
```

The point of origin cannot be moved as in other languages. It is always equal to zero.

Of course, an array may have several dimensions, in which case the definition is as follows:

```
<Type> <Name of the variable> [<Nmax1>] [<Nmax2>] [...],
...;
```

for example:

```
int number[20][40];
```

Access the different elements by mentioning each of the indexes affected. For example:

```
first=number[0][0];      last=number[19][39];
middle1=number[18][8];   middle2=number[2][4];
```

Here we have to make a very important statement: The compiler does not verify whether the indexes used are within valid limits. Any time you go beyond them, you are likely to suffer the consequences.

You could easily modify essential memory areas without realizing it. It isn't unusual for this kind of error to cause a system failure (crash).

The most frequently used array is a character array, better known as a string array, which has only one index. A string array can be defined and have values assigned at the same time. Just enclose the string in quotation marks (and not between apostrophes like you would for a *char* constant). Here's an example:

```
static char file[7]="test.c";
```

The key word *static* is absolutely essential. We'll explain why later.

The array index sets the maximum capacity (be very careful). When you estimate the length of a given string (in our example, the string has 6 characters), always consider the null character that is required at the end of the string.

This null character, is represented by '\0'. The size of our array in this example must be at least 7. But, you could also allow for a higher value.

In fact, the compiler would have just as easily accepted the array definition without any mention of its size, since it's capable of estimating the length of the string by itself. You're perfectly correct in writing:

```
static char file[]="test.c";
```

Generally speaking, conventional operators cannot link or manipulate strings. Even assignments using the = sign are only allowed when the variable is initialized. It's not permitted as an executable instruction. Manipulations of strings are done using special functions that we'll discuss in detail later.

Example

The program PARABOLA.CPP draws a parabola using the *printf()* function:

```
/*************************************************************
**        PARABOLA.CPP                                     **
**               Copyright (c) 1990 Micro Application      **
**               Copyright (c) 1992 Abacus Software, Inc.  **
*************************************************************/

#include <stdio.h>

void main()
{
  float x = -7, par[21];    /* Define variables */
  static char espace[] = "                 ";
  int n, Y;
  for (n = 0; n < 21; ++n)
                                   /* Calculate the parabola  */
  {
     par[n] = x * x;
     x += 0.7;
  }
  printf("Parabola:\n");
  for (n = 0; n < 21; ++n) /* Display the graphic */
  {
     Y = par[n];
     espace[Y] = 'X';
     printf("%s\n", espace);
     espace[Y] = ' ';
  }
}
```

At the beginning of the program, two arrays are defined: *par[21]* is an array of 21 real numbers and *space[]* is a string of characters initialized by a string containing a large number of spaces.

In the first *for* loop the program calculates the different values of the parabolic function that are stored in the *par[]* array.

The second loop displays the results on the screen. The parabola appears horizontally. First, *Y* is assigned one of the parabolic values from the array (for example, 16). Then you write an 'X' into the 16th element of the *space[]* string. The string is then displayed by the *printf()* function (using the %s format specification), which causes an 'X' to appear in the 16th column of the screen. After that, you delete the 'X' in the string and the loop begins again.

Note that you have to write character string variables without square brackets when you use them as parameters for the *printf()* function. With the *scanf()* function, you eliminate the & signs. We'll explain these rules in Chapter 7.

Let's go back to initializing the arrays.

❶   For character type arrays, you have selected the way the initializing process will proceed. For example:

```
Static char address[ ] = "125 North State St";
Static char city[8] = "Detroit"
```

❷   For integer (int) type arrays, the technique is almost the same:

```
Int response[4] = {27,38,55,62};
```

or:

```
Int response[4];
response[0] = 27;
response[1] = 38;
response[2] = 55;
response[3] = 62;
```

❸   Initializing a multi-dimensional int type array is just as easy:

```
int matrix[2][4] = {
                    {10,20,30,40},
                    {15,25,35,45}
                    };
```

For example, matrix[0][2] has a value of 30.

Σ   Lesson Summary

- Definition of a array:

  ```
  <Type> <Name of the variable> [<Nmax1>] [<Nmax2>]
  [...],...;
  ```

- Initialization of a string of characters:

  ```
  static char <Name of the variable> [] = <Text>;
  ```

- The compiler doesn't verify whether indexes used are included within the authorized limits.

- Character string constants are text strings enclosed by quotation marks.

- Strings end with the character '\0'.

- To display strings with the printf() function, use the format specification %s.

Exercises:

❶ Indicate which of the following array definitions are incorrect:

```
unsigned int matrix[3,3];
int vector[6];
char computer[]='IBM PC';
float measure[2][1000];
int des[3][3][3];
char name[8]="Isabelle";
char month[14]="June";
```

❷ How do you define an array of strings of characters? Define such an array that will store the names of the twelve months of the year.

❸ Define an array initialized by the following matrix:

```
2 0 3
4 2 8
```

❹ Write a program that sorts 5 integer numbers in ascending order. Use the following method:

```
Element   n [0]   [1]   [2]   [3]   [4]
Contents      3     1     5     7     2
```

[0] is compared to [1]. If [0] > [1], the two elements are switched. Then [1] is compared to [2], and the procedure repeats itself. When you get to [4], start over at the beginning. This time go up to [3]. The next time around go to [2], and then to [1]. The numbers are now sorted. (This procedure is called a "Bubble Sort" and can also be applied to larger tables.)

6.2   Pointers

When programming with a high level language, you can often forget that the computer's memory is made up of a series of numbered cells. High level languages adapt the variables they use to this system without requiring users to be aware of the consequences. These variables take up a number of bytes, the size depends on the variable type, starting at a specific address. A pointer is a variable intended to store this address. By pointing to variables of a given type, pointers allow accessing memory with a great deal of flexibility.

LESSON

You can define a pointer variable by:

```
<Type> *<Name of the pointer>,...;
```

for example:

```
int *ptr;
```

Here *ptr* points to an *int* type variable. At this point in the game *ptr* doesn't have an address, so truthfully speaking, it doesn't point anywhere unless it falls by chance on some location in the memory. To really use a pointer, you must assign the address of an ordinary *int* variable to *ptr*. For example:

```
int var;          ptr=&var;
```

& is the addressing operator. When applied to any variable it returns its address.

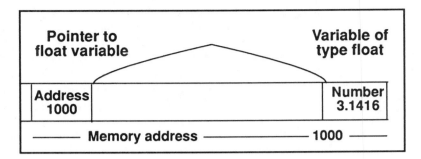

Pointer to a float variable

The pointer *ptr* is directed to the variable *var*. To access the contents of the variable, use the * operator which has already appeared in the definition stage of the pointer. For example:

```
*ptr=45;
```

At the same time, this statement assigns the value 45 to the variable *var*. **ptr* and *var* are identical. They access the same locations in the memory.

Let's go over it again:

❶   For example, you indicate a Pointer variable by *int *ptr*. So then:

```
int var = 100;
ptr = &var;
```

means that *ptr* contains an address which stores a value of 100. It returns the memory address of a variable.

❷   **ptr* returns the value contained in the memory space designated by *ptr*. Therefore, **ptr* returns a value of 100.

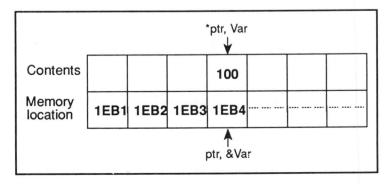

Now we can see why the *scanf()* function uses the addressing operator *&*. During input, a value is read from the keyboard and stored in a variable. This operation is only carried out when the function knows the corresponding memory location.

The greatest advantage that pointers have is that they can receive varied assignments during the course of a program. A single pointer variable can access a multitude of ordinary variables, one after the other, simply by knowing their locations.

But along with this power there's a trap. It wouldn't be very wise for you to write:

```
int *ptr,var = 100;
*ptr = 345
ptr = &var
```

Do you know why?

We have just put the number 345 in the memory location to which *ptr* pointed. But which location? That's the problem. We don't really know where *ptr* was pointing at that particular moment. You can imagine what headaches this could cause. That's why you must systematically assign an address to a pointer before using it.

It's important for you to understand the relation between pointers and arrays. When you eliminate the square brackets of an indexed variable, the result becomes an object that C treats as a pointer to the first variable of the array. The following statements are entirely legitimate:

```
char field[20],*ptr;
ptr=field;
```

With arrays having only one index, this equivalence even lets you use an index with the pointer to access an element in the table. For example:

```
ptr[13]=20;
```

There is still one important difference: You can't reassign the address of an array variable like you can with a pointer.

Let's review the distinction between an integer and an array:

❶   A pointer variable points to an address containing an integer:

```
Int var, *ptr;     /* <--Initialization */
Var = 100;         <--Var is a variable. It contains
                   the value 100 */
ptr = &Var;        /* <--ptr points to the address
                   where the
                   value 100 is stored(for
```

```
                                   example 1E3) */
             *ptr = 50;            /* <--This assignment stores the
                                   value 50 in the memory place
                                   designated by the address 1E3. */
```

Conclusion : Var now contains the value 50.

❷   A pointer variable points to an address containing the first
       element of an array:

```
             static char table[5] = "aaaa";   <--Initialization
                                              of an array
             char *ptr;                        <--Definition of
                                              the pointer
             ptr = table;                      <--ptr points to
                                              the address where
                                              table[0] is located
             ptr[2] = 'V';                     <--From now on the
                                              3rd element
                                              contains 'V'
```

Conclusion: The array now contains "aaVa". The array
                     indicated an address where the value *table [0]*
                     is stored.

Notice that the assignments are not identical in the two modes.

Example:

The program POINTER.CPP gives you several examples of
pointer- and array-based operations:

```
/****************************************************************
**     POINTER.CPP                                            **
**             Copyright (c) 1990 Micro Application           **
**             Copyright (c) 1992 Abacus Software, Inc.       **
****************************************************************/

#include <stdio.h>

void main()
{
  int var[3], *iptr;       /* Define variables */
  static char *Word1 = "Hello", Word2[20] = "friends";
  int n;
  for (n = 0; n < 3; ++n)
    /* iptr skims over all the elements of var[] */
  {
    var[n] = n;
    iptr = &var[n];
    printf("var[%d] = %d\n", n, *iptr);
  }
printf("\n%s %s\n", Word1, Word2);

    /* Display pointer and array */
```

```
printf("\nEnter your name (max. 19 letters): ");
    /* Prompt for input   */
scanf("%s", Word2);
printf("%s %s\n", Word1, Word2);
    /* Display */
Word1 = Word2;
    /* Assign a pointer */
printf("%s %s\n", Word1, Word2);
    /* Display */
}
```

The program begins by defining the pointer and array variables used. The equivalence of these two types is particularly clear in the initialization stage of the char variables. In fact, it is identical in both cases. At the end of the program, the two variables *word1* and *word2* appear in the same way as parameters of the *printf()* function.

In the *for* loop, the *iptr* pointer points to all the successive elements of var. The *&* operator carries out the assignment of the address of *var*. There's another way this could have been down:

```
iptr=var;
for (n=0;n<3;++n)
{
  var[n]=n;
  printf("var[%d]=%d\n",n,iptr[n]);
}
```

Remember that in the case of the program example, *iptr* is a pointer to an address containing an integer (*var[n]*), which means that *printf()* uses **iptr* to restore the value of *var[n]*. On the other hand, in the case previously described, *iptr* points to an array. So *printf()* uses *ptr[n]* to restore the value of *var[n]* (and not **ptr[n]*).

Here the base address of the table is first assigned to the pointer. After that, *iptr* and *var* designate identical variables. The assignment in the loop also counts for *iptr*, even though it is executed on *var*.

After the loop, the two initialized strings are displayed. Then you select a new value for *word2*. You don't have to put *&* operators before the parameters of *scanf()* because *word2* is a pointer and as such, it already represents an address (*table* refers to the memory address where the *table[0]* values are stored). Since you can focus your selection on a string that is longer than the initial one, we've been careful to let you have enough space when you're at the point of defining *word2*.

In the next to the last line, the base address of the *word2[]* array is assigned to the *word1* pointer. Consequently, the address of the initialization string "Hello" is lost and you'll no longer be able to locate this text. The inverse assignment would not have been possible since addresses of arrays cannot be changed.

Lesson Summary

- Pointers indicate addresses of variables of a given type.

- Definition of a pointer:
  ```
  <Type> *<Name of the pointer>,...;
  ```

- Accessing pointers:
  *<Name of the pointer> = Contents of the variable referenced by the pointer.
  <Name of the pointer> = Address of the variable referenced by the pointer.

- Operator giving the address of a variable: &

- Pointers and arrays have similar properties.

Exercises:

❶ What are the final values of the variables *a*, *b* and *c* after executing the two sequences of the following programs:

```
int a,b,c,*ptr;        char a,b,c,*ptr;
ptr=&a;                a=b=3;
*ptr=4;                ptr=&a;
b=a+5;                 c=*ptr+=2;
ptr=&b;                ptr=&c;
c=*ptr;                ++(*ptr);
```

❷ If field represents an array and *ptr* is a pointer of the same type, why are the following statements equivalent?

```
ptr=field;                      ptr=&field[0];
```

❸ Find the errors appearing in the two excerpts of the following program:

```
static char x[]="abcd";    int number1,number2;
static char y[]="efgh";    int *ptr=&number1;
char *ptr=x;               ptr=25;
x=y;                       number2=ptr+6;
y=ptr;                     ptr=&number2;
```

6.3   Pointer Arithmetic

Pointers contain addresses. Addresses are numbers and using numbers you can do calculations. There is a kind of arithmetic

especially intended for pointers and created to access data fields.
You can manage arrays without resorting to indexing. Accessing
with pointers is generally faster than using indexed arrays.

LESSON

Depending on its type, each variable occupies a certain number of
bytes in the memory. If you increment a pointer of the same type,
its address does not increase by 1, but rather by the length of the
type:

```
Int field[3] = {1,2,3},*ptr;
ptr = field;
```

In our figure, FFDC is the starting address for the field. This
means that, at that particular moment, *ptr* is equal to FFDC (in
hexadecimal notation).

```
++ptr;
```

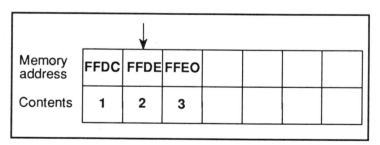

Increment the address designated by *ptr*. Now *ptr* points to the
address FFDE. The difference between FFDE and FFDC is 2,
which, in hexadecimal, represents 2 bytes or 16 bits. 16 bits is
exactly the size of the *int* type.

One last piece of information: You know that for the *int* type, %d
displays it in the way it is normally represented (base 10). You can
use %x in its place to display the hexadecimal representation
(base 16).

Let's condense the preceding example:

```
int field[3],*ptr;
ptr=field;              /* ptr points to field[0] */
++ptr;                  /* ptr points to field[1] */
```

We're using an *int* type, so its length is 2 bytes. After the first assignment, *ptr* points to the base of the *field* array. Since *ptr* references an *int* type integer, incrementing the last statement increases the address by 2.

You should know that the arrays in the memory are arranged like linear strings. Their elements are lined up one directly on top of the other.

When you increase the *ptr* pointer by two bytes, you make it point to the second element of the *field* array. Therefore, you can access the corresponding data by using the * *operator*.

Study the following example so you'll understand once and for all how this incrementation works:

```
main ()
{
int a[3] = {1,10,20},*ptr;
ptr = a;
printf("value1 %d address1 %x\n",*ptr,ptr);
++ptr;
printf("value2 %d, address2 %x\n",*ptr,ptr);
}
```

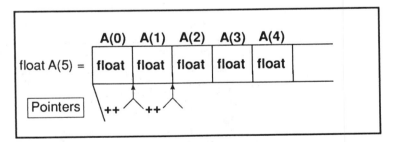

Example of incrementing a pointer

Of course, the mechanism is the same for the decrement operator. By writing the statement:

```
--ptr;
```

you could negate the preceding action. So it's possible for you to skim over the arrays, element by element, and access their contents using pointers.

You can also carry out more important moves by adding any number you wish to a pointer.

For example:

```
float value[20],*ptr;
ptr=value;                /* ptr points to value[0] */
ptr+=10;                  /* ptr points to value[10] */
```

Subtraction works in a similar way. It's even possible to point to fields without altering the pointer:

```
*(ptr+10) is equal to ptr[10] (if ptr[10] is initialized!)
```

The implicit result of this arithmetic is that pointers can be compared. This comparison focuses on the addresses:

```
ptr1=ptr2;
ptr2+=50;
if (ptr1<ptr2) ...
```

In this example, the condition tested is obviously not met. Each time that you use the pointers you have to be conscious of their dangers because pointers allow you to directly access memory.

If you make mistakes in programming, it might cause you to write over zones in the memory that contain sensitive data. To put it plainly, this means that using pointers could quite easily lead you to a system failure.

Most of the time, any errors committed don't, strictly speaking, go against the rules of syntax for pointers. That's why the compiler generates warnings in places that seem suspicious.

When you program with pointers, it is particularly unwise to ignore these warnings. It's better to have to interrupt your compilation than to reboot the system.

Example

The file PTRPAR.CPP performs the same function as the program PARABOLA.CPP we looked at in Section 6.1. It draws a parabola:

```
/*******************************************************
**      PTRPAR.CPP                                    **
**             Copyright (c) 1990 Micro Application   **
**             Copyright (c) 1992 Abacus Software, Inc. **
*******************************************************/

#include <stdio.h>

void main()
{
  float x = -7, par[21];   /* Define the variables */
  float *ptr = par, *fin = &par[20];
  char *espace = "                          ";
```

```
        int Y;

        do                              /* Calculate the parabola */
        {
           *ptr = x * x;
           x += 0.7;
        }
        while (ptr++ < fin);
        ptr = par;
        printf("Parabola:\n");
        do                              /* Display the graphic */
        {
           Y = *ptr;
           *(espace + Y) = 'X';
           printf("%s\n", espace);
           *(espace + Y) = ' ';
        }
        while (ptr++ < fin);
}
```

Pointers carry out the operations on the arrays whereas in PARABOLA.CPP indexes did it. At the outset the program initializes two float type pointers: *ptr* and *fin*. *ptr* points to the first element in the *par* array and *fin* points to the last one. It's also a pointer that references the space string.

A *do-while* loop now corresponds to the *for* loop of PARABOLA.CPP. The most important point in relation to our pointer arithmetic is the condition in parentheses.

That's where the *ptr* is incremented the length of one element and the loop is tested. The ++ operator is placed after *ptr*, which means that the comparison focuses on the address before incrementation.

If this comparison is still equal when it gets to the last element, the loop is interrupted.

The second *do-while* loop functions in the same manner. But before it begins, *ptr* has to point back to the beginning of the *par* table.

You also access the space string using pointers. In fact, the space variable is not directly incremented, but it indirectly points to each element thanks to a * type addition (*space+Y*).

Σ

Lesson Summary

- Operations on pointers: ++, --, +, -, =, +=, -=

- Indirect access: *(<Pointer> +/- <Expression>)

- The pointers can be compared.

> • Watch out for errors when you program with pointers.

Exercises:

❶   *ptr* is a pointer to an *int* type variable. Initially *ptr* points to the base of an *int* array. Which element of the table is referenced by each of the three following expressions:

    ptr[1]   *(ptr+1)   *(++ptr)

Which of these operations modifies the pointer?

❷   Write a program capable of finding a specified letter inside any word of 20 characters. The result displayed should indicate the index of the first occurrence in the event that the letter is found.

❸   Find the error hidden in the following program sequence:

```
int table[20], *ptr=table,n;
for (n=0; n<20; --n) *(ptr++)=2;
```

6.4   Structures

The arrays have the advantage of grouping together data of the same kind (for example, measurement or text results, etc.) in the same variable. But these variables have to be of the same type. To get around this restriction, C language lets you define hybrid arrays called structures.

LESSON

It's up to you, as the user, as to how you define the struct type. Here's the syntax:

```
struct <Name of the structure>
    {
      <TypA> <Member A>, ...;
      <TypB> <Member B>, ...;
      ...
    };
```

for example:

```
struct person
    {
    char name[20];
    int age;
    };
```

In this example, *struct person* is the name of the new type. It contains two elements called "members": the string *name* and the variable *int age*. Contrary to what happens with arrays, individual elements are not indexed but are simply designated by their name.

When you introduce a defined type variable, use the same syntax as for defining an ordinary variable.

For the type you simply indicate:

```
struct <Name of the structure> <Name of the variable>,...;
```

for example:

```
struct person friend;
```

In this example, *friend* is a variable of the *struct person* type. Once you're in a program you can individually access the different members of a structure by writing:

```
<Name of the variable> . <Name of the member>
```

for example:

```
friend.age=15;
```

The name of the variable is followed by the name of the member and separated from it by a period. In our example, you assign the number 15 to the *age* element of the *friend* variable.

We could compare the structure of our example to an ordinary array of the same dimension:

Definition of the variable:

```
struct person friend;              int table[2]
```

Elements:

```
friend.name                        table[0]
friend.age                         table[1]
```

This comparison shows that the members of a structure correspond to the elements of an array. But they have the great advantage of being able to be of different types while the elements of an array must have the same type.

Example

STOCK.CPP is an example of a simple inventory control program.

```
/*****************************************************
**     STOCK.CPP                                    **
**        Copyright (c) 1990 Micro Application      **
**        Copyright (c) 1992 Abacus Software, Inc.  **
*****************************************************/

#include <stdio.h>

void main()
{
    struct article                  /* Define a structure */
    {
        int         quantity;
        float       price;
    };

    struct article bolt, screw;     /* Define variables */

    int bpiece, spiece;
    char response;

    bolt.quantity = 0;                    /* Initialization */
    bolt.price = .20;
    screw.quantity = 0;
    screw.price = .10;

    do
    {
        printf("Input/Output\n------------\n\n");
                /* Prompt for input */
        printf("Bolts: ");
        scanf("%d",&bpiece);

        printf("Screws: ");
        scanf("%d",&spiece);

        bolt.quantity += bpiece;
            /* Calculations */
        bolt.price *= 100. / bolt.quantity;
        screw.quantity += spiece;
        screw.price *= 100. / screw.quantity;

        printf("\nStock\n--------\n\n"); /* Display */
        printf("Bolts : %d items at $%g a
        piece.\n",bolt.quantity,bolt.price);
        printf("Screws: %d items at $%g a
        piece.\n",screw.quantity,screw.price);

        printf("\nDo you want to make another entry?
        (Y/N)");
        scanf("%s",&response);
    }
    while (response != 'n');
}
```

The *struct article* type is defined at the very beginning. It contains two members: *quantity* and *price*, the one being *int*, the other *float*. The two variables *bolt* and *screw* are next defined as variables of this new type.

You could have defined these variables at the same time as the structure by writing:

```
struct article
  {
    int quantity;
    int price;
  } bolt, screw;
```

In the initialization lines that follow, you see how to access the different members. The name of the member is obviously the same with both variables, since it is a part of the type.

In the *do-while* loop you can select article inputs and outputs by typing positive or negative numbers. The quantity in question is updated.

The price is modified as well. If you increase the quantity, the per unit price decreases and vice versa. The "neutral" stock mark is located at 100 pieces. Therefore, in this case the quotient:

```
100./xxxx.quantity
```

is equal to 1 and the multiplication is of no consequence. At the end the display shows the quantity and the stock of each article. Again, it's obvious that you access the different members using:

```
<Name of the variable>.<Name of the member>
```

Σ

Lesson Summary

- Definition of the struct type:

```
struct <Name of the structure>
{
        <TypA> <Member A>, ...;
        <TypB> <Member B>, ...;
        ...
};
```

- Definition of a struct type variable:

```
struct <Name of the structure> <Name of the
variable>, ...;
```

or put the <Name of the variable> directly after the definition of the struct.

> • Access the struct variables:
>
>   <Name of the variable> . <Name of the member>

Exercises:

❶ Design a type of structure whose variables can be used as files in a bibliography giving:

>   the title
>   the editor's name
>   the editor's number (int)
>   the price

Use the author's name as one of these struct variables.

❷ Overlaid structures. Examine the following structure types:

```
struct person              struct family
  {                          {
  char first name[20];       char last name[20];
  int age;                   struct person father, mother;
  };                         struct person son daughter;
                             }
```

What information can be stored in a struct *family* type variable? Given that *fam1* is a variable of this type, how can you access the age of the father?

❸ Write a program that calculates the functions:

>   f (x) =x   (straight line)

and:

>   f (x) =x*x   (parabola)

or *x* going from -10 to +10 by steps of 0.5. Put the results in two struct variables that each have the name of the function and include an array intended for receiving the *f(x)* values calculated.

6.5   Combination of Types and Typedef

So far we have studied some very different types: standard types, arrays, pointers, and structures. It's possible to combine these types. You can also construct types to fit your needs by adapting them to any given problem.

You can even give any name you choose to types you've created.

  LESSON

You can name the types that you have defined by using the keyword: typedef. The syntax is similar to the one you use to define a variable:

a) Standard types:	`typedef <Standard type> <Name of the type>;`
for example	`typedef int BOOLEAN;`
b) Arrays:	`typedef <Stand. type> <Name of the type> [<Nmax>];`
for example	`typedef char STRING[80];`
c) Pointers:	`typedef <Standard type> * <Name of the type>;`
for example	`typedef int *INTPTR;`
d) Structures:	`typedef <Definit. of the structure> <Name of the type>;`

for example	`typedef struct`
	`{`
	`char name[20];`
	`int age;`
	`} PERSON;`

<Name of the type> is the name of the new type. For example, *STRING* is the name of a type that refers to a table of 80 characters.

Note that you can give the name of a variable right after defining a structure.

The user can define, as ordinary standard variables, those having a type that he or she has defined:

```
<Name of the type> <Name of the variable>, ...;
```

for example:

```
STRING last name, first name, street, city;
```

The variables introduced are 80 character strings (including the ending '\0'). Any combination of the 4 categories is possible. Let's study the following definition as an example:

```
typedef struct          /* Definition of the type */
    {
    char day,month;
    int year,
    } *DATE[100];
DATE appointments;      /* Definition of the variable */
```

appointments is an array of structure pointers. Although this definition may seem strange, at least it shows that in this area you can let your imagination run wild.

Experience shows that a large variety of types is needed when you solve complex problems. In practice, it isn't unusual to meet definitions similar to the one mentioned here.

Example:

The following example CHESS.CPP draws a chess board on the screen.

```
/*************************************************************
**      CHESS.CPP                                           **
**          Copyright (c) 1990 Micro Application            **
**          Copyright (c) 1992 Abacus Software, Inc.        **
*************************************************************/

#include <stdio.h>

void main()
{
  typedef int BOOLEAN;                /* Define types */
  typedef BOOLEAN TABLE[8][8];
  int m,n;                            /* Define variables */
  BOOLEAN one = 1;
  TABLE chess_board;
  for (n = 0; n < 8; ++n)
                                /* Calculate the chessboard */
  {
    for (m = 0; m < 8; ++m) chess_board[m][n] = one = !one;
    one = !one;
  }
  for (n = 0; n < 8; ++n)            /* Display */
  {
    for (m = 0; m < 8; ++m)
    {
      if (chess_board[m][n])
        printf("%c%c", 219, 219);
      else
        printf("  ");
    }
    printf("\n");
  }
}
```

The *BOOLEAN* type is defined as the equivalent of the *int* type. This means that all *BOOLEAN* type variables are also *int* variables.

You may think that this definition is superfluous, but it is useful for understanding the rest of the program. The variable *one* is a logical or Boolean variable.

The second *typedef* defines a two dimensional *BOOLEAN* type array. The new type is called *TABLE*. Next you define a variable of this type called *chess_board*.

TABLE is a logical array with a dimension of 8x8. In reality, a chess board has 8x8 squares that can only be black or white, either 0 or 1.

The first loop calculates the distribution of the squares whose state is stored in the *chess_board* variable. The second loop manages the display. The first *printf()* function displays the special IBM ASCII code character 219 twice. This displays a little rectangle the size of a letter.

The next example is called EXCHANGE.CPP and you can use it to convert foreign currencies into US dollars.

```
/***************************************************************
**        EXCHANGE.CPP                                      **
**          Copyright (c) 1990 Micro Application           **
**          Copyright (c) 1992 Abacus Software, Inc.       **
***************************************************************/

#include <stdio.h>

void main()
{
  typedef struct currency     /* Define new type */
  {
     char        code;
     float       exchange;
  } CTABLE[3];

  CTABLE cur;                  /* Define the variables */
  char incur, n, response;
  float amount, amount_dollars;
  for (n = 0; n < 3; ++n) /* Get today's exchange rate. */
  {
     printf("\ncurrency %d: ", n + 1);
     scanf(" %c", &cur[n].code);
     printf("exchange      : ");
     scanf("%g", &cur[n].exchange);
  }
  do                           /* Calculate the conversion */
  {
     printf("\nAmount and currency : "); /* Display */
     scanf(" %g %c", &amount, &incur);
     n = 0;                    /* Look for currency */
     while (n < 3 && cur[n].code != incur) ++n;
     if (n != 3)      /* Conversion */
     {
        amount_dollars = amount * cur[n].exchange;
        printf(" %c %g = F %g\n", incur, amount,
amount_dollars);
     }
```

```
        else
          printf("Unknown currency \n");
        printf("\nContinue? (Y/N) ");   /* End the program? */
        scanf(" %s", &reponse);
      }
    while (response != 'n');
  }
```

CTABLE is defined as a structure array. The *cur* variable belongs to this type. You access the members of the *n* index structure using the following formulas:

```
cur[n].code          for the code of the currency
cur[n].exchange      for the exchange rate of the currency.
```

n indicates which of the three structures are to be used, in other words, the currency in question. The data input loop also shows this kind of access with the *&* operator.

After the input loop, the program does the conversion. It begins by identifying the currency. When its code is recognized, the calculation is executed.

When entering data, only one character should be entered at the "currency x:" prompt to represent the type of currency. The exchange rate should then be entered at the "exchange:" prompt. For example:

```
currency 1: C
exchange : .8
```

Σ

┌───┐
│ **Lesson Summary**   │
│   │
│ •   Types defined by the user may use any name chosen and must │
│   be introduced by typedef.   │
│   │
│ •   It is possible to combine different types.   │
│   │
│ •   Types defined by the user may be overlapped.   │
└───┘

Exercises:

❶   Replace the two *typedef* sequences by two definitions uniquely yours:

```
typedef float ftablo[20];    typedef char String[80];
typedef ftablo *fmatrix;     typedef struct person
                             {
                             String name;
                             String address;
                             int age;
                             } Person;
```

❷   Define a type of variable that manages a telephone directory of 50 correspondents using the following input:

correspondent's name
telephone number
city
zip code (long int)

❸   What is the difference between?

a pointer to an integer array int
and a pointer to an integer int

If you need help, think about pointer arithmetic.

Chapter 7

Functions And Structure Of Programs

Functions

Parameters and Return Values

The main() Function

Initializing Global Variables

Recursion

7.   Functions And Structure Of Programs

7.1   Functions

Until now our programs have been made up of a simple *main()* function. The instructions were inside a unique body between brackets. This form is very simple and really isn't suitable for large programs because it wouldn't be easy to read. It is preferable to divide long and complicated programs into small functions that are easy to manage.

LESSON

A function is a small isolated program which, like a variable, has a name and can be called up. You can pass input parameters to it, which are used to carry out various calculations. The function can return values as results of operations. For example, *printf()* and *scanf()* are predefined functions of C. As with the *main()* function, a function consists of a header and a body.

First let's examine the header which is written as:

```
<Type> <Name of the function> (<List of the parameters>)
```

for example:

```
int sum(int beginning, int end)
```

<List of the parameters> is a list of "formal" variables, each one being preceded by its type and separated by commas. You must indicate the type individually for each variable even if it is repeated. Formal variables let you access parameters transmitted while the function is being called up (these are the "arguments").

<Type> means the type of the value returned. In our example the function would return an int value.

The body of the function may be set up like *main()* using definitions of variables and instructions. Include it between two brackets:

```
{
/* Declaration of the variables */
...
/* Statements */
...
}
```

for example:

```
{
   int n,sum=0;
   for (n=beginning; n<=end; ++n)
   sum=n;
   return(sum);
}
```

The following statement returns the result of the function:

```
return(<return-expression>);
```

Unless the function return type is void, it must contain one return statement.

This statement interrupts the execution of the function. Here is the complete way of writing our example with the definition of the sum function:

```
/**********************************************************
**         SUM2.CPP                                      **
**               Copyright (c) 1990 Micro Application    **
**               Copyright (c) 1992 Abacus Software, Inc. **
**********************************************************/

#include <stdio.h>

/* Definition of the function Sum */
int Sum(int start,int finish)                 /*Header*/
{                                             /*Body*/
 int n, Sum=0;
 for (n=start;n<=finish;++n)
  Sum+=n;
 return(Sum);
}

/* Main Program */
void main()
{
 int value1,value2,total;
 printf("Enter two numbers:");
 scanf(" %d %d",&value1,&value2);
 total=Sum(value1,value2);     /* Call the Sum function */
 printf(" The  Total of all numbers between %d and %d is
%d\n",value1,value2,total);
}
```

The program calculates the sum of all whole numbers included between the first and second parameter. For instance, the numbers 4 and 8 would be used as follows:

```
x=sum(4,8);
```

In this example the function calculates the sum of all numbers in the range from 4 to 8 and the result is assigned to the *x* variable.

If the function shouldn't return the result, you have to introduce a new type called a *void*. This type reserves, as it were, a place reduced to "nothing". *Void* functions do not return any value. You've seen this type in every previous example where *main()* has been a *void* type.

You may also find that the function does not need an input parameter. In this case place an empty parentheses after the name of the function. For example:

```
int sum()
```

Parentheses generally make up the distinctive mark in a function's name. They allow distinguishing a variable name from a function name. Parentheses are acceptable when defining or calling a function.

Here are two other points to remember:

☞　You absolutely must define functions outside of any other function. Functions must also be defined before being called.

☞　The parameters of the function as well as the variables defined in the body of the function only have a local range. This means that they are only available inside the function.

Example

The program ROUND.CPP consists of four functions. It takes any decimal number and calculates:

a)　The number rounded off to the nearest whole number.

b)　The number rounded off to the nearest specified place after the decimal point.

```
/*******************************************************
**        ROUND.CPP                                   **
**              Copyright (c) 1990 Micro Application  **
**              Copyright (c) 1992 Abacus Software, Inc. **
*******************************************************/

#include <stdio.h>

/* Function: Round to a whole number */
int round_whole_number(double number) /* Function Header*/
{   /* Function Body */
```

```
      int orig_number = number;          /* Define variables */
      if (number < orig_number + 0.5)
                                    /* Round to whole number */
          return(orig_number);
      else
          return(orig_number + 1);
  }

  /* Function: Round to a specified decimal position */
  double round_decimal(int position, double number)
  {
      double cnumber, power = 1;        /* Define variables */
      while (position-- != 0) power *= 10;
                              /* Calculate the power of 10 */
      cnumber = number * power;
      cnumber = round_whole_number(cnumber) / power;
                      /* Call round_whole_number function */
      return(cnumber);
  }

  /* Function: Display */
  void display(int enumber, double cnumber)
  {
      printf("Rounded whole number: %d\n", enumber);
                                            /* Display */
      printf("Rounded decimal number: %lg\n", cnumber);
  }

  /* Function: Main() */
  void main()
  {
      double number, nnumber;        /* Define variables */
      int position = 2, orig_number;
      printf("Enter a floating point number: ");
                                    /* Prompt for input */
      scanf("%lg", &number);
      orig_number = round_whole_number(number);
                      /* Call round_whole_number function */
      nnumber = round_decimal(position, number);
                          /* Call round_decimal function */
      display(orig_number, nnumber);
                              /* Call display function */
  }
```

Let's first examine the *round_whole_number()* function. It rounds off a number with a floating decimal to the nearest whole number. When you initialize the whole number, *orig_number*, a type conversion is carried out. This conversion shortens the number, which is eventually adjusted thanks to the comparison which follows. Notice that the *return()* statement occurs twice in the function, although it can only return a single value. Remember: as soon as a *return()* statement appears, execution is interrupted. If the *if* statement is met, then the second *return()* is not reached.

The *round_decimal()* function rounds a number off to a decimal place specified by the *position* variable in *main()*. You can change the value of *position* to specify the number of digits to keep after the decimal point. The operation consists of first multiplying the number by the corresponding power of ten, rounding off the result to the nearest whole number, then dividing the number obtained. Calculating the powers of ten is done in a *while* loop.

Remember that the *round_whole_number()* function is called by the *round_decimal()* function. Generally speaking, you can call functions from any place in the program.

The *display()* function is the *void()* type. This function does not return a value. When you call you cannot make an assignment. Although in *main()* the *round_whole_number()* and *round_decimal()* are assigned to variables, the *display()* function is an instruction by itself.

Here is a comment about variables: certain names appear in several functions. For example, the *cnumber* variable is used as an argument in *display()* and as an internal variable in *round_decimal()*.

Within a function, a variable is local. It has nothing to do with a variable having the same name in another function. Types are also independent. Communication between functions is established only when the function is called with arguments.

Σ

Lesson Summary

- Function definition:

```
<Type <Name of the function (<List of the parameters>)
{
...
/* Body of the function */
...
}
```

- Calling a function:

```
<Name of the function> (<Param1>,<Param2>,...);
```

- Assignment of the returned value and interruption of the function:

```
return(<return-expression>);
```

- Functions which do not return a value should be the *Void* type.
- Variables within a function are only valid within that function.
- A function must be defined outside of any other function.

Exercises:

❶   In the following functions, pick out the headers that are wrong:

```
void printline(int number)
int lis();
char codage(char letter, int code)
double maximum(double x, y, z)
void nothing(void)
int printer(int model)
```

❷   Define a function that calculates the whole powers of a number x:

$$f(x)=x^n \qquad n \text{ positive integer}$$

Then test the function.

❸   Write a program to determine the initial height from which an object is dropped and the length of time it falls given the speed (s) of impact on reaching the ground. Apply the following:

```
t=s/9.81        h=4.905*t*t
```

(*t* in seconds, *h* in feet, *s* in meters/second). Besides *main()*, use the following functions:

a.) calculate *t*

b.) calculate *h*

c.) display the result

Use a constant factor of $32ft/sec^2$ as the velocity at which the object falls.

7.2   Parameters and Return Values

In the last lesson we used only standard types as function parameters or as values returned by functions. Other types may be used. However, arrays can't be passed directly between functions. It's necessary to use pointers. This section will discuss methods for passing parameters and return values.

LESSON

Let's begin by examining the definition and the call of a function whose list of parameters contains a pointer. For example:

```
void divide(int *ptr)
     {
        *ptr/=2;
     }
```

You can call this function like this:

```
int number=18;
divide(&number);
```

The argument of the function is the address of the number variable, that is to say a pointer to *int*. This value corresponds exactly to the type anticipated for the **ptr* variable in the function definition. You can directly access the contents of *ptr* by using the notation **ptr*. The variable in question is divided by two at this point.

Once the function has been executed, *number* possesses a new value, 9. That's the advantage of the pointer; used as an argument, it lets you transform the variable transmitted. Until now, with ordinary variables, this wasn't possible because only the occasional value of the argument was transmitted to the function. In other words, the function had access to the value of the variable but not to its address.

In technical terms, this is how you distinguish the call "by value" from the call "by reference" (reference is used here as a synonym for "address").

In C++, you can pass the parameters by reference without needing to manipulate pointers. Simply put the sign "&" in front of the name of the variable. The divide function becomes:

```
void divide(int &i)
     {
        i/=2;
     }
```

From now on, you can call it like this:

```
int number=18;
divide(number);
```

But with arrays, only references may be passed. We already saw (Section 6.2) that arrays and pointers share certain characteristics. That's why the object obtained as a result of

eliminating the brackets of an array is a pointer. If you call a
function like this:

```
char text[100];
coding(text);
```

the coding argument is a character pointer. You must anticipate
the appropriate definition in the header of the function:

```
void coding(char *word)
```

C would also accept the following definition:

```
void coding(char word[])
```

There is no restriction in passing parameters for a structure. You can
carry out a call by value or a call by reference. But this is as far as
the similarity between arrays and structures goes.

The values returned by the functions are also capable of taking on
nonstandard types. Structures and pointers are allowed, but arrays
are not.

Here is one characteristic of the definition of a function header.
Along with the form that we've already described, you could
define the parameters like this:

```
<Type> <Name of the function> (<NameVar1>,<NameVar2>,...)
    <Type> <NameVar1>,...;
    <Type> <NameVar2>,...;
    {
    ...
    }
```

for example:

```
int rounded(position,number,number)
    int position, number;
    double number;
  {
  ...
  }
```

This syntax has been handed down from the early days of the C
language and it is still in use today.

Example

The program BUBBLES.CPP uses a *sort()* function that lets you sort
the numbers stored in an integer table in ascending order. The
method used is called a "Bubble Sort".

```
/*************************************************************
**        BUBBLES.CPP                                       **
**            Copyright (c) 1990 Micro Application          **
**            Copyright (c) 1992 Abacus Software, Inc.      **
*************************************************************/

#include <stdio.h>

void sort(int *table,int nelem) /* Bubble Sort function */
{
  int m, n, temp;                      /* Define variables */
  while (--nelem > 0)                  /* Comparison loops */
  {
     for (n = 0; n < nelem; ++n)
     {
       if (table[n] > table[n+1]) /* Compare 2 elements */
       {
            temp = table[n];
                        /* If necessary, swap positions */
            table[n] = table[n+1];
            table[n+1] = temp;
       }
     }
  }
}
void main()
{
  int val[100],nelem,n;                /* Define variables */
  printf("Number of elements : ");
  scanf("%d",&nelem);
  printf("\n");
  for (n = 0 ; n < nelem ; ++n)         /* Select values */
  {
     printf("Value %d: ", n+1);
     scanf("%d", &val[n]);
  }
  sort(val,nelem);                      /* Call Sort function */
  printf("\nValues after sorting....\n\n");  /* Display */
  for (n = 0; n < nelem; ++n) printf("Number %d: %d\n", n+1, val[n]);
}
```

The way that this sorting algorithm works is similar to the one found in Section 6.1.3. We are essentially interested in passing parameters. The sort function expects to receive a pointer to the array to be sorted and an indication of the size of the array. Accessing different elements is done using an index, which is justified in the case of one dimensional arrays.

It's important to understand that *table* is a local pointer, but after you call the function:

```
tri (val, nelem);
```

it points to the *val* data in the *main()* function and is identified with this variable. All the modifications carried out on *table* by the *sort()* function also assign the elements of *val*. It follows that *val* is modified and its contents go from being disorganized to sorted.

Before you try the program, remember that when you are asked for the "Number of elements: _" you should answer with a whole number between 0 and 100. The upper limit is 100 because the *val[]* array was given those dimensions.

The second example is the program VECTOR.CPP which calculates the product of two vectors. (The mathematical theory involved is of no importance to us.)

You'll probably recall that a vector is 3 numbers.

```
Vector 1 = (2, 5, 11)
Vector 2 = (3, 8, 10)
```

The vectorial product of the first two is:

```
Vector 3 = (5*10-11*8, 11*3-2*10, 2*8-5*3)
```

Which results in:

```
(-38, 13, 1)
```

```
/***********************************************************
**       VECTOR.CPP                                      **
**                Copyright (c) 1990 Micro Application   **
**                Copyright (c) 1992 Abacus Software, Inc. **
***********************************************************/

#include <stdio.h>

typedef struct
     /* Definition of a global variable for type Vector */
{
  float x, y, z;
} vector;

vector pv(vector a, vector b)
                        /* Calculate the vectorial product */
{
  vector sum;                          /* Define variables */
                             /* Calculate the components */
  sum.x = a.y * b.z - a.z * b.y;
  sum.y = a.z * b.x - a.x * b.z;
  sum.z = a.x * b.y - a.y * b.x;
  return(sum);          /* Return a vector type variable */
}
void main()
{
  vector a, b, c;     /* Define variables */
  printf("Vector A: (x,y,z) = ");    /* Prompt for input */
  scanf(" ( %g , %g , %g )", &a.x, &a.y, &a.z);
  printf("Vector B: (x,y,z) = ");
```

```
scanf(" ( %g , %g , %g )", &b.x, &b.y, &b.z);
c = pv(a, b);      /* Call function */
printf("A x B = (%f,%f,%f)\n", c.x, c.y, c.z);
                              /* Display results */
}
```

First note that the *vect type* is defined by a *typedef* keyword outside of any function. Consequently, the functions in their entirety, without exception, can use this type since it possesses a general reach.

The function *pv()* calculates the vectorial product of two vectors called *a* and *b*. Since these two variables are structures, you can pass them to the function using a "by value" call. The result returned is also a structure. The function itself is a *vect type*.

Then, assign the vectorial product of *a* and *b* to *c* using the simple instruction:

```
c= vp(a,b);
```

When you select vectors to multiply, notice that the syntax for the *scanf()* function is written:

```
"( %g, %g, %g)"
```

Each vector should be a series of 3 components separated by commas, with parentheses around the entire expression. Here, for example, is a vector as it should be entered:

```
(2.4,5,0.5)
```

Σ

Lesson Summary

- The parameters of a function (=arguments) may have any types.
- The values returned may have any type except the array type.
- The "By value" call sends only the value of the argument to the function.
  The "By reference" call sends only the address of the argument to the function.
- Only "by reference" calls are allowed for arrays.
- Alternate syntax for function headers:

```
<Type> <Name of the function> (Var1>,<Var2>,...)
<Type> <Var1>,...;
<Type> <Var2>,...;
```

Exercises:

❶   Explain what the following functions do by examining the arguments used and the returned value:

```
char find(char text[], char letter)
int index(char *text, char letter)
void output(double *value)
struct file lookfor( struct file *list, char *person)
float measure(int channel_input)
```

❷   Devise a function that can locate a specified letter in a given word.

❸   Write a program capable of encoding and decoding a word entered from the keyboard. To encode a letter, use its ASCII value increased by 1. To decode it, do just the opposite. Define an appropriate function for each of the two operations.

7.3   The main() Function

In comparison to the other functions, the only thing that makes *main()* unique is that it is executed first when you start the program. The *main()* function is capable of using parameters which are passed to it. However, these parameters come from outside the program.

LESSON

To execute a program from DOS, you must use the following syntax (which is set up, not by C, but by the operating system being used):

```
<Name of the program> <Parameter1> <Parameter2> ...
```

for example:

```
lookfor Hi letter.txt
```

The *main()* function can take as many parameters as you wish from the DOS command line. Just use a header such as:

```
main(int argc, char *argv[])
  {
  ...
  }
```

The parameter *argc* receives the number of arguments from the command line (including the *<Name of the program>*). *argv* is an array of pointers to character strings. When you call a program, the strings receive the parameters indicated in the command line, which means that in our example:

```
argc=3      argv[0]="lookfor"
            argv[1]="Hi"
            argv[2]="letter.txt"
```

Thus, it is possible to store the command line parameters and use them in the rest of the program. Notice that the names of the *argc* and *argv* variables are universally used but you are under no obligation to do so.

In order to be able to test the parameters passed to *main()*, you must run the program from DOS. Theoretically, you should leave the programming environment (the IDE).

Example

CODE.CPP lets you encode a word entered as a parameter in the command line.

```
/***********************************************************
**        CODE.CPP                                       **
**              Copyright (c) 1990 Micro Application     **
**              Copyright (c) 1992 Abacus Software, Inc. **
***********************************************************/

#include <stdio.h>
#include <stdlib.h>

void exit(int status);

void main(int argc, char *argv[])
{
  int n = 0, status;
  if (argc != 2)    /* Verify the number of parameters. */
  {
    printf("Number of parameters is incorrect");
                                        /* Error Message */
    exit(status - '0');
  }
  while (argv[1][n] != 0)          /* Encoding loop */
  {
    if (argv[1][n] > 96 && argv[1][n] < 123)
      argv[1][n++] = 219 - argv[1][n];
                          /* Encode a letter */
    else
      argv[1][n++] = '\a';  /* Character not permitted */
  }
  printf(argv[1]);                      /* Display results */
}
```

The two parameters *argc* and *argv* are in the header of the *main()* function. If you call up the program from DOS by typing, for example:

```
code trial
```

the variables have as their value:

```
argc=2      argv[0]="code"
            argv[1]="trial"
```

First the program verifies whether the number of arguments is two. If that isn't the case, it displays an error message and the *exit(status-'0')* instruction ends the execution. The parameter of the *exit()* function indicates a state of interruption that DOS in turn exploits. The value zero we've used here is a standard value.

For the time being, you can ignore the new items like *<STDLIB.H>* and *exit()* introduced in this example. They will be explained later in this book.

The *do-while* loop carries out the encoding. Each letter is changed like this:

```
ASCII new = 219 - ASCII old
```

The alphabet is "reflected" as in a mirror: the first letter (a) becomes the last (z), the second (b) becomes the next to the last (y), and so on:

```
a->z  b->y  c ->x  d->w  etc...
```

To avoid any problems with the special characters, the program only uses lowercase letters. You can test this restriction by using an *if* statement. As soon as an unauthorized letter appears, it is replaced by '\a' (i.e., an audible beep).

Let's take another look at the *argv* table. Its first index indicates which of the pointers of the table is affected. But this pointer points in turn to a character table because the second index lets it position itself on a character. In our example, you get:

```
argv[1][2]='y'  because of argv[1]="try"
```

The loop is interrupted when it discovers a string terminator '\0'. In our example it is reached in *argv[1][3]*.

The coding method that we've chosen has a great advantage: after encoding a name, the same program can decode it. After being run twice, the character string is exactly as it was before encoding.

Σ

> ## Lesson Summary
>
> - Arguments of the main() function:
>
>   main(int argc, char argv[])
>   argc= number of DOS arguments
>   argv= table of pointers to DOS arguments (strings
>   of characters)

Exercises:

❶   If a program will be run with the DOS command:

```
prog notbeaut.c pretty.c
```

What indexes do you have to supply to *argv* to get the
letters '*b*', '*p*', '*c*'?

❷   Write a program that finds out how many times a given
letter appears in a word. You should run this program from
DOS using the command:

```
<Name of the program> <Word> <Letter>
```

for example:

```
Findlet computer u
```

7.4   Initializing Global Variables

We have already seen that the variables defined within functions
only have a local range. Consequently, communication between
functions is limited to the parameters that are passed. It is
necessary to have certain variables available during the course of
a program. These variables are made available by an operation
called global definition.

LESSON

Global variables are defined at the very beginning of the program,
outside of any function. The syntax is identical to that of an
ordinary declaration. For example:

```
int nb;
char function()
{ ... }
main()
{ ... }
```

In this example, *nb* is a global variable that can be accessed from *function()* as well as from inside of *main()*.

Types can also be subjected to a global definition. We've already done this in VECTOR.CPP. The syntax is the same as for a local definition.

You can initialize global variables. Unlike ordinary local variables, global variables can receive an initial assignment even if they are tables or structures. The syntax is written as follows:

```
<Type A/S> <Name of the variable> = {<Elem1>, <Elem2>, ...};
```

for example:

```
typedef double VECTOR[3]; VECTOR vector = { 1.5, 2.7, -3.2};
```

<Type A/S> represents an array or structure type. The initial values are in brackets. In our example the vector array is initialized with three floating decimal numbers. It's also possible to initialize a *<Type A/S>* variable with a number of values less than the maximum number of elements. The forgotten elements are automatically set to zero.

The form for initializing structures is the same. However, the initial values should correspond to each of the members, since they will eventually be of different types:

```
typedef struct
{
  int age;
  char first_name, last_name[20];
} PERSON;
PERSON father={25, 'B', "Smith"};
```

When the array or structure possesses several dimensions, the brackets can be overlapped. For example:

```
typedef int MATRIX[2][3];
MATRIX mat = { {2,5,3}, {8,23,14} };
```

The last index refers to the numbers located the farthest to the right inside the brackets.

Example

The program HEX.CPP converts a decimal number into its hexadecimal representation.

```
/*************************************************************
**        HEXA.CPP                                         **
**            Copyright (c) 1990 Micro Application         **
**            Copyright (c) 1992 Abacus Software, Inc.     **
*************************************************************/

#include <stdio.h>

/* Initialization */
char hex_number[16] = {'0','1','2','3','4','5','6','7',
                       '8','9','A','B','C','D','E','F'};
/* Conversion function */
void convert(char *hexstring, unsigned int dec)
{
  int n = 3;                       /* Define variable */
  do                               /* Conversion loop */
  {
     hexstring[n] = hex_number[dec % 16];
     dec /= 16;
  }
  while (n-- > 0);
}
void table()               /* Display the conversion table */
{
  int n;
  for (n = 0; n < 16; ++n) printf("%c Hex = %d Decimal\n",
hex_number[n], n);
  printf("\n\n");
}
void main()
{
  unsigned int decimal;        /* Define variable */
  char *hex = "0000";
  table();                     /* call the function */
  printf("Convert Decimal -> Hexadecimal (End by entering
0)\n\n");
  do
  {
     /* Prompt */
     printf("Decimal number: ");
     scanf("%d", &decimal);
     convert(hex, decimal);        /* Conversion */
     /* Display results */
     printf("Hexadecimal: %s\n\n", hex);
  }
  while (decimal != 0);
}
```

The *table()* function displays a hexadecimal conversion table for the first 16 numbers. The conversion of any number is handled by the *convert()* function.

At the beginning of the program a global variable called *hex_number* is defined. It represents the conversion table: the corresponding hexadecimal number is associated with each index.

You could have also initialized this array as a character string:

```
hex_number[]="0123456789ABCDEF";
```

The result would have been the same. The global *hex_number* variable is accessible from any function. The *convert()* and *table()* functions make the most of this possibility. Since *table()* doesn't need any parameter other than *hex_number*, its parentheses do not contain an argument.

The program's progress appears in the *main()* function. First you display the hexadecimal conversion table. Then a loop lets you convert any number selected on the keyboard. The loop ends when you enter the value 0.

In our second example, DAY.CPP, a global structure array is initialized in the first lines of the program. The object of the program is to calculate the day of the week corresponding to any date.

```
/**************************************************************
 **        DAY.CPP                                          **
 **             Copyright (c) 1990 Micro Application        **
 **             Copyright (c) 1992 Abacus Software, Inc.    **
 **************************************************************/

#include <stdio.h>

typedef struct          /* Define the type */
{
  char *name;
  int days;
} MONTHS[12];
        /* Initializations */
MONTHS ms = {{"January", 31}, {"February", 28},
            {"March", 31}, {"April", 30},   {"May", 31},
            {"June", 30}, {"July", 31}, {"August", 31},
            ("September", 30}, {"October", 31},
            {"November", 30}, {"December", 31}};
char *dweek[] = {"Monday", "Tuesday", "Wednesday",
            "Thursday", "Friday", "Saturday", "Sunday"};
int cday(int day, int month, int an)
/* calculate the day of the week */
{
  int m = 0, sum = day, remainder;  /* Define variables */
  while (m < month - 1) sum += ms[m++].days;
  remainder = an % 4;
  sum += an + 4 + (an - 1) / 4;
  if (remainder == 0 && month > 2) sum++;
  return(sum % 7);    /* return calculated value */
}
void main()
{
  int day, month, an, day_of_week;
  printf("Enter Date: mm/dd/year ");
```

```
        scanf("%d/%d/%d", &month, &day, &an);
        day_of_week = cday(day, month, an);
                                /* Display results */
        printf("%s %d, %d is on %s\n",ms[month - 1].name, day,
    an, dweek[day_of_week]);
    }
```

You first define a new type called *Month* which is a 12 item table. Initializing creates overlapped brackets. The inside brackets let you initialize the individual structures (name of the month and number of days), while the outside brackets surround the table as a whole.

The *dweek* variable contains the names of the days of the week. So *dweek* is a character pointer table which references the strings indicated.

The function *cday()* calculates the day of the week. It returns a number between 0 and 6 which can be used as an index of the *dweek* table. This last "conversion" is carried out inside the *main()* function as a parameter of the *print()* function.

When entering data, the full year must be given. Also, leading zeros should not be entered for a one digit month or day. For example, January 1, 1992 would be entered as 1/1/1992.

Σ

Lesson Summary

- Variables and global types, defined inside any function are accessible from all the functions.

- Initializing tables and structures:

      <Type A/S> <Var> = {<Elem1>, <Elem2>, ...};

- Initializing tables and structures with several dimensions: use overlapped brackets.

Exercises:

❶   Mark the incorrect initializations:

```
int number[8]={12, 14, 25, -13, 2};
char *season[4] = {"spring", "summer", "autumn",
                   "winter"};
        double value[4]={3.2,2,5.3,2.7,35.2};
        int mat[4][2]={2,3},{4,1},{8,4},{2,6};
        float function[2][2]={{0,2.45},{1,3.14}};
```

❷   Why is the following initialization correct even though no
index appears between the square brackets of the tool
variable?

```
char *tool[]={"Hammer","Pliers","Screwdriver"};
```

❸   Write a program which converts numbers between 1 and 100
into words.

7.5   Recursion

It is also possible for a function to call itself. In certain cases it is
necessary to have the value returned by a function passed back to
the same function as input. Such a function is called a recursive
function.

LESSON

As a general rule, it is possible to create a non-recursive equivalent
of the function, a function whose value is explicitly calculated
from parameters. However, this non-recursive version is quite
often more complicated.

Example

Let's consider a sequence of numbers defined as follows:

•   The first two equal 1.
•   Another number in the sequence is obtained by taking the
sum of the two numbers that precede it.

The program SEQUENCE.CPP contains two ways of calculating a
number located anywhere in this series. A non-recursive and a
recursive function are used.

```
/*************************************************************
**      SEQUENCE.CPP                                       **
**           Copyright (c) 1990 Micro Application          **
**           Copyright (c) 1992 Abacus Software, Inc.      **
*************************************************************/

#include <stdio.h>


/* FUNCTION: Calculate non-recursive version */
int non_recurs_seq(int index)
/* index = place of the number to calculate */
{                               /* Body of the function */
    int i,number_1,number_2,number;
    /* Define variables */
    number_1=number_2=1;
```

```
        /* Values of the first terms in the sequence */
           for ( i = 1 ; i <= index-2 ; i++)
                   /* Loop until index */
           {
               number = number_1;
                       /* Save the value of number_1 */
               number_2 = (number_1 = number_2) + number;
                           /* Assign number_2 to number_1
                                     and find the sum. */

           }
           return number_2;            /* Return the final sum */
        }


        /* FUNCTION: Recursive calculation for sequence */
        int recurs_seq(int index)
        {
           if ((index == 1) || (index==2))
                       /* First terms of the sequence */
               return 1;                       /* return 1 */
           else
               return recurs_seq(index-1)+recurs_seq(index-2);
          /* If not, return the sum of the two preceding terms. */
        }

        void main()
        {
           int i;
               printf("Index  Recursive  Non-Recursive\n");
           for (i=1 ; i<=10 ; i++)
                   /* Display the first terms of each sequence */
               printf("  %2d       %2d
        %2d\n",i,recurs_seq(i),non_recurs_seq(i));
        }
```

You can see that the recursive function *recurs_seq* is more compact
and easier to understand. This is because the problem to be solved
was presented in recursive form.

Recursive functions should follow strict rules. If not, they could
very well cause the program to crash.

Example

```
/*****************************************************
**      SEQ_ERR.CPP                                **
**          Copyright (c) 1990 Micro Application   **
**          Copyright (c) 1992 Abacus Software, Inc. **
*****************************************************/

#include <stdio.h>


/* FUNCTION: Calculate non-recursive version */
int non_recurs_seq(int index)
     /* index = place of the number to calculate */
{       /* Body of the function */
```

```
        int i,number_1,number_2,number;
                            /* Define variables */
        umber_1=number_2=1;
        /* Values of the first terms in the sequence */
        for ( i = 1 ; i <= index-2 ; i++)
                            /* Loop until index */
        {
           number = number_1;
                        /* Save the value of number_1 */
           number_2 = (number_1 = number_2) + number;
                        /* Assign number_2 to number_1 and
                           find the sum. */
        }
        return number_2;        /* Return the final sum */
}

/* FUNCTION: Recursive calculation for sequence */
int recurs_seq(int index)
{
  return recurs_seq(index-1)+recurs_seq(index-2);
     /* return the sum of the two preceding terms. */
}

void main()
{
   int i;
       printf("Index  Recursive  Non-Recursive\n");
   for (i=1 ; i<=10 ; i++)
     /* Display the first terms of each sequence */
       printf("  %2d       %2d
%2d\n",i,recurs_seq(i),non_recurs_seq(i));
}
```

 This example loops without stopping. You must interrupt it by pressing Ctrl+Break. Since you didn't define when the loop should be interrupted, the function can never return a final result. To avoid this, in certain cases, the function must furnish a result without calling itself. Most often, a recursive function is presented as follows:

```
<Type> <Name of the function> (<List of the parameters>)
{
      If <Condition>
      return <Value>;    /* Value calculated explicitly */
   else
      return <Value calculated with other parameters>;
      /* Value obtained by making recursive calls */
}
```

Always verify that your recursive functions are equipped with conditions specifying when the search for elements needed to calculate the result should stop.

Σ

Lesson Summary

- Recursive functions are functions which call themselves.
- Recursive functions are often simpler and more understandable than their non-recursive counterparts.
- Every recursive function must contain a condition whose purpose is to interrupt recursive calls.

Exercises:

❶ Write two functions, one recursive and the other non-recursive, calculating the factorial of a positive whole number n (i.e., the product of all the whole numbers included between 1 and *n*).

❷ Write two functions giving the maximum element of a table of integers chosen at random. One of these functions should be recursive.

You should use the C functions *randomize()*, which initializes the random number generator, and *random()* which generates a random number between 0 and its argument. Both of these functions are defined in *<stdlib.h>*.

Chapter 8

Modular Structure

Programs and Modules

Declarations and Header Files

Standard Library Header Files

Range and Duration of a Variable, Storage Classes

Turbo C++ Preprocessor Directives

8. Modular Structure

8.1 Programs and Modules

The C language allows dividing a program into several individually compiled .CPP files which the linker can join together to create an executable program. This can be a real advantage. Once you have created and thoroughly debugged a new function, it's no longer necessary to create it again for every program you write. It's also not necessary to recompile every module of every program constantly.

LESSON

Compiling and linking two or more .CPP files into an executable program takes place in two stages:

a) First, each .CPP file must be compiled into an .OBJ file. This interim step is accomplished automatically by the Turbo C++ IDE.

b) Next, the linker combines all specified .OBJ files to create an executable program (.EXE).

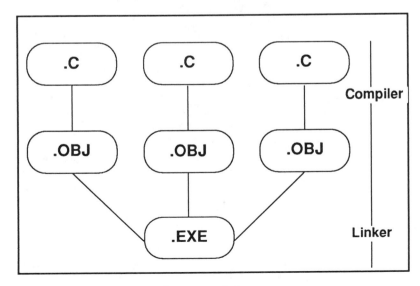

Compiling a modular program

This used to be a very complex and mysterious process, one which many beginning programmers shied away from. The Borland Turbo C++ IDE has greatly simplified the process of creating program modules and linking them to create executable programs.

A program which requires several .CPP files to be compiled and linked when creating executable code is called a "project". The list of project modules is stored in a file with the extension .PRJ.

Of course, the IDE must know which project you want to work on. Activate the *Project* menu by pointing and clicking with your mouse or by pressing the [Alt]+[P] keys. Select the *Open Project* menu item and select the name of the .PRJ file as shown in the following figure.

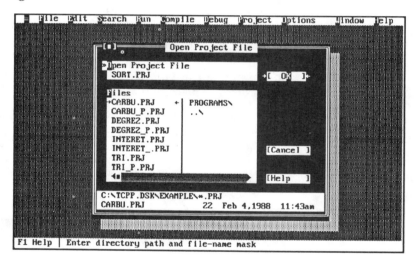

The Open Project File Selector

Selecting the *Close Project* menu item closes the project. Once this menu item has been selected, any compilation is done only to the file in the current active window.

In order to manage the list of files in the project, a special utility program called MAKE is used. MAKE is a utility used by many C programmers. When using the Turbo C++ IDE, you only need to be aware that it exists. The IDE takes care of managing everything.

MAKE is actually rather complicated, even though it simplifies programming in C. Fortunately, it's not necessary for us to go into detail. If you do want to know more about using MAKE, refer to your Borland Turbo C++ Users Guide for information. It's explained in detail in your manual.

Example

Here's a sample of how you can use Projects to simplify your programming efforts in Turbo C++. Let's go back to the BUBBLES.CPP example in Section 7.2 and divide that program into two .CPP files. The first file, SORT.CPP contains the *sort()* function:

```
/*****************************************************************
**      SORT.CPP                                              **
**          Copyright (c) 1990 Micro Application             **
**          Copyright (c) 1992 Abacus Software, Inc.          **
*****************************************************************/

void sort(int *table,int nelem)    /* Bubble Sort function */
{
  int m, n, temp;              /* Define variables */
  while (--nelem > 0)          /* Comparison loops */
  {
      for (n = 0; n < nelem; ++n)
      {
        if (table[n] > table[n+1])
             /* Compare 2 elements */
             /* If necessary, swap positions */
        {
             temp = table[n];
             table[n] = table[n+1];
             table[n+1] = temp;
        }
      }
  }
}
```

MAINSORT.CPP is the main program:

```
/*****************************************************************
**      MAINSORT.CPP                                          **
**          Copyright (c) 1990 Micro Application             **
**          Copyright (c) 1992 Abacus Software, Inc.          **
*****************************************************************/

#include <stdio.h>
/* Bubble Sort function prototype*/
extern sort(int *table,int nelem);


void main()
{
  int val[100],nelem,n;                /* Define variables */
  printf("Number of elements : ");
  scanf("%d",&nelem);
  printf("\n");
  for (n = 0 ; n < nelem ; ++n)        /* Select values */
  {
      printf("Value %d: ", n+1);
```

```
      scanf("%d", &val[n]);
   }
   sort(val,nelem);                     /* Call Sort function */
   printf("\nValues after sorting....\n\n"); /* Display */
   for (n = 0; n < nelem; ++n) printf("Number %d: %d\n",
n+1, val[n]);
   }
```

In order to create an executable program, each of these programs must be compiled to create an .OBJ file, then the .OBJ files must be linked.

The Turbo C++ IDE makes creating a project file easy. Use the mouse or press the [Alt]+[P] [O] keys to select the *Open Project File* selection box. Enter the name of the project to be created (e.g., enter SORT_P.PRJ).

A new window will open. This window is titled *Project: SORT_P*. Press the [Ins] key to open a file selector and choose the files to include in the project list. In this case select SORT.CPP and MAINSORT.CPP. After both files are selected, press [Alt]+[D] or select *Done* with the mouse pointer to close the file selector.

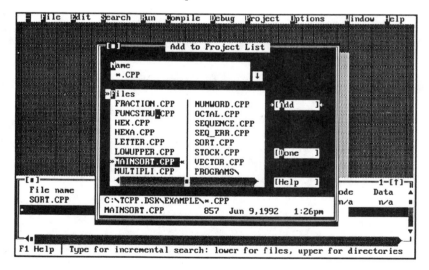

Adding a file to the Project List

The names of the selected .CPP files are displayed in the Project window. Notice the Lines, Code and Data fields all contain the entry *N/A*. This information is not available yet. Open the *Compile* menu and select *Make* from the menu. (You can also choose *Make* by pressing the [F9] key.) Now the information is displayed.

When the IDE compiles and links the selected files, the resulting executable file is not named SORT.EXE or MAINSORT.EXE, but is assigned the name of the project file. In this case, the executable file is named SORT_P.EXE.

To learn more about the Project Window, make it the current active window, and press [F1] to call the Turbo C++ Help system.

Lesson Summary

- Programs can be divided up into several modules.

- To create an executable program from .CPP modules:

First, create a new project file, then add the necessary modules by using the [Alt]+[P] [A] or [Ins] keys to add the necessary items.

➡   **Exercises:**

❶   Why do you execute a program translation in two stages, compilation and link edition?

❷   The standard library of the C compiler is made up of OBJ files which are compiled versions of the standard C language functions. Is there a fundamental difference between functions written by the user and these standard functions?

8.2   Declarations and Header Files

When we divided the program into several modules, we ignored one problem: When the compiler processes a file, how can it know if all the functions used really exist? That is, whether they are available in an .OBJ file or in some other .CPP file? While compiling MAINSORT.CPP, why did the compiler accept the *sort()* function when it didn't even know this name?

Actually, it didn't. You must explicitly tell the compiler about all the functions to use when they are defined before the first call of the module concerned. This is called "prototyping" and is satisfied by the following line:

```
EXTERN sort(int *table, int nelem);
```

   LESSON

A function declaration looks exactly like the header of the function. Its syntax is written like this:

```
<Type> <Name of the function> (<List of the parameters>);
```

for example:

```
int maximum( int *table, int size);
```

The only difference is the semicolon that ends the function declaration.

External function declarations are generally done at the beginning of the module. Their goal is not only to make the existence of the functions known, but to allow the compiler to verify the types of the parameters passed.

You don't have to assign names to the parameters of the declaration. Simply indicating their type is good enough.

```
<Type> <Name of the function> (<List of the parameter types>)
```

for example:

```
int maximum(int *, int);
```

External or global variables defined in other files, also have to be declared (the compiler tolerates no carelessness on this point). The syntax of this declaration is the same as for defining variables, except that you must use the keyword *extern*:

```
extern <type> <Name of the variable>
```

for example:

```
extern char letter, *string;
```

Once you've taken care of this declaration, you can access the variable from any place in the module. The variable is treated as a normal global variable.

When programs consist of several source files, some functions are likely to be called from any module and should be declared everywhere. To avoid continually rewriting the same declarations, make a special file that groups the declarations. This file is named with the filename extension .H. It is included in each module by using the following:

```
#include "<Name of the header file>"
```

for example:

```
#include "HEADER.H"
```

This tells the compiler that when the file is compiled, the contents of the header file should be inserted here. Functions and variables declared in the header file will be accessible by the rest of the module.

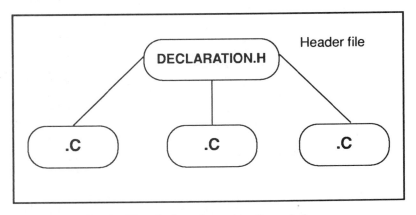

The header file: declarations for the whole program

Example

The program DEGRE2.CPP calculates the solutions of a second degree equation. It is made up of four source files:

DEGRE2.CPP   Main program, calculates solutions.
ROOT.CPP   Function for calculating a square root.
ERR.CPP   Error function with interruption of the program.
ERRMSG.CPP   Definition of a table of strings of characters with error messages.

The project file is called DEGRE2.PRJ.

A header file DEGRE2.H contains the declarations of the *root()* and *error()* functions. The contents of DEGRE2.H are as follows:

```
/* Header file DEGRE2.H */

void error(int errnum);

double root( double number );
```

In the main program the header file is included by an *#include* instruction:

```
/************************************************************
**    DEGRE2.CPP                                          **
**            Copyright (c) 1990 Micro Application        **
**            Copyright (c) 1992 Abacus Software, Inc.    **
************************************************************/

#include <stdio.h>
```

```
#include "c:degre2.h"          /* Include the header file */
void main()
{
  double p, q;              /* Define the variables */
  double a1, a2;
  printf("Solve the second degree equations of this
form:\n\n");
  printf("\tx*x + px + q = 0\n\n");
  printf("Enter values for p, q : ");  /* Prompt*/
  if (scanf("%lg , %lg", &p, &q) != 2 ) error(1);
                            /* Check for valid input */
  a1 = p / 2;                          /* Calculate */
  a2 = a1 * a1 - q;
  a2 = root(a2);           /* Call the square root function */
  printf("\n\nx1 = %g    x2 = %g\n", a1 - a2, a1 + a2);
                                        /* Display */
}
```

Because of this including "degre2.h", both the *root()* and *error()* functions are available to the program. The *error()* function is called when the *scanf()* function returns a value other than 2.

The *root()* function is called in the next to the last line. It is defined in ROOT.CPP:

```
/*************************************************************
**      ROOT.CPP                                            **
**           Copyright (c) 1990 Micro Application           **
**           Copyright (c) 1992 Abacus Software, Inc.       **
*************************************************************/
#include <stdio.h>
#include "c:degre2.h"

double root(double number)          /* Newton's Iteration */
{
  double x, temp;                      /* Define variables */
  if (number < 0) error(0);  /* Is the number positive? */
  if (number == 0) return(0);
                        /* No calculation if equal to zero */
  x = number / 2;       /* Beginning value for iteration */
  do
  {
    temp = x * x - number;
    x = x - temp / 2 / x;
    if (temp < 0) temp = -temp;
  }
  while (temp / number > 1.e-8);
                              /* Condition for interrupt */
  return(x);                         /* Return result */
}
```

The header file also must be included in ROOT.CPP, since this module calls up the error() function. Moreover, this call is done with a parameter other than the one used in DEGRE2.CPP.

To calculate the root, you use an algorithm called Newton's method. The iteration is interrupted as soon as it has reached a sufficient degree of accuracy.

The ERR.CPP file contains an example of an external variable declaration:

```
/*************************************************************
**      ERR.CPP                                            **
**          Copyright (c) 1990 Micro Application           **
**          Copyright (c) 1992 Abacus Software, Inc.       **
*************************************************************/

#include <stdio.h>
#include <stdlib.h>

extern int *errmsg[];     /* Declare external variable */
void error(int errno)     /* Displays an error message */
{                         /* and interrupts the program */
  printf("error: %s\n", errmsg[errno]);
  exit(0);                /* Interruption */
}
```

The external variables are defined in the ERRMSG.CPP file:

```
/*************************************************************
**      ERRMSG.CPP                                         **
**              Copyright (c) 1990 Micro Application       **
**              Copyright (c) 1992 Abacus Software, Inc.   **
*************************************************************/

#include <stdio.h>

char *errmsg[] = {"The Root of a negative number not
possible.", /* Define the variables*/
            "Selection error"};
```

As you can see, it is possible to create CPP files strictly for defining variables. You can efficiently separate programs and data.

To finish the previous example, simply create a project file, DEGRE2.PRJ, to bring this information together. After the project is created, select *Make* and create the executable file.

If you have any problems:

 Check the current directory settings using the *Directories* menu item from the *Options* menu. The settings may have changed when the project was loaded.

☞ When C++ has been installed following the standard procedure, the .H files are searched for in the INCLUDE directory. Put DEGRE2.H in this directory.

☞ Also, all .CPP files in the project generally should be in the same directory. This is true in this case. All of our files are in the \EXAMPLE directory.

Σ

Lesson Summary

- Declaring a function:

      ```
      <Type> <Name of the function> (<List of the parameters>);
      <Type> <Name of the function> (<List of the types of the
      parameters>);
      ```

- Declaration of a variable:

      ```
      extern <Type> <Name of the variable>, ...;
      ```

- A header file contains declarations and includes the filename extension of .H.

- Including a header file:

      #include "Name of the header file" in the current directory.
      #include <Name of the header file> from the INCLUDE directory.

⟹ **Exercises:**

❶ Indicate which of the following declarations are correct for defining the header of a function or an external variable:

```
int minimum(int *,int)
char *find(char *string);
extern int number;
double pi=3.14;
float measure(float x, float y, float z);
unsigned int age (struct person)
```

❷ Is the include directive, #include, an executable instruction? In other words, does it perform operations during the execution of the program? To which part of C does it address itself?

❸ Write a program that lets you do statistics on the grades of a class of 6 students. The program should be made up of two modules:

```
average.cpp    Calculate the class average
class.cpp      Main program, input/output
```

Use a header file CLASS.H.

8.3   Standard Library Header Files

Most of the functions you've used so far are defined in the <STDIO.H> file. These are functions like *printf()*, *scanf()* and *exit()*. Other headers are available, too.

LESSON

The C++ compiler includes some files with the extension .LIB. These files contain, in a compacted form, all the C functions available. We call these "libraries". When the linker is called, it looks in these libraries for the functions used by the application program. These functions are then incorporated into the .EXE file.

All the functions implemented in C language are processed in the same way as the functions defined by the user. Consequently, they must be declared. The procedure is the same as previously presented. You include header files in the source code.

However, remember that a compiled program may consist of several hundred functions. It would take a lot of time and energy to include header files as bulky as those needed to declare so many functions.

That's why we've divided the available functions into several groups. Each group has a specific .H file. These header files are located in the INCLUDE subdirectory of the C++ compiler. When you need to know the header file that corresponds to a specific function, just refer to the User's Guide or examine the .H file. Another simpler option with Borland is to call the on-line Help and look up the function in question. All necessary information will be displayed.

Here are the most important files:

stdlib.h   Contains the declarations of the primary standard functions, for example *exit()*.

math.h   Contains the declarations of the math functions.

string.h   Contains the declarations of the functions that process strings of characters.

stdio.h   Contains the declarations of the main input-output
            functions, in particular *printf()*, *scanf()*.

conio.h   Contains the declarations of the input-output functions
            concerning the keyboard and screen.

You can include these header files in the source code by using a
simplified form of the #include instruction:

```
#include <<Name of the header file>>
```

for example:

```
#include <string.h>
```

Write the name of the file between the less than (<) and greater
than (>) symbols. These symbols tell the compiler that it should
look for the corresponding files in the INCLUDE subdirectory (or
in the directory established by the environment parameter SET
INCLUDE), regardless of the directory of the source module.

Example

The program RAND.CPP generates random numbers included
between 0 and 99.

```
/*********************************************************
**       RAND.CPP                                       **
**           Copyright (c) 1990 Micro Application       **
**           Copyright (c) 1992 Abacus Software, Inc.   **
*********************************************************/

#include <stdio.h>
#include <conio.h>
                  /* Include header file for input/output */

void main()
{
  unsigned int n;                      /* Define a variable */
  printf("To generate a random number, press any
key...\n\n");
  while (!kbhit()) n += 7;    * Increment and wait loop */
  n %= 100;
  printf("The number generated is %d\n", n); /* Display */
}
```

The principle of this program is as follows: The *kbhit()* function
returns a Boolean value: 1 (=TRUE) if you have just pressed a key,
0 (=FALSE) if you haven't. The *while* loop then runs until you
press a key (the operator '!' lets you reverse the value returned by
kbhit()). During this phase the variable *n* increases by 7 with
each execution of the loop. As soon as the loop is interrupted, *n* is

divided by 100 and you assign to it the remainder from the whole division. Since the loop turns an undetermined number of times, *n* finally contains at random a value included between 0 and 99. The program uses the two external functions *printf()* and *kbhit()*. The declarations of these functions appear in the header files *<stdio.h>* and *<conio.h>*.

There is also a built-in randomize function for generating random values:

```
/************************************************************
**      RANDOM.CPP                                        **
**           Copyright (c) 1990 Micro Application         **
**           Copyright (c) 1992 Abacus Software, Inc.     **
************************************************************/

#include <stdlib.h>
#include <stdio.h>
#include <time.h>

void main(void)
{
    int n;                  /* Define a variable */

    randomize();
    printf("Here are 20 random numbers from 0 to 99\n\n");
    for(n=0; n<10; n++)
        printf("%d\n", rand() % 100);
}
```

Here is another example: the program INTEREST is made up from two .CPP files:

```
/************************************************************
**      INTEREST.CPP                                      **
**           Copyright (c) 1990 Micro Application         **
**           Copyright (c) 1992 Abacus Software, Inc.     **
************************************************************/

#include <stdio.h>
#include <stdlib.h>

double time(double, double, double);   /* Declaration */
void main()
{
    double x, x0, z, t;        /* Define variables */
    printf("Length of time for investment plan:\n\n");
    printf("Beginning Investment : ");
    scanf(" %lg", &x0);
    printf("Ending Value : ");
    scanf(" %lg", &x);
    printf("Rate of Interest : ");
    scanf(" %lg", &z);
    t = time(x0, x, z);        /* Call function */
    printf("Length  = %lg years\n", t);
}
```

```
/*************************************************************
**      INTERET1.CPP                                       **
**                  Copyright (c) 1990 Micro Application   **
**                  Copyright (c) 1992 Abacus Software, Inc.**
*************************************************************/
#include <stdio.h>
#include <math.h>         /* Include the Math Lib header */
double time(double start, double finish, double interest)
{
     double q, t;                     /* Define variables */
     q = 1 + interest / 100;
                          /* Calculate the length of time */
     t = log(finish / start) / log(q);
     return(t);
}
```

This program calculates the length of time an investment plan will take to reach a predetermined level based on the starting value and a constant rate of interest. The actual calculation is carried out by a function called *time()* in the INTERET1.CPP file. Since this module calls the *log()* function (natural logarithm), you must include the header file *<math.h>*.

The main program INTEREST.CPP uses the *printf()*, *scanf()* and *time()* functions. The first two functions are declared by including the header file *<stdio.h>*. On the other hand, *time()* is explicitly declared before the start of the *main()* function.

☞   When entering the "rate of interest" a whole number should be entered. For example, if the interest rate is 12%, enter 12.

Σ

Lesson Summary

- Header files (files included) of all the standard functions are in the subdirectory INCLUDE.

- To include a standard header file:

      #include <<Header file>>

- Main header files:

stdlib.h	Standard basic functions
math.h	Math functions
string.h	Manipulating character string functions
stdio.h	Standard inputs-outputs
conio.h	Keyboard-screen inputs-outputs

Exercises:

❶   By consulting the reference documents of your version of C++, locate the header files in which the following functions are declared:

```
strcpy()     sin()       ceil()
atof()       putch()     fprintf()
```

❷   Write a program consisting of a single .CPP file that determines the length of a three-dimensional vector. Hint, here is the mathematical solution:

```
l=sqrt(x*x + y*y + z*z)     (square root)
x,y,z = components of the vector
```

❸   Write a program that allows you to test your reaction speed. To do this, use the *kbhit()* loop from the program RAND.CPP, and assign *n* the unsigned long type. Increment *n* by a single unit for each execution of the loop. Count the number of times the loop is executed before you can react and press a key.

8.4   Range and Duration of a Variable, Storage Classes

We've seen that by placing the EXTERN keyword before a variable we indicate that this variable is defined in another .CPP file. There are still additional keywords to influence the range and the duration of variables. These are storage classes.

LESSON

The storage class of a variable is specified at the time it is defined according to the following syntax:

```
<Storage class> <Type> <Name of the variable>,...;
```

for example:

```
extern char *errmsg[];
```

The storage class is described by one of the following keywords:

```
extern
static
auto
```

These keywords have different meanings depending on whether the variable affected is local or global (i.e., whether it's a question of a variable defined inside or outside of a function).

Global variables can belong only to external or static classes.

a)   A variable is declared *external* if it is defined in another file and if it should be considered as a global variable inside the file in consideration.

b)   The keyword *static* determines the range of the variable in the .CPP file considered. As far as other modules are concerned, the variable is "invisible". None of them can access it.

Local variables can belong to three classes.

a)   *Extern* has the same effect as a *global* variable. You can declare variables defined in another file, but you can only access them for the function in with the declaration.

b)   An *auto* variable is reallocated and reinitialized each time the function with its declaration is called. Its contents are lost between two successive calls of the function.

c)   *Static* variables keep their contents when the execution of the function has ended. If you indicate an initialization, it is only carried out the first time the function is called. This class has an interesting characteristic in that *static* tables can be initialized inside of functions. (This is why we used the *static* class in Section 6.1.)

Example

FUEL.CPP calculates how much fuel a car consumes. It records the "fill-ups" (up to twenty) and draws the corresponding diagram.

Create a project file named FUEL.PRJ and add FUEL.CPP and CONSUM.CPP to create FUEL.EXE.

```
/************************************************************
**      FUEL.CPP                                          **
**              Copyright (c) 1990 Micro Application      **
**              Copyright (c) 1992 Abacus Software, Inc.  **
*************************************************************/

#include <stdio.h>
#include <stdlib.h>    /* Include standard headers */
double consume(long mi, double gal);
void statistic();
void main()
{
  long mi;              /* Define variables*/
  double gal, cons;
  char response;
```

```
                    do
                    {
                       printf("\n\n\nFuel Consumption\n\n");    /* Input*/
                       printf("Miles since last Fill-up : ");
                       scanf("%ld", &mi);
                       printf("Number of gallons of fuel added : ");
                       scanf("%lg", &gal);
                       cons = consume(mi, gal);
                                         /* Calculate Miles per Gallon */
                       printf("\nConsumption = %lg Miles/Gallon\n\n", cons);
                       statistic();              /* Display statistics */
                       printf("\nContinue (Y/N)? ");  /* End or continue? */
                       scanf(" %c", &reponse);
                    }
                    while (response != 'n');
                 }
```

The main program contains calls to two functions called *consume()* and *statistics()*, and which are defined in the CONSUME.CPP module:

```
/**********************************************************
**    CONSUME.CPP                                        **
**            Copyright (c) 1990 Micro Application       **
**            Copyright (c) 1992 Abacus Software, Inc.   **
**********************************************************/

#include <stdio.h>

static double stat[20];        /* Define static variable */
static int Nmax = 0;
double consume(long mi, double gal)
{
   static long anc_mi = 0, n_gal = 0;
   auto long d_mi, d_gal;
   double cons;

   d_mi = mi + anc_mi;
   d_gal = gal + n_gal;         /* Calculate */
   cons = d_mi / d_gal ;
   anc_mi = mi;
   n_gal= gal;
   if (Nmax < 20) stat[Nmax++] = cons;
   return(cons);               /* Return the calculated value */
}

void statistic()
{
   auto int n = 0, index;       /* Define variables */
   char *col =
"**********************************************************";
   while (n<Nmax)                    /* Construct diagram */
   {
       index = stat[n] * 3;
       col[index] = '\0';
       printf("Fill %d : %s\n", ++n, col);
       col[index] = '*';
```

```
      }
    }
```

We've already explained the external storage class in the preceding examples. Here we use static and auto classes.

Let's examine the *consume()* function. Its arguments are: the number of miles since the last fill-up and the number of gallons of fuel added. The variable *anc_mi* is a long type and is initialized at zero at the first call of the function. As soon as the consumption has been calculated, the variable contains the new mileage and keeps this value until the next function call. The number of miles traveled is d_mi=mi - anc_mi.

To underline how the keyword *auto* is used, we set up the storage class *d_km* variables of the *consume()* function and the *n* variables and *index* of the *statistic()* function. In fact, it really isn't necessary to specify this class, since it is automatically assigned by default. Therefore, all variables without indication of class are implicitly *auto* variables. They are redefined and eventually reinitialized at each function call.

The *statistic()* function calls a double type *stat* array with the integer variable *Nmax*. These variables are defined at the very beginning of the file as *global* and *static* variables. Their access is strictly reserved to this file. You cannot use them from the FUEL.CPP file, even if you declared them there as *extern*. A graph can be drawn following the principle presented in Section 6.1 for the PARABOLA.CPP program.

Compile (using a project file) and then run FUEL.EXE. Enter the following values and the program will respond as follows:

```
Fuel consumption
Miles since last fill-up:  300
Number of gallons of fuel added:   12
Consumption = 25 miles/gallon
Fill-up 1: ************* Do you want to continue (Y/N) ? Y
Fuel consumption
Miles since last fill-up:  200
Number of gallons of fuel added:   7
Consumption = 26 miles/gallon
Fill-up 1: *************
Fill-up 2: ******************
```

Σ

Lesson Summary

- Syntax of the assignment of storage classes during the definition of the variables:

    ```
    <Storage class> <Type> <Name of the variable>,        ...;
    ```

- Meaning of the classes in the case of global variables:

extern	Declaration of the external variables.
static	Limited range of a single .CPP file.

- Meaning of the classes in the case of local variables:

extern	Declaration of the external variables.
static	The contents of the variable are kept from one call to another.
auto	The contents of the variable are lost when you leave the function (Class by default).

Exercises:

❶ What is the difference between *extern* class local variables and *global* variables?

❷ It is possible to assign the *static* class to functions. What are the consequences of this allocation?

❸ Define a function that returns the number of times it has been called.

8.5 Turbo C++ Preprocessor Directives

Turbo C++ uses a single pass compiler for its IDE and command line versions. However, it's sometimes useful to understand the terminology from earlier multi-pass compilers. Although Turbo C++ really doesn't use a preprocessor, as was required with earlier primitive forms of C, we will include a brief explanation of this earlier terminology. These directives can also be used in Turbo C++ as the need arises.

The *#include* directive only addresses the compiler. Instructions of this type are sometimes called compiling directives. They let you exercise a certain amount of control over compilation of a file.

LESSON

Here are two other directives often used in C:

```
#define
```

and:

```
#ifdef...#else...#endif
```

The directive *#define* tells the compiler that before any compiling is done, it must replace certain names by strings of characters. The syntax is as follows:

```
#define <Name> <String of characters>
```

for example:

```
#define TRUE 1
```

A directive absolutely must be placed at the beginning of the line. Directives do not end with the usual semicolon.

In our example the name *TRUE* is replaced by the number *1* each time that it appears in the text of the program. Generally, *#define* directives are placed at the beginning of a file since they activate substitutions throughout the file.

For instance, in a function, *<Name>* can contain parameters:

```
#define <Name> (<List of symbols>) <String of characters>
```

for example:

```
#define add(x,y) (x+y)
```

This category of directives is called a "macro". The *<List of symbols>* contains symbols without any indication of their type. When the compiler finds the *<Name>* in the text, it automatically replaces it with the *<String of characters>*. All parameters appearing in the file at the place of the *<List of symbols>* are inserted in the *<String of characters>*. If, according to the directive given beforehand, the compiler discovers the directive:

```
add(p+2,n)
```

it substitutes in its place the expression:

```
(p+2+n)
```

you can also use a *#define* directive without indicating its *<String of characters>*, as in this example:

```
#define ABC
```

This simply means that you have defined *ABC*. You can test the existence of this definition later on by using the *#ifdef* directive whose syntax is written like this:

```
#ifdef <Name>
   ...
   <Program>
...
#endif
```

for example:

```
#ifdef ABC
   printf("ABC defined\n");
   f=F+1;
#endif
```

#ifdef tells the compiler to compile the lines that follow (up to *#endif*) only if *<Name>* is defined. Just like a normal *if* statement, you can combine this directive with an alternative introduced by *#else*:

```
#ifdef <Name>
   <Sequence of program 1>
#else
   <Sequence of program 2>
#endif
```

for example:

```
#ifdef ABC
   printf("ABC defined\n");
#else
   printf("ABC not defined\n");
#endif
```

Σ

➥

Exercises:

❶   *#ifndef* ("if not defined") is another compilation directive. It is used in the same way as *#ifdef*. What is it used for?

❷   The *#define* directive is often used in header files to put certain general definitions at the disposal of the whole program. Create a header file containing the following macros:

Macro	Operation
NEWLINE	Starts a new line
BEEP	Emits a sound signal (by '\a')
STOP	Interrupts the program
PROD(x,y)	Multiplies x by y

Chapter 9

C++ Function Libraries

Access to the Files

Keyboard and Screen Management

Mathematical Functions

Manipulating Strings

Memory Models

9.   C++ Function Libraries

9.1   Access to the Files

To store data, you must have some permanent storage media such as floppy diskettes or a hard disk available. Any language should provide input-output instructions for accessing these storage devices.

LESSON

Basic accessing is always done through the operating system. The user doesn't need to worry about the internal characteristics of the hardware or the physical modes of the recording process. The interface between a C++ program and DOS is a *FILE* type pointer. For example:

```
FILE *fileptr;
```

This type is defined in the standard header file *<stdio.h>*, which is always included in the modules that process the files.

Although the structure of the *FILE* pointer is not very simple, you should have some understanding of it. A file is an object consisting of sequential data arranged as a list. The *FILE* pointer points to this list. When you open a file, the pointer points to the beginning of the file. When you read a character, the pointer moves forward a position, and so on until the end of the file.

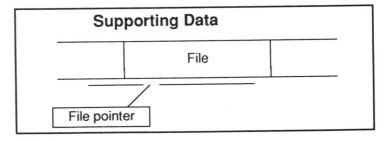

Diagram of a file pointer

Once the pointer has been defined, you must assign to it the address of the *FILE* object. This is done by the *fopen()* function:

```
FILE *fopen(char *<File name>, char *Access>);
```

for example:

```
fileptr=fopen("data.dat","rt");
```

In the following table, *<Access>* represents the method of opening the file by DOS:

<Access>	Method
r	Read only
w	Write (create text)
a	Write at the end of the file
r+	Read and write (pre-existing file)
w+	Read and write (create text)
a+	Read and write (write only at the end of the file)

To these methods, you can add a *t* for the "text" mode and a *b* for the binary mode. The "text" files are series of characters, generally grouped together in lines.

For example, a C++ source file is a text file. A binary file is made up of a series of bytes placed end to end. An executable file is a binary file. Text mode is suitable for ASCII files, but other files must be processed in binary mode.

You might find that calling *fopen()* causes an error. For example, if you try to open a file that doesn't exist. The address returned by the function is equal to zero. This is the "null pointer".

Once the *FILE* pointer has received an acceptable value, you must refer to it when processing each command of the file. Let's examine the most important commands.

```
*int fgetc(FILE *<File pointer>)
```

This line reads the characters of the file one at a time.

```
*int fputc(char <Character>,
FILE *<File pointer>)
```

This sample will write a *<Character>* in the file. In case there's an error, the function returns the value *EOF* (End of File, defined in *<stdio.h>*).

```
*char *fgets(char *<String>, int <LongMax>),
FILE *<File pointer>)
```

Reads a line of text from the file and assigns it to the *<String>* parameter. *<LongMax>* gives the maximum length of the line. If the value returned is a null, you have reached the end of the file.

```
*int fread(void *<Pointer>, int <Size>,
int <Num>, FILE *<File pointer>)
```

Reads a block of data made up of *Num* elements of size *<Size>* (in bytes). The block of data is written at the *<Pointer>* address. In return, you get the number of elements actually read. If there's an error, this value is less than *<Num>*.

 A pointer to null is a pointer to any object.

```
*int fwrite(void *<Pointer>, int <Size>,
int <Num>, FILE *<File pointer>)
```

Writes a block of data of *<Num>* elements of size *<Size>* (in bytes). *<Pointer>* gives the starting address of the data block. The value returned is the number of elements actually written in the file.

```
*int fscanf(FILE *<File pointer>, char *<Format>,
<List of parameters>)
```

Reads the text and the data the way that *scanf()* does, but from a file. The value returned is the number of parameters read correctly.

```
*int fprintf(FILE *<File pointer>, char *<Format>,
<List of parameters>)
```

Writes text and data in the way that *printf()* does, but to a file. The value returned is the number of bytes written correctly.

```
*int feof(FILE *<File pointer>)
```

Indicates whether you have reached the end of the file. If that's the case, a value other than zero is returned. If not, a value of zero is returned.

Finally, every file opened must be closed with the function:

```
int fclose(FILE *<File pointer>)
```

Example

The first example is named CHARCNT.CPP. This program can be called from the DOS command line and counts the number of times a specified character occurs in a file.

```
/*******************************************************
**     CHARCNT.CPP                                    **
**            Copyright (c) 1990 Micro Application    **
**            Copyright (c) 1992 Abacus Software, Inc. **
*******************************************************/

#include <stdio.h>
#include <stdlib.h>

void error(char *message)
/* To interrupt the program in case of an error */
{
  printf("Error: %s\n", message);   /* Error Message */
  exit(0);
}
void main(int argc, char *argv[])
                        /* Arguments from DOS command line */
{
  int cnt = 0;                              /* Define variable */
  FILE *pfich;
  char chara;                              /* Verify arguments */
  if (argc != 3) error("Syntax : CHARCNT <Filename>
<character>");
  chara = argv[2][0];
  if (argv[2][1] != '\0') error("Incorrect Character");
  pfich = fopen(argv[1],"rt");   /* Open the file */
  if (pfich == 0) error("Cannot open file");
  while (!feof(pfich))     /* Search and count loop */
     if (fgetc(pfich) == chara) ++cnt;
  fclose(pfich);                           /* Display the result */
printf("The character %c occurs %d times in the file
%s\n", chara, cnt, argv[1]);
}
```

Run this program by entering:

```
CHARCNT <File> <Character>
```

for example:

```
CHARCNT test.txt x
```

Begin by defining the *pfich* file pointer. Assign the initial address using the *fopen()* function which opens the file. Then pass the parameter *argv[1]* to the *fopen()* function. *argv[1]* contains the name of the file given in the command line.

The file access mode is described by "rt" which means to open the file as read-only in text mode. If the value returned by *fopen* is zero, an error message interrupts the program.

The search procedure itself is executed in the *while* loop. The *fgetc()* function reads the file character by character. How the loop continues depends on the value returned by the *feof()* function.

As long as this value is greater than zero, you haven't yet reached the end of the file.

The following example program, TELDISK.CPP creates a sample telephone directory.

```
/*****************************************************
**     TELDISK.CPP                                 **
**            Copyright (c) 1990 Micro Application  **
**            Copyright (c) 1992 Abacus Software, Inc.  **
*****************************************************/

#include <stdio.h>                /* Include header files */
#include <stdlib.h>

typedef struct                    /* Type definition */
{
  char last_name[20], first_name[20];
  char telephone[20];
} DIRECTORY[30];
DIRECTORY directory;
int Nmax = 0;
void error(char *message)         /* Error routine */
{
  printf("Error : %s\n", message);  /* Error Message */
  exit(0);
}
void save()              /* Save the directory to disk */
{
  FILE *fp = fopen("tel.dat", "wb");
                                     /* Open for writing */
  if (fp == 0) error("Write Error in file 'tel.dat'");
  fwrite(directory, sizeof(DIRECTORY), 1, fp);
                                     /* Writing directory */
  fputc(Nmax, fp);
  fclose(fp);
}
void open()                   /* Open the directory */
{
  FILE *fp = fopen("tel.dat", "rb"); /*Open for reading */
  if (fp == 0) error("Read Error in 'tel.dat'");
  fread(directory, sizeof(DIRECTORY), 1, fp);
                                     /* Read directory */
  Nmax = fgetc(fp);
  fclose(fp);
}
void select()     /* Select a new last name */
{
  printf("\n\nSelect\n\n");
  printf("Last  name : ");
  scanf(" %s", directory[Nmax].last_name);
  printf("First name : ");
  scanf(" %s", directory[Nmax].first_name);
  printf("Telephone  : ");
  scanf(" %s", directory[Nmax].telephone);
  ++Nmax;
}
```

```
void list()           /* Display the file */
{
  int n;
  printf("\n\nList\n\n");
  for (n = 0; n < Nmax; ++n)
  {
    printf("%s, %s  Tel.: %s\n",
    directory[n].last_name, directory[n].first_name,
directory[n].telephone);
  }
  printf("\n");
}
void main()           /* Main Program */
{
  char response;
  do                  /* Function Menu */
  {
    printf("\n\n(1) Save    (2) Load  (3) Enter Data  (4)
List  (X) to Quit\n\n");
    printf("Enter choice:   ");
    scanf(" %c", &reponse);
    switch (response)  /* Execute the selected function */
    {
      case '1' : save(); break;
      case '2' : open(); break;
      case '3' : select(); break;
      case '4' : list(); break;
    }
  }
  while (response != 'x');
}
```

We're especially interested in looking at the *save()* and *load()* functions. The TEL.DAT data file is opened using the "b" (binary) mode, as soon as the *fp* file pointer is initialized. This file is not a text file.

After checking to make sure that all has gone well when the file is opened, the directory structure table is recorded or read in its entirety on the diskette.

The *fwrite()* or *fread()* functions see that these operations are carried out correctly. The first parameter is obviously the table itself.

The second parameter which corresponds to the size of the table in bytes is evaluated by the operator:

```
sizeof(<Type>)
```

The number of elements is 1, since we are only sending a single table. At the end of the file, the *putc()* or *fgetc()* files lets you record or read the data.

Σ

> **Lesson Summary**
>
> - Header file: <STDIO.H>
>
> - A FILE type pointer manages access to the files.
>
> - Methods for opening a file:
>   r w a r+ w+ a+
>
>   Additional parameters:
>   t(ext) or
>   b(inary)
>
> - Commands for accessing files:
>   ```
>   fopen(), fgetc(),  fputc(),  fgets(),  fputs()
>   fread(), fwrite(), fscanf(), fprintf(),
>   feof(),fclose()
>   ```
>
> - sizeof() operator:
>   ```
>   sizeof(<Type>)
>   ```

Exercises:

❶ How do you determine the memory location occupied by the directory table in the TELDISK.CPP program?

❷ Write a program that generates a .CPP file (for example, HELLO1.CPP) identical to the HELLO.CPP in Section 2.3.

If you need help, remember that quotation marks inside a string are represented by \". For example:

```
text = "He said, \"It is chilly this morning\" ";
```

❸ Modify the program TELDISK.CPP in such a way that you don't record all of the directory table but only the elements that have actually been selected.

9.2 Keyboard and Screen Management

So far we have used the *printf()* and *scanf()* functions to control input and output for the keyboard and the screen. Let's examine these important functions more closely.

There are other input/output functions available for more specialized tasks. One example would be for reading an isolated character or for displaying an unformatted string.

LESSON

If you've been entering the various examples into your computer, you should be familiar with the syntax of *printf()* pretty well by now. We are going to look at some other ways for formatting the screen. Here is the complete list of the possible specifications for *printf()*:

Format specification	Type	Representation
%d	int	decimal
%u	unsigned int	decimal
%o	unsigned int	octal
%x	unsigned int	hexadecimal
%f	float	decimal, floating point decimal
%e	float	exponential
%g	float	Like %f or %e
%c	char	ASCII characters
%s	char *	string of characters

You can add the letter "l" to each of these specifications, for example "%ld" or "%lf". The parameter type is changed from *int* to *long*, or from *float* to *double*.

You can use all *int* type specifications with a *char* type parameter, in which case the value of the ASCII code is displayed.

If the representation of a number uses letters (for example, FE in hexadecimal = 254 decimal), either upper or lowercase letters are displayed depending on whether the specification is itself written in upper or lowercase.

Therefore:

    = %x

could display:

    2fe4

while:

    %X

might display:

    2FE4

It is also possible for you to specify the number of positions of the display. You should put the number you want between the % symbol and the letter of the format. For example, use:

```
%6d
```

to display an *int* type parameter occupying 6 positions aligned to the right. Any positions not used are replaced by blank spaces.

With numbers having a floating decimal, you can also set the number of digits after the decimal point. Thus:

```
%8.3f
```

displays a number occupying a total of 8 positions, three of which follow the decimal, and the entire number aligned at the right.

All these specifications are also valid for the *scanf()* function, except for the number of digits after the decimal point. Don't forget to select all the characters appearing in the command string (except for the "blank characters" described in Section 3.2).

There are still several very specialized input/output statements that we need to mention. The following list shows the header files that must be included when declaring them:

*int getch()   <conio.h>

Reads a character typed on the keyboard without displaying it on the screen.

*int getche()   <conio.h>

Reads a character typed on the keyboard and displays it on the screen.

*char *gets(char *<String>)   <stdio.h>

Reads a string typed on the keyboard and places it in the *<String>* variable.

*int kbhit()   <conio.h>

Verifies whether a key has been typed. If so, it returns a number other than zero (logically "true"). If not, it returns 0.

*int putch(int <Character>)   <conio.h>

Displays a character on the screen.

*int puts(char *<String>)   <stdio.h>

Displays a string on the screen, goes to the next line and adds the character '\n'.

Σ

Lesson Summary

- Header files:

      <stdlib.h>
      <stdio.h>

- New format specifications:

      %o   unsigned int   octal
      %x   unsigned int   hexadecimal
      %f   float   decimal, floating decimal point
      %e   float   exponential

- Keyboard and screen management functions:

      getch(), getche(), gets(), kbhit()
      putch(), puts()

Exercises:

❶ Explain how you will display the decimal number 46 if you use the following format specifications:

      %d, %e, %X, %o, %u, %3x, %4u

Do the same for the number 13.52 with the following formats:

      %f, %e, %g, %6.2f, %8.1E, %5.2G

❷ Why is it sometimes more useful to use the *puts()* function instead of *printf()* when you want to display static text? (Think of what happens when this text is extremely large.)

❸ Write a program that displays a table of all the ASCII characters (decimal code greater than 32). The table should give the decimal and hexadecimal code of each character.

9.3   Mathematical Functions

Computers are very good at doing complicated mathematical calculations. Let's take a look at what C++ has to offer to assist with "Number crunching".

LESSON

When a module uses math functions, it is necessary to include the header file *<math.h>*. Not using this header will cause errors, since conversion of parameters is not handled automatically. If you send an *int* type value to a function which expects a *double* type parameter, the compiler does not convert the parameter without *<math.h>*.

The number and the variety of math functions differ from one compiler to another. The following list provides the most important functions which are standard implements in all C compilers.

```
double sin(double <Value>)
double cos(double <Value>)
double tan(double <Value>)
```

Calculate the sine, cosine, and tangent of *<Value>*. The *<Value>* must be expressed in radians.

```
double asin(double <Value>)
double acos(double <Value>)
double atan(double <Value>)
```

Are inverse functions of *sin()*, *cos()* and *tan()*. The result is expressed in radians.

```
double fabs(double <Value>)
```

Returns the absolute value of *<Value>*. You shouldn't confuse this function with *abs()*, which only works for whole arguments.

```
double exp(double <Exp>)
```

Calculates the exponential function e to the x power (e=2.71828...).

```
double log(double <Value>)
```

Is the inverse function of *exp()* and calculates the natural logarithm of *<Value>*.

```
double log10(double <Value>)
```

Returns the decimal logarithm of *<Value>*.

```
double pow(double <Base> , double <Exponent>)
```

Calculates *x* to the *y* power, *x* being the *<Base>* and *y* the *<Exponent>*.

```
double sqrt(double <Value>)
```

Gives the square root of *<Value>*.

Example

The program SCALE.CPP calculates the frequency of the twelve notes of the musical scale.

```
/**************************************************************
**      SCALE.CPP                                           **
**              Copyright (c) 1990 Micro Application        **
**              Copyright (c) 1992 Abacus Software, Inc.    **
**************************************************************/

#include <stdio.h>
#include <math.h>
#include <stdlib.h>
char *scale[] = {"A","A#","B","C",   /* Initialize */
                 "C#","D","D#","E",
                 "F","F#","G","G#",
                 "A"};
void main()
{
  double factor, freq;                /* Define variables */
  int n;
  factor = pow(2., 1. / 12.);
  for (n = 0; n < 13; ++n)
  {
     freq = 440. * pow(factor, n);
     printf("%s\t= %lg Hz\n", scale[n], freq);
  }
}
```

To move from one note to the next, multiply the frequency by a constant factor. This factor is calculated using the *pow()* function. The loop calculates all the frequencies one after the other beginning with A at 440 Hz and executing a multiplication by the factor to the *n* power.

We should point out that the *pow()* function waits for a double type value as its second parameter, while the loop uses *int* variables. If you hadn't done a declaration using the *<math.h>* file included, the compiler wouldn't have known that it should convert the value sent to it. By neglecting to include the header file, you would have a wrong value calculated by the *pow()* function.

The second program called GAUSS.CPP calculates a function called the "Gauss function" and draws its graph.

```
/**************************************************************
**      GAUSS.CPP                                           **
**              Copyright (c) 1990 Micro Application        **
**              Copyright (c) 1992 Abacus Software, Inc.    **
**************************************************************/
```

```
#include <stdio.h>
#include <conio.h>
#include <math.h>
#include <stdlib.h>

void main()
{
  int a, b;                             /* Define variables */
  float x;
  clrscr();
  printf("Gauss Curve");
  for (x = -10; x <= 10; x += 0.5)   /* Calculation Loop */
  {
    a = x * 3.5 + 40.;
    b = 23. - 20. * exp(-x * x / 10.);   /* Exponential */
    gotoxy(a,b);
    printf("*");
  }
  gotoxy(1,24);
}
```

The loop uses the *exp()* function. In fact, the Gauss distribution function that you see represented here is written as: (-x*x/10) f(x) = e.

Σ

Lesson Summary

- The *<math.h>* header file is mandatory for math functions.

- The math functions are:

```
sin(), cos(), tan(), asin(), acos(), atan()
fabs(), exp(), log(), log10(), pow(), sqrt()
```

Exercises:

❶   Explain why the following program doesn't produce the expected result:

```
#include <stdio.h>
main()
{
  double s2;
  s2=sqrt(2);
  printf("Square root of 2 = %lg",s2);
}
```

❷   Write a program that calculates the value acquired from an investment when you know: the starting capital, the interest rate, and the length of time in years.

9.4   Manipulating Strings

 Processing strings of characters is something computers spend a lot of time doing. Since the standard operators in the C language (+,=,==,etc...) are not applied directly to strings but to pointers, it is necessary to introduce a series of special functions which are manipulation functions for strings of characters.

 LESSON

String manipulation function declarations are defined in the *<string.h>* header file.

Remember that functions cannot return tables and that they are incapable of returning strings of characters.

The following kind of call:

```
text0=strcat(text1,"0123456789");
```

assigns a string pointer to the *char* type *text0* variable but it does not make a copy of its contents.

To modify a string or change its contents, you must move it as an argument "by reference" to the appropriate function. In other words, you send it to the pointer which addresses it. Then the function concerned can access the contents of the string and submit it to processing. This principle is valid for all the functions that modify strings in any possible manner.

```
char *strcpy(char *<Destination>, char *<Source>)
```

The preceding line copies the contents of the *<Source>* string into the *<Destination>* string. Be sure to reserve enough space in memory for the *<Destination>* string to store the *<Source>*. A pointer to the *<Destination>* string is also returned.

```
char *strncpy(char *<Destination>, char *<Source>,
int<LongMax>)
```

This line will copy exactly *<LongMax>* characters from *<Source>* into the *<Destination>* string. If the *<Destination>* string is initially longer than the *<Source>*, no null ('\0') is inserted at the end. In other words, the surplus is left "hanging".

```
int strcmp(char *<String1>, char *<String2>)
```

This line compares *<String1>* to *<String2>* according to alphabetical order:

Comparison	Value returned
<String1> > <String2>	>0
<String1> = <String2>	=0
<String1> < <String2>	<0

```
char *strcat(char *<Destination>, char *<Source>)
```

Appends the *<Source>* string to *<Destination>*, that is, it adds the *<Source>* string onto the end of the *<Destination>* string.

```
int strlen(char *<String>)
```

Returns the length of the *<String>*.

```
char *strchr(char *<String>, char <Character>)
```

Provides a pointer at the first occurrence of *<Character>* in the *<String>*.

The functions *sprintf()* and *sscanf()* are also useful for manipulating strings. Their declarations are in the *<stdio.h>* header file.

```
int sprintf(char *<Output string>, char *<Command string>,
<List of parameters>)
```

sprintf() functions exactly like *printf()*, except that the text formatted is placed in *<Output string>* instead of being displayed.

```
int sscanf(char *<Input string>, char *<Command string>)
```

sscanf() is used like *scanf()*, but instead of being typed on the keyboard, the text entered is read in the *<Input string>*.

Example

Here is an interesting subject for readers who like poetry. The program POEM.CPP is capable of writing poems which you should find interesting, although the poems it creates may not rhyme, or even make very much sense.

```
/************************************************************
**      POEM.CPP                                          **
**           Copyright (c) 1990 Micro Application         **
**           Copyright (c) 1992 Abacus Software, Inc.     **
************************************************************/

#include <stdlib.h>     /* Include necessary headers */
#include <string.h>
#include <stdio.h>
#include <conio.h>
```

```
#define ALTMAX 6          /* Define dimensions of tables */
#define STRMAX 60

typedef char STRING[STRMAX];    /* Definition of types */
typedef STRING ALTERNATIVE[ALTMAX];
                                /* Possible phrases */
ALTERNATIVE subject   = {"the old tree", "a satin
butterfly" , "the blazing sun", "a song bird", "the clear
blue sky", "the trembling grass"};
ALTERNATIVE verb = {"shimmers", "sings", "shines",
"whispers", "rocks", "leans"};
ALTERNATIVE prep_phrase   = {"in the morning light", "in
the soft breeze", "between the dew covered twigs", "in the
midst of a field of flowers", "above the crystal lake",
"near the burbling brook"};

/* Combine the expressions */
void combine(char display[80], int n1, int n2, int n3)
{
  char result[80];              /* Define the variables */
  unsigned int order;
  order = rand() % 2;
                   /* String order: subject-verb-phrase */
  if (order)
    strcpy(result, subject[n1]);
                                  /* Copy instruction */
  else
    strcpy(result, prep_phrase[n1]);
  strcat(result, " ");           /* Concatenation */
  strcat(result, verb[n2]);
  strcat(result, " ");
  if (order)
    strcat(result, prep_phrase[n3]);
  else
    strcat(result, subject[n3]);
  strcat(result, ".");
  result[0] -= 32;              /* Make the first letter
                                an upper case character. */
  strcpy(display, result);
                            /* Copy the text into display */
}

void main()
{
  char text[80]; /* Define and initialize the variables */
  unsigned int n1, n2, n3, n = 0, m;
  do
  {
    printf("\n\n\nSummer Dreams\n\n"); /* Title */
    for (n = 0; n < 2; ++n)
    {
      for (m = 0; m < 4; ++m)
      {
        n1 = rand() % ALTMAX;  /* Set the combinations */
        n2 = rand() % ALTMAX;
        n3 = rand() % ALTMAX;
        combine(text, n1, n2, n3);
        printf("%s\n", text);
```

```
                    }
                  printf("\n");
                }
              printf("\n\n\nCreate another poem? (Y/N) ");
          }
        while (getch() != 'n');
    }
```

The principle behind this program is really very simple. First the string tables called *subject*, *verb* and *prep_phrase* are initialized with the standard expressions.

These expressions are then combined using the *rand()* function which, by generating random numbers, lets you assemble any sentence by chance. The *rand()* function is declared in the *<stdlib.h>* header.

The *combine()* function is used for manipulating the strings. The standard expressions are placed end to end in the *result* variable. *strcpy()* copies the first string (its type - subject or prepositional phrase - depends on the *order* variable), and then the two other strings are linked to it by *strcat()*.

It's important to understand that you could not have replaced the *strcpy()* function by the following assignment:

```
result=subject[n2];
```

This type of assignment would result in two errors. First of all, the assignment does not send the string of characters but sends only the pointer to the *subject* string. Next, *result* is not a pointer it's a table.

Therefore, its address cannot be modified by an assignment.

Another example is an application of a Bubble Sort.

```
/****************************************************
**      SORTSTRI.CPP                              **
**             Copyright (c) 1990 Micro Application **
**             Copyright (c) 1992 Abacus Software, Inc.  **
****************************************************

#include <stdio.h>
#include <string.h>


typedef char STRING[20][30];        /* Define type */
void sort(STRING txt, int nelem)    /* Bubble sort strings
*/
{
  int m, n;                         /* Define variables */
  char temp[30];
```

```
        while (--nelem > 0)
          {
            for (n = 0; n < nelem; ++n)
              {
                if (strcmp(txt[n], txt[n+1]) > 0)
                  {
                        strcpy(temp, txt[n]);
                        strcpy(txt[n], txt[n+1]);
                        strcpy(txt[n+1], temp);
                  }
              }
          }
      }

    void main()
    {
      int nelem, n;                         /* Define variables */
      STRING txt;
      printf("Number of strings: ");
      scanf("%d", &nelem);
      printf("\n");
      for (n = 0; n < nelem; ++n)    /* Input loop */
      {
          printf("String #%d: ", n+1);
          scanf("%s", txt[n]);
      }
      sort(txt, nelem);                /* Call sort */
      printf("\nList sorted:\n\n"); /* Display */
      for (n = 0; n < nelem; ++n) printf("String #%d: %s\n",
    n+1, txt[n]);
    }
```

 It is interesting to compare this program with the program BUBBLE.CPP in Section 7.2. The *sort()* function executes the permutation of two strings by using the *strcpy()* function instead of assignments.

You also execute the comparison of the elements to be sorted in a different way:

```
BUBBLE.C        if (tablo[n]>tablo[n+1]) ...
SORTSTRI.C      if (strcmp(txt[n],txt[n+1])>0 ...
```

As a matter of fact, you can't compare two strings like you compare two numbers. If you wrote:

```
if (txt[n]==txt[n+1]) ...
```

you would compare the corresponding pointers.

Σ

> **Lesson Summary**
>
> • Header file for string manipulations: <string.h>
>
> • Strings of characters cannot be processed by the standard operators + = == < > etc.
>
> • String manipulation functions:
>
> ```
> strcpy(),   strncpy(),   strcat(),   strcmp()
> strlen(),   strchr(),    sprintf(),  sscanf()
> ```
>
> • Other functions:
>
> ```
> rand()      Generates random numbers.
> getch()     Reads a character typed on the keyboard.
> ```

Exercises:

❶   What do you risk doing if you send a *<Destination>* string that is too small to contain a copy of the *<Source>* to the *strcpy()* function?

❷   Write a program capable of indicating whether a given string is in a text (or a file).

9.5 Memory Models

When a variable is defined, the compiler reserves space in the memory for it. The biggest disadvantage of this is that it establishes needs in the program's memory before analyzing them.

There are times when it isn't possible to anticipate the need in advance. For example, if you want to read and process files having different sizes.

The appropriate amount of memory can be reserved only when the program is executed.

C helps in these situations by using memory management functions which allow it to be precise in reserving space while the program is being executed.

LESSON

To reserve (or "allocate") space in the memory, use the function:

```
void *malloc(unsigned <Nbyte>)
```

The parameter *<Nbyte>* contains the number of bytes to be allocated. Therefore, to reserve space for an *int* type variable, assign a value of 2 to the parameter.

Of course, you can also use the *sizeof()* function when you don't know the exact size of the type in question.

malloc() supplies a pointer at the beginning of the allocated memory block. If there isn't enough space available, the value returned is the null pointer (a value of 0 is returned).

Once you've assigned this result to a pointer variable the allocated memory can be accessed. For example:

```
int *ptr;
ptr=malloc(2);
*ptr=1234;
```

There is also another function that plays the same role as *malloc()*, but it has different parameters:

```
void *calloc(unsigned <Nelem>, unsigned <Nbyte>)
```

calloc() allocates memory space for *<Nelem>* elements having a size of *<Nbytes>* (in bytes).

The allocations carried out can be checked and canceled when the reserved memory is no longer necessary. This memory can be released by using the *free* function:

```
void free(void *<Pointer>)
```

The *<Pointer>* variable must contain the starting address of the allocated block.

To adapt the size of a memory block to new requirements, use the function:

```
void *realloc(void *<ForPtr>, int <Nbyte>)
```

<ForPtr> represents the pointer previously used for referencing the block. *<Nbyte>* is the number of bytes you want. *realloc()* returns a new pointer. The contents of the former block are not lost in this procedure.

All memory management functions are declared in the header file *<alloc.h>*.

Example

The program ENCODE.CPP allows you to encode files similar to the method used by CODE.CPP in Section 7.3.

```c
/**********************************************************
**      ENCODE.CPP                                      **
**              Copyright (c) 1990 Micro Application    **
**              Copyright (c) 1992 Abacus Software, Inc. **
**********************************************************/

#include <stdio.h>           /* Include necessary headers */
#include <stdlib.h>
#include <io.h>              /* Prototype for filelength() */

void error( char *message )   /* In case of an error... */
{
    printf( "Error: %s\n" , message );
    exit( 0 );
}

void code( unsigned char *txt )       /* Encode the text */
{
    unsigned char    *ptr = txt;   /* Define a pointer */

    while( *ptr != '\0' )                    /* Encode it */
    {
        if ( *ptr > 31 && *ptr < 128 )
            *ptr = 159 - *ptr;
        ++ptr;
    }
}

void main( int argc, char *argv[] )
                    /* Get input from DOS command line */
{
    FILE    *file;                   /* Define variables */
    char    *text,
                    temp;
    int         size;

    /* Verify valid parameters entered */

    if( argc != 2 )
            error( "Proper Syntax :  encode <Filename>" );

    file = fopen( argv[1] , "rb" );
                                /* Open file for reading */
    if( file == 0 )
            error("Cannot open file");

    size = filelength( fileno( file ) );
                                /* Calculate the file size */
    text = (char *) malloc( size );
                                /* Allocate memory for file
                                    and return pointer */
    fread( text , 1 , size , file );
```

```
                                    /* Read the file */

        temp = text[ size - 1 ];
        text[ size - 1 ] = '\0';

        fclose( file );                      /* Close the file */
        code( text );
                /* Call the function to generate the code */

        printf("%s\n", text);

        file = fopen( argv[1] , "wb" );
                                        /* Record encoded text. */
        text[ size - 1 ] = temp;

        fwrite( text , 1 , size , file );
        fclose(file);

        free(text);              /* Release memory allocated */
    }
```

 Run this program from DOS by indicating the file to be processed. Once the file is open, a special instruction determines its size. (For an explanation of the *filelength()* and *fileno()* functions, consult the manual that came with your compiler.)

Next, *malloc()* reserves the necessary memory and assigns the address of the start of the block to the text character pointer. When the file has been read, the *code()* function encodes its contents. *printf()* then displays the resulting text.

Finally, the encoded text is rewritten to the original file and *free()* releases the allocated memory.

Decoding works the same as with CODE.CPP. Just run the program a second time on the encoded file.

Test this program thoroughly before entrusting a valuable file to it.

Σ

Lesson Summary

- Header files for managing memory:

    `<alloc.h>`

- Memory management functions:

    `malloc(), calloc(), free(), realloc()`

Exercises:

❶ What inconveniences do the usual array variables present when you try to store lists of data of different sizes?

❷ Give the appropriate statements (with their parameters) for allocating the necessary memory for the following user defined types.

```
typedef int TABLE[20];
typedef int *INTPTR;
typedef char STRING[30];
typedef struct
{
   int x,y,z;
   char *name;
} VECTOR;
```

❸ Write a program that lets you select a variable number of lines (with a maximum of 80 characters per line) and record them as a text file. Anticipate indicating the number of lines just before you select them.

Chapter 10

Turbo C++: Better Than C

The Concept of Class

Object Oriented Programming

Data Abstraction

10. Turbo C++: Better Than C

10.1 The Concept of Class

C++ is an improvement over the original C language. That's why the ++ increment operator used in C language has been added to the name. You've already been exposed to some of the enhanced features of Turbo C++ in the preceding sections of this book. Other important additions for C++ include Object Oriented Programming and data abstraction.

LESSON

The basis for these two programming techniques is the concept of *Class*. A class is a predefined type in C++. Each class represents a set of objects, operations and conversions available for creating, changing, and destroying the objects. Derived classes can be declared to inherit the members of one or more parent class. When you define a class you are adding a new data type to C++. This new data type is treated exactly the same as built-in data types.

Structures and unions in C++ are considered as classes. A simplified class definition may appear as:

```
class-key class-name<:base-list>{<member-list>}
```

class-key is either class, struct, or union.

Base-list is optional and may be used to list the base classes from which the class *class-name* inherit or derive objects and operations. This base-list has access specifiers that can modify access rights of the derived classes.

Member-list is also optional. It declares the data and function class members with default and optional access specifiers.

Class-name is any unique identifier within the scope. Class names can be omitted.

The class type is very similar to the struct type. The main difference is that the class type can contain functions or operators as well as data.

For example, let's examine CLASSPOS.CPP which represents a screen position class:

```
/***********************************************************
**   CLASSPOS.CPP                                        **
**          Copyright (C) 1990 Micro Application         **
**          Copyright (C) 1992 Abacus Software, Inc.     **
***********************************************************/

#include <stdio.h>

class Screen_pos                    /* Screen Position class */
{
    int ln,col ;                         /* Line and column */
public:
    Screen_pos( int l = 1, int c =1)      /* Constructor */
        { ln = 1 ; col = c ; }
    int line ()                          /* Return the line */
        { return ln ; }
    int column ()                      /* Return the column */
        { return col ; }
    void place(int l , int c)
        { ln = 1 ; col = c ; }
    void deplace( int dl =0, int dc =0)      /* Displace */
        {
        ln += dl;
        col += dc;
        }
};

void main ()
{
    Screen_pos pos;
    int line, column, dis_line, dis_column;
    printf("Enter a screen position : (line,column) = ");
    fflush(stdin);
    scanf("%d,%d",&line,&column);
    pos.place(line,column);
    printf("Enter a displacement : (line,column) =");
    fflush(stdin);
    scanf("%d,%d",&dis_line,&dis_column);
    pos.deplace(dis_line, dis_column);
    printf("Result of displacement : ( %d,%d
)",pos.line(),pos.column());
}
```

The *Screen_pos* class is similar to a structure. First, it is made up of two integers, *ln* and *col*, which represent the line and column for the screen position. But then other functions are added: *line()*, *column()*, *place()*, *displace()* and a special function that has the same name as the class: *Screen_pos()*. These functions are called *member* functions of the *Screen_pos* class. They have access to all the members of this class. More generally speaking, all the elements defined in a class are called members of that class.

Let's examine with the *line()* and *column()* functions which simply return the line and column of a *Screen_pos* type variable. Notice how you can call them by putting the name of a *Screen_pos* type variable and a period in front of them, just as you would to access the members of a structure. *pos.line()* returns the line of the *pos* variable.

The *place()* function lets you modify the values of the line and column numbers. In the same way, the *displace()* function adds the displacement values *dl* and *dc* to the line and column.

Screen_pos(), is a little different. Here, there's a question of a *constructor* of the *Screen_pos* class. Beginning with two integers (*l* and *c*), a *Screen_pos* type variable is created. The *pos* variable is automatically "constructed" when it is declared at the beginning of the *main()* function. The line and column values are default values specified in the header of the constructor, in this case, the values 1 and 1. However, we could have written:

```
Screen_pos pos(20,5)
```

or:

```
Screen_pos pos(18)
```

In the first case, *pos* would have had 20 and 5 as the numbers for the line and column, and in the second case, 18 and 1 (1 being the default value of the constructor).

You recognize a constructor by the fact that it carries the same name as the class of which it's a member. There may be several constructors in a class, in which case you differentiate them by the list and type of their parameters. A constructor is a particular function. It doesn't return a value, not even void, and cannot be called like an ordinary function.

The keyword *public* specifies that all the members that follow it are public and can be used outside the class. This is the case for all the member functions that we have defined. However, we could have written private functions by putting the keyword *private* in front of them.

When the functions or data are private, they are members of a class and can only be used within that class. More precisely, they can only be used by other member functions. This is an important point to remember in C++. Data from a class can be hidden from functions outside of the class.

You can see that this has a great influence on how easily programs can be transferred to other computers, and to the maintenance of these programs.

The *ln* and *col* data from the *Screen_pos* class is private. In fact, by default, the first part of a class declaration is private. That's why the class includes functions returning the line and column. This data is not accessible otherwise.

Finally, notice the default values in the headers of the *place()* and *displace()* member functions. They can be called with one or two parameters, or with none at all.

Σ

Lesson Summary

- Declaration of the class:

```
class <Class name>
{
        <Private data>
public:
        <Interface>
}
```

- Definition of a class constructor:

```
<Class name> (<Parameters>)
```

- Access to a member or calling a class member function:

```
<Class name>.<Member's name>
<Class name>.<Function name>(<Parameters>)
```

➡

Exercises:

❶   What modifications do you have to consider in the *Screen_pos* class in order to be able to eliminate the *line()* and *column()* member functions?

❷   Define a vector class based on VECTOR.CPP, as presented previously. This class should permit calculating the product of two vectors.

10.2 Object Oriented Programming

LESSON

Programs written in C++ usually include several classes. Often different classes have some part in common. Let's go back to the example in the preceding section. In general, any position on the screen is associated with a character that is displayed at that position. A second class can be created consisting of a line number, a column number and a character code.

This second class has the same data as the *Screen_pos* class from CLASSPOS.CPP, but adds a character. Turbo C++ takes this into account by using *inheritance,* one of the foundations for Object

Oriented Programming. Examine the following program,
CLASCHAR.CPP:

```
/***********************************************************
**   CLASCHAR.CPP                                        **
**              Copyright (C) 1990 Micro Application      **
**              Copyright (C) 1992 Abacus Software, Inc.  **
************************************************************/

/* This example requires installing ANSI.SYS from your
CONFIG.SYS file */

#include <stdio.h>              /* Include standard headers */
#define cls()       printf("%c[2J", 27)   /* Clear screen */
#define goto(x,y) printf("%c[%d;%dH", 27, y, x)
                                        /* Move cursor */

class Screen_pos                    /* Screen position class */
{
    int ln,col ;                        /* Line and column */
public:
    Screen_pos( int l = 1, int c =1)     /* Constructor */
       { ln = l ; col = c ; }
    int line()                          /* Return the line */
       { return ln ; }
    int column()                      /* Return the column */
       { return col ; }
    void place( int l , int c)
                               /* Put a space on the screen */
       { ln = l ; col = c ; }
    void move( int dl =0 , int dc =0)         /* Move */
       {
      ln += dl;
      col += dc;
       }
};

class Char_Pos : public Screen_pos
{
    char ch;                      /* Associated character */
public:
    Char_Pos(int l=1,int c=1,char chr=' ')
                        : Screen_pos( l ,c ) /* Constructor */
    {
      ch = chr ;
    }
    void new_char( char chr )    /* Change the character */
    {
      ch = chr ;
    }
    char character                 /* Return the character */
    {
      return ch;
    }
    void display()                       /* Display character */
    {
        goto(column(),line());
```

```
                        printf("%c",ch);
                   }
               void remove()                           /* Erase character */
               {
                  goto(column(),line());
                  printf("%c",' ');
               }
               void move ( int , int );                      /* Move */
          };

          void Char_Pos::move ( int dl , int dc )
                                             /* call Function move() */
          {
                  remove();
                  place( line() + dl , column() + dc );
                  display();
          };

          void main ()
          {
              Char_Pos pos;
              int line, column, new_line, new_column;
              char character;
              cls();
              printf("Enter a screen position : (line,column) = ");
              fflush(stdin);
              scanf("%d,%d",&line,&column);
              printf("Enter a character : ");
              fflush(stdin);
              scanf(" %c",&character);
              pos.place(line,column);         /* Place at position */
              pos.new_char(character);     /* Change the character */
              pos.display();                            /* Display */
              goto(1,3);               /* Move cursor to position */
              printf("Enter the displacement : (line,column) = ");
              fflush(stdin);
              scanf("%d,%d",&new_line,&new_column);
              pos.move(new_line, new_column);           /* Move it */
              goto(1,4);
              printf("Result of the displacement: ( %d,%d)" ,
          pos.line() , pos.column());
          }
```

The *Screen_pos* class has remained unchanged. However, we've
added a new class: *Char_Pos*. This class is derived from the
Screen_pos class. It inherits the features of the original class, and
can add new features of its own. We decided this when we defined
it as:

```
: public Screen_pos
```

By specifying it this way, we are saying that the *Char_Pos* class
inherits all the public members of the *Screen_pos* class. In other
words, the public members of *Screen_pos* are also members of
Char_Pos. However, Private members of *Screen_pos* (*ln* and *col*)

remain inaccessible. This limitation has nothing to do with the fact that Screen_pos was defined as public. *Char_Pos* is a class derived from *Screen_pos*, so the latter is a base class of *Char_Pos*.

The *Char_Pos* class has some supplementary member data (a character) and adds it to *Screen_pos* along with member functions for manipulating this character. We're referring to the functions that let us modify the character, display it at the position specified by *ln* and *col*, and delete it. Notice that these new member functions do not have direct access to the private *ln* and *col* data, but can modify it only through the member functions defined in *Screen_pos*.

The *constructor* of the new class is much more interesting. As a constructor of a derivative class, it calls the constructor of the base class. Remember that a direct call from a constructor isn't possible. That's why this new constructor is declared as it is:

```
: Screen_pos ( l , c )
```

This declaration specifies how to use the base class constructor. This isn't required. If we hadn't mentioned the *Screen_pos* constructor, it would have been implicitly called without any parameter. The default values would have been assigned to the *ln* and *col* data. However, by doing it this way, we guarantee that this data really gets the values that we give it in a *Char_Pos* type variable declaration. For example:

```
Char_Pos pos(2,3,'A');
```

It's also possible to execute multiple inheritances, which means that one class may very well derive from several base classes. All that's necessary is to indicate several class names separated by commas after the public keyword. In this case, the derivative class inherits from all the public members of each base class.

The fact that *Char_Pos* possesses supplementary data causes changes in the *move()* function. It isn't only a question of adding the displacement values to *ln* and *col*. You also have to take the display into account. The *Char_Pos* class redefines this member function. But the writing of the function is now outside the class. Only the header stays inside. It is possible to define a function in a class and write it outside the class. To do this, declare the function as you normally would by only writing the parameter types:

```
void displace ( int , int );
```

Then, take this declaration and write it like the function. You must place the name of the class followed by two colons (:) in front of the name of the function:

```
void Char_Pos::move( int dl , int dc )
                                        /* call Function move() */
{
    remove();
    place( line() + dl , column() + dc );
    display();
};
```

This double character :: shows that the *move()* function belongs to the *Char_Pos* class.

Why do it this way? There are two reasons. First, class definitions rapidly become very difficult to read if all the entries of member functions are included. The definition of a function alone can tell what that function does. You just have to add a comment to it.

Secondly, any member function written inside a class is implicitly considered as inline, which means that the compiler inserts its entry each time it is called. When inline functions are very long, the length of the executable program can increase considerably. When member functions are really long, think about putting their body outside your classes. On the other hand, you could write a member function outside its class and specify it as inline. But this should be done only for short and frequently used functions.

You're probably wondering what's so interesting about programming with classes that inherit from each other. What is the use of Object Oriented Programming?

In some programs, you'll frequently find types of variables that are quite similar. Consider the Turbo C++ programming environment. It consists of windows, pull-down menus, dialog boxes, etc. Isn't there a basic relationship between these elements? Basically all of them are made up of a framework for building a user interface for an application.

Imagine how you would program an interface in traditional C language. You would need a type for each of the elements and you would probably use more or less identical procedures for getting them to appear on the screen, moving them around, and closing them. With Object Oriented Programming, you only need to create a base class and define derivative classes which inherit the characteristics of the base class, while also adding specific elements to the menus, dialog boxes, or windows.

Therefore, you would have to write far fewer functions. This is an area in which Object Oriented Programming is superior to traditional programming. It considers existing relationships between computer objects or between objects in the real world.

Nonetheless, inheritance doesn't work without some problems. You need to know what these problem areas are and how to solve them. Here is an example inspired by what we have seen regarding structures: CLPERERR.CPP.

```
/**********************************************************
**      CLPERERR.CPP                                     **
**           Copyright (c)  1990  Micro Application      **
**           Copyright (c)  1992  Abacus Software, Inc.  **
**                                                       **
**   This example requires ANSI.SYS to be installed on  **
**   your computer.                                      **
**                                                       **
**********************************************************/

#include <string.h>          /* Include standard headers */
#include <stdio.h>
#define cls()      printf("%c[2J", 27)
                             /* Define Clear screen function */
#define goto(x,y) printf("%c[%d;%dH", 27, y, x)
                             /* Define cursor movement function */

class person                              /* Class person */
{
   char nameper[20];               /* Name of the person */
   int ageper;                     /* Age of the person */
public:
   person(char nm[20] = "" , int ag = 0) /* Constructor */
   {
      strcpy(nameper , nm);
      ageper = ag;
   }
   void display()    /* Display last name and first name */
   {
      goto(1,1);
      printf("The person's name is %s, Who is %d years
old.",nameper,ageper);
   }
   void changename(char nm[20] = "")/* Change the name */
   {
      cls();
      strcpy(nameper,nm);
      display();
   }
   char *name()                          /* Return the name */
   {
      return nameper;
   }
   void changeage(int ag)                /* Change the age */
   {
      cls();
      ageper = ag;
      display();
   }
```

```
       int age()
       {
           return ageper;
       }
};

class associate : public person
{
    char firstnameper[20];
public:
    associate( char nm[20]="" , int ag = 0 , char
frstnm[20] ="")
          : person ( nm , ag )
       {
         strcpy(firstnameper , frstnm);
       }
    void display()
                    /* Display last name, age and first name */
       {
          person::display();
          printf(" The first name is : %s",firstnameper);
       }
    void changefirstname( char frstnm[20] )
                                    /* Change the first name */
       {
         cls();
         strcpy(firstnameper, frstnm);
         display();
       }
    char *firstname()                    /* Return first name */
       {
         return firstnameper;
       }
};

void main()
{
    char name[20], firstname[20];
    int age;
    cls();
    printf("What is your friend's first name? ");
                                      /* Get the first name */
    scanf(" %s",&firstname);
    printf("How old is your friend? ");    /* Get the age */
    scanf(" %d",&age);
    {
    associate friend1("",age,firstname);
                                    /* Construct the variable */
    friend1.display();
            /* Display the last name, first name and age */
    goto(1,2);
    printf("What is your friend's last name? ");
                                       /* Get the last name */
    scanf(" %s",&name);
    cls();
    friend1.changename(name);            /* Change the name */
    }
}
```

The base class is called *person*. Its data is made up of the name and age of the person. It contains member functions for modifying and displaying this data. From the *person* class we derive the *associate* class, where we add the first name and the member functions to modify it. We also need a new display function. Notice that this new *display()* function calls the former *display()* function. In order to do this, use the line:

```
<Class name>::<Function name>
```

As when writing a member function outside its class, the double colon :: is used to indicate that the function belongs to the class. Here, *person::display()* means the *display()* function defined in the *person* class should be called.

The main program first asks for the first name and age of one of your friends. At that point, the *friend1* variable is constructed from the values that you have given and an empty name. Next, you are asked for the last name of your friend. The *changename()* function redisplays the class data after it has modified the person's name.

During the second display, only the name and age appear on the screen. The new display of the data requested by the *changename()* function is done, not by the *friend::display()* function, but by the *display()* person function.

The explanation for this apparent phenomenon is really quite simple. Determining which procedure should be called is performed during compilation. When the *changename()* function is compiled, only the *person::display()* function is defined and the compiler doesn't know that there will be a derivative class redefining the *display()* function. It uses *person::display()*. Obviously, this poses a problem. Regardless of the class of the variable whose name precedes the name of the *changename()* function, the *display()* function of the *person* base class is always called instead of that function in the class of the variable.

There are two solutions for this problem. You can probably guess one but the other one may not be so obvious.

The first method is to rewrite the *changename()* function in each derivative class. Then the *display()* function of the derivative class is used. However, you can immediately see the disadvantage. Since the *changename()* function is identical for all derivative classes, you would write the same thing several times. If this function is lengthy the size of the program would increase considerably.

The other solution is much wiser. Since problems arise during compilation, why not do something when the program is executed? You would have to be able to determine which *display()* function to call according to the class of the variable concerned. This is a preferred method with C++. Let's modify the preceding program:

```
/*****************************************************
**      CLASSPER.CPP                                **
**          Copyright (c)  1990  Micro Application  **
**          Copyright (c)  1992  Abacus Software, Inc.  **
**                                                  **
**      This example requires ANSI.SYS to be installed  **
**      on your computer.                           **
**                                                  **
*****************************************************/

#include <string.h>           /* Include standard headers */
#include <stdio.h>
#define cls()      printf("%c[2J", 27)
                             /* Define Clear screen function */
#define goto(x,y) printf("%c[%d;%dH", 27, y, x)
                             /* Define cursor movement function */

class person                              /* Class person */
{
   char nameper[20];                 /* Name of the person */
   int ageper;                       /* Age of the person */
public:
   person(char nm[20] = "" , int ag = 0) /* Constructor */
   {
      strcpy(nameper , nm);
      ageper = ag;
   }
   void display()    /* Display last name and first name */
   {
      goto(1,1);
      printf("The person's name is %s, Who is %d years
old.",nameper,ageper);
   }
   void changename(char nm[20] = "" )
                                       /* Change the name */
   {
      cls();
      strcpy(nameper,nm);
      display();
   }
   char *name()                         /* Return the name */
   {
      return nameper;
   }
   void changeage(int ag)               /* Change the age */
   {
      cls();
      ageper = ag;
      display();
   }
   int age()
```

```
        {
          return ageper;
        }
};

class associate : public person
{
   char firstnameper[20];
public:
   associate( char nm[20]="" , int ag = 0 , char
frstnm[20] ="")
       : person ( nm , ag )
     {
       strcpy(firstnameper , frstnm);
     }
   void display()
                /* Display last name, age and first name */
     {
       person::display();
       printf(" The first name is : %s",firstnameper);
     }
   void changefirstname( char frstnm[20] )
                                   /* Change the first name */
     {
       cls();
       strcpy(firstnameper, frstnm);
       display();
     }
   char *firstname()                /* Return first name */
     {
       return firstnameper;
     }
};

void main()
{
   char name[20], firstname[20];   /* Declare variables */
   int age;
   cls();
   printf("What is your friend's first name? ");
                                   /* Get the first name */
   scanf(" %s",&firstname);
   printf("How old are they? ");        /* Get the age */
   scanf(" %d",&age);
   {
   associate friend1 ("",age,firstname);
                             /* Construct the variable */
   friend1.display();
           /* Display the last name, first name and age */
   goto(1,2);
   printf("What is your friend's last name? ");
                                   /* Get the last name */
   scanf(" %s",&name);
   cls();
   friend1.changename(name);       /* Change the name */
   }
}
```

Our modification isn't easy to find. We simply added the keyword *virtual* before the header of the *display()* function, which becomes virtual, which means that this function should be defined in each derivative class and that every call to this function is determined at the moment of execution.

What really happens when a class contains virtual functions? During the construction of a variable of this class, in other words when the variable is mentioned for the first time in the program, a table containing information about each virtual function is created. When a virtual function is called, this table indicates which version of the function should be used.

Σ

Lesson Summary

- Inheritance between classes:
  ```
  class <Name of the derivative class>
  : public <Name of the base class>,<Name of the base
  class>,...
  {
          <Definition of the class>
  }
  ```

- Constructor of a derived class:
  ```
  <Name of the derivative class> (<List of parameters>)
  : <Constructor of a base class> (<List of
  parameters>)
  : <Constructor of a base class> (<List of
  parameters>)
  : ...
  {
          <Writing the constructor>
  }
  ```

- Every function defined inside a class is automatically inline, so its code is inserted every place that it is called.

- A member belongs to a class:
  ```
  <Class name> :: <Member's name>
  ```

- Declaration of a virtual member function (function dependent on each derivative class):
  ```
  virtual <Function declaration>
  ```

Exercises:

❶   Let's suppose that you could possibly test the class of a variable within a member function called by:

```
<Variable name>.<Member function>
```

It would be a way of avoiding having to resort to using virtual functions.

But what major disadvantage would this present?

10.3 Data Abstraction

In the previous examples, the member data of each class was private. It couldn't be accessed from outside the class. How can it be useful to prevent access to data and force the programmer to use member functions?

One of the main justifications for this method is that C++ was intended to allow programs to be easily ported from one operating system to another. A program written for a specific computer should be easily adaptable to a different computer. The data that we have described in a certain way (by strings, integers, etc.), using such and such a computer, could all be introduced in another way on a different computer. In the simple cases that we've previously seen, there is obviously no confusion possible. But, you could assume that every programmer might feel lead to write things in several different ways according to the performances and capacities of each computer.

If a program never directly accesses the data of a class, it won't need to be modified when you change the organization of the data and adapt the software to another computer. You could be satisfied by simply transforming what is inside each class, in particular, the member functions.

However, it's also possible that the data from a class would have to be carefully checked before being used. If a class uses pointers as member data, you don't want the program to touch them without using the member functions that test the validity of the parameters.

Finally, you can justify using private data by considering how programs are debugged. If a program passes systematically through member functions to reach the data of a class, you only need to verify that these member functions are written correctly to be sure that the program doesn't contain an error regarding the use of that class.

This theory, which recommends that you reach the data of a class only by member functions, is called *data abstraction*. To put it plainly, the data is no longer defined by the way it is set up as variables, but by the operations that you can carry out on it.

Here's an example of data abstraction:

```
/****************************************************************
**   FRACTION.CPP                                             **
**              Copyright (C) 1990 Micro Application          **
**              Copyright (C) 1992 Abacus Software, Inc.      **
****************************************************************/

/* This example requires installing ANSI.SYS from your
CONFIG.SYS file */

#include <stdio.h>                    /* Include standard headers */
#include <stdio.h>
#include <math.h>

#define cls()      printf("%c[2J", 27)   /* Clear screen */
#define goto(x,y) printf("%c[%d;%dH", 27, y, x)
                                         /* Move cursor */

class fraction
{
     int num, den;
public:
     void simplify();                    /* Reduce the fraction */
     fraction(int numerator = 0., int denominator = 1.)
                                         /* Constructor */
     {

       num=numerator;
       den=denominator;
       simplify();
     }
     int numerator()
     {
       return num;
     }
     int denominator()
     {
       return den;
     }
     friend fraction
       operator+( fraction , fraction );
                                    /* Sum of two fractions */
     friend fraction
       operator*( fraction , fraction );
                                  /* Product of two fractions */
};

     void fraction::simplify()    /* Reduce the fraction */
     {
       int r, s, t;
       if (den != 0)
       r=( (abs(num)>=abs(den)) ? abs(den) : abs(num) );
       s=( ((r=abs(den))!=0) ? abs(num) : abs (den) );
       while (r)
       {
         t = s % r;
         s = r;
         r = t;
       }
```

```
                          if ( num*den >= 0 )
                          {
                             num = abs(num) / s;
                             den = abs(den) / s;
                          }
                           }
                  }

            fraction operator+( fraction f1, fraction f2 )
            {
                  fraction f(f1.num * f2.den + f2.num * f1.den,
        f1.den * f2.den);
                  f.simplify();
                  return f;
            }

            fraction operator*( fraction f1, fraction f2)
            {
                  fraction f(f1.num * f2.num , f1.den * f2.den );
                  f.simplify();
                  return f;
            }

     void main ()
     {
            int d1, d2, n1, n2;
            cls();
            printf("Express fraction #1 in the form num / den :
     ");
            scanf(" %d / %d",&n1,&d1);
            printf("Express fraction #2 in the form num / den :
     ");
            scanf(" %d / %d",&n2,&d2);
            {
                  fraction f1(n1,d1), f2(n2,d2);
                  printf("f1 + f2 = %d / %d\n",(f1+f2).numerator(),
                                          (f1+f2).denominator());
                  printf("f1 * f2 = %d / %d\n",(f1*f2).numerator(),
                                          (f1*f2).denominator());

            }
     }
```

 This example introduces a number of new things. First, notice that the fraction class redefines + and * operators. We say that the + and * operators are overloaded. To do this, you just have to declare something like this inside a class:

```
<Name of the type> operator<Operator> ( <List of
parameters>)
```

Then an operator appears as a particular member function. That greatly facilitates writing operations on fractions. In the main program, we can write f1+f2 or f1*f2 exactly as if f1 and f2 were real or integer types. Therefore, it becomes possible to make types as easily usable as the predefined types of the language itself.

The keyword friend precedes the declarations of the overloaded + and * operators. Use this keyword to specify that a function is a friend function of a class. A friend function can access all the members of the class without even being a member function of that class. What's the advantage in using friend functions?

In this example, it is possible for us to combine fractions or integers by using the + or * operator, and Turbo C++ does all the necessary conversions to guarantee a correct result. If we had specified that the + operator was a member of the fraction class, a program like the following would cause an error:

```
main()
{
  int k=2;
  fraction f1(1,2),f; /* f1 = 1/2 ; f =1 */
  f=k + f1;
}
```

In fact, the compiler considers that the + operation is a member of *k* and, since *k* is an integer, it is not a class type and, therefore, has no member.

You see that the way a fraction is represented has little importance. We could have opted to use a real quotient of the numerator and denominator instead of two integers. While this would have facilitated writing the addition and multiplication operations, it would have made calculating the numerator and denominator more difficult. However, the main program, which only uses member functions of the fraction class, would not have been modified in spite of it all. The fraction class, as well as its mathematic analog, is defined by the operations that you can apply to it. You can ignore its real nature.

During an inheritance between classes, we can choose to show, outside of the derived class, that it contains the members of the base class. This is the method that we chose in the previous section when we wrote:

```
class Char_Pos : public Screen_pos { ... }
But if we had put:
class Char_Pos : private Screen_pos { ... }
```

The members of *Char_Pos* inherited from *Screen_pos* would have been private. This is a convenient way to conceal the fact that one class is derived from another.

> **Lesson Summary**
>
> - Operator surcharge in a class:
>
>   ```
>   <Type returned> operator<Operator> (<List of
>   parameters>);
>   ```
>
> - Friend functions of a class:
>
>   ```
>   friend <Function declaration>
>   ```
>
> - Private inheritance:
>
>   ```
>   class <Derivative class> : private <Base class> {...}
>   ```

Exercises:

❶   Modify the preceding main program so that it calculates the sum and the product of a whole number and a fraction.

Chapter 11

Utilities

The Integrated Debugger

Turbo Profiler

11. Utilities

11.1 The Integrated Debugger

Turbo C++ has an integrated debugger. This tool allows rapidly detecting errors when a program is executed. Unlike syntax errors, which are indicated by the compiler and which are generally easy to correct, execution errors often show up only when the program behaves abnormally. Sometimes these errors are hidden so well that they only appear after a long time. You can see how important it is to use a debugger for examining values of a variable in order to see how a program is progressing, etc.

LESSON

The integrated debugger Turbo C++ can do several things. It can display the value of several variables, trace a program, or put break points into a program. The options for these features are located in the *Run* and *Debug* menus of the Turbo C++ IDE.

A debugging session is the stage during which, once the program has been freed from syntactical errors, you can determine the cause of execution errors or abnormal program behavior. The main idea behind this part of program development is to examine the program a little at a time to more precisely zero in on any errors. The integrated debugger lets you move the run bar around in the program. This bar is a highlighted area covering a line indicating the area of the program being executed.

All the ways for moving this run bar are located in the *Run* menu. The first one is the option *Go to Cursor*. By selecting this menu item or by pressing F4, you make the bar move from where it is correctly located to the place where the cursor is located in the source program. If the program has not been executed yet, it is first compiled and linked. The *Trace Into* menu item (accessed also by pressing F7) moves the run bar forward one instruction. The *Step Over* menu item, (F8), is a variation of this. If the bar reaches a function call, it stays within the current function, and does not go into the function called. Use *Step Over* if you are interested in a particular function and don't want to be disturbed or slowed down by calls to other parts of the program.

You can also put stopping points (breakpoints) in your program. A breakpoint is a place where your program absolutely must stop during its execution. You can make it stop at strategic moments so you can view the contents of a variable or ask for the evaluation of an expression. The *Go to Cursor* command is affected by breakpoints. If there is a breakpoint between the run bar and the cursor, the program stops at the breakpoint.

To put a breakpoint on a precise line, put the cursor on this line and select the *Toggle Breakpoint* menu item in the *Debug* menu. You can also press the Ctrl+F8 keys.

Every line containing a breakpoint is marked by a bar in inverse video, or by a red background color. To delete a breakpoint, place the cursor on the line in question and activate the *Toggle Breakpoint* option again.

Turbo C++ uses a Breakpoint dialog box which contains all information about breakpoints that you have already set and contains ways to modify them or add others. This dialog box also permits activating a breakpoint only if a precise condition is met. The condition in question is expressed like any C language condition.

Besides being able to move and stop the run bar, you need a way to verify that the program is really doing what you want it to do. Turbo C++ allows you to examine the contents of certain variables and evaluate expressions as soon as the run bar is placed somewhere.

The *Evaluate/modify* menu item (in the *Debug* menu or the shortcut Ctrl+F4) allows checking the value of an expression. In this way, you can briefly verify that certain variables or expressions are indeed taking the desired values. You can even modify the contents of a variable in order to give it the desired value and verify the rest of the program. On the other hand, you can also determine the behavior of a function if a variable does not take the right value. Move between editable fields by using Tab to move ahead or Shift+Tab to move backwards. When you are in the part called Evaluate, you can press the ⬇ key to view a list of the last expressions that have been calculated.

A more practical way of watching the contents of a variable is to use the Watch window. To verify the value of a variable at each breakpoint of the run bar, add it to the list of variables in this window. Choose the *Add Watch* option in the *Watches* submenu of the *Debug* menu, and specify the name of the variable. If you place the cursor on the name of a variable and press Enter when the *Add Watch* option is selected, this variable is added to the list. You can call the *Add Watch* option quicker by pressing Ctrl+F7. If there is no run bar, or if it hasn't yet reached the place where the variable is declared, or very simply if you haven't declared the variable anywhere, the Watch window displays the message, *undefined symbol*, which means that the variable is not defined. The Watch window is brought up to date each time the run bar stops.

You can remove a variable from the Watch window with the *Delete watch* option in the *Watches* submenu. Activate the Watch window by pressing F6, by clicking on it or by selecting the *Watch* option in the *Window* menu. Move the inverse video bar to the variable that you want to delete and select the *Delete Watch* option.

The integrated debugger also provides a symbolic stack which displays all the functions that have been called from the beginning of the program up to the instruction at which the run bar is pointing. You use this window with the *Call stack* option in the *Debug* menu or by pressing Ctrl+F3. You can only activate it when the run bar is present.

Example:

This program, EXDEBUG.CPP, has a deliberate error.

```
/*****************************************************
**     EXDEBUG.CPP                                **
**           Copyright (c) 1990 Micro Application  **
**           Copyright (c) 1992 Abacus Software, Inc. **
*****************************************************/

#include <stdio.h>

void main()
{
    int i=0;
    while (i<10)
        printf("Hello!");
}
```

If you run this program, your screen is filled with "Hello!". How can you find the mistake easily?

Place the cursor on the line:

```
int i=0;
```

and select the *Go to Cursor* option by pressing F4. If necessary, the file is compiled and linked and the run bar is placed on the line. Continue by selecting *Trace Into* (F7). The run bar will execute the loop several times. Perhaps we should examine the contents of the variable *i*, which is the only variable in this program and is the condition for the *while* loop. Select *Add Watch* (Ctrl+F7), and type the name of this variable, *i*. The "Watch" window now contains a message something like this:

```
i : 0
```

If you execute *Trace Into* several times by pressing F7, the value of *i* is not changed. That's where the error is. We forgot to increment *i* each time the loop is executed.

Σ

Lesson Summary

- Move the run bar:
  to the cursor (Go to Cursor):   F4
  instruction by instruction, by going into the
  functions called (Trace Into):   F7
  instruction by instruction, by jumping over the
  functions called (Step Over):   F8

- Breakpoints:

  Place a breakpoint at or remove it from the current
  line (Toggle Breakpoint):   Ctrl + F8

- Breakpoints dialog box:

  Evaluation of expressions followed by variables:
  evaluation of expressions (Evaluate):   Ctrl + F4
  followed by variables (Add Watch):   Ctrl + F7

- Symbolic stack:
      Ctrl + F3

➡ ## Exercises:

❶   How would you go about finding the error in the *seqrec()* function of the program in Section 7.5?

11.2 Turbo Profiler

The Turbo Profiler, included with Version 2.0 of Turbo Debugger and Turbo Assembler, and with Borland C++ and Applications Frameworks, is a performance analyzer. Its goal is to find which parts of your program are the most ineffective. Then you can improve these sections to make your program faster.

LESSON

Turbo Profiler can suggest several ways to optimize your program. Among the most important ones are: determining the time spent executing a part of the program, calculating the number of times a function is called, calculating the number of open files, and lots of other information.

You can begin analyzing a program by entering:

```
tprof <Name of the program>
```

Example: We're going to analyze the program EXPROFIL.CPP found on your companion diskette.

Run Turbo C++ and compile this program, then return to the DOS command line. Change to the directory which has EXPROFIL.EXE and type:

```
tprof exprofil
```

The environment of Turbo Profiler is similar to that of the Turbo C++ IDE. The source program is displayed in a window. Another window, which is blank for the time being, collects the results of the analysis.

To begin the analysis, open the *Run* menu and select the *Run* option. Our sample program is executed and the numbers from 0 to 99 are displayed in pairs. Then Turbo Profiler takes control and displays:

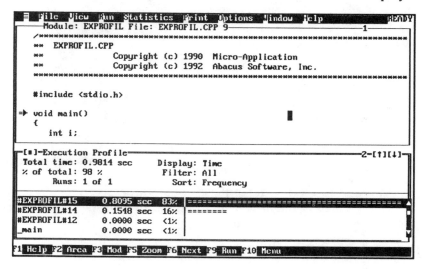

The Turbo Profiler

Line number 15 consumes most of the time. Second place goes to line 14. To view the lines in the analysis window, move the highlighted area with the cursor keys in the list of these lines and press (Enter).

These two lines are:

```
printf(" %g",(float)i);
```

and:

```
printf(" %d",i);
```

Thus, the Turbo Profiler shows you that displaying data on the screen takes the most time. All the other lines require an insignificant amount of time. You can also see that displaying real numbers is much slower than displaying whole numbers.

When a program is loaded into the Turbo Profiler for the first time, all executable lines of the program are displayed. You can only examine the functions of your programs, or only specific lines. Here's how: choose the "module" window by pressing (F3) and then select the local menu for this window by pressing (Alt)+(F10). Two options are of particular interest to us: (Add areas) and (Remove areas).

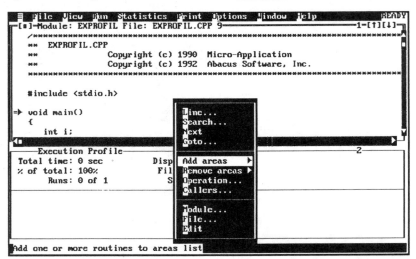

The first of these options allows you to add analysis areas to those that are already present. By selecting it, you can call a submenu as shown in the following figure.

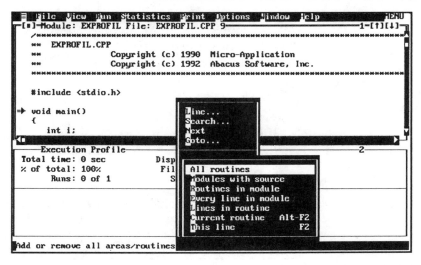

All Routines: All the functions and procedures of the program, including those for which no source is available. This is handy for analyzing the performances of the libraries.

Modules with source:
All the functions having a source.

Routines in module:
All the functions of the part of the program located in the "module" window.

Every line in module:
All the lines.

Lines in routine: All the lines of the function where the cursor is located.

Current routine: The function where the cursor is located.

This line: The line where the cursor is located.

It is also possible to obtain statistics other than the time spent executing areas. You may access these other options in the local menu of the "Execution Profile" window. Activate this window by pressing (F6), then press (Alt)+(F10). Choose the *Display* option. A dialog box is displayed and you can select other analysis options.

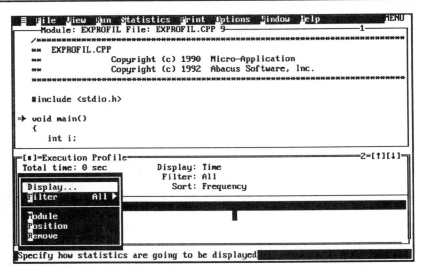

Time: Total time spent in each area. This is the option by
           default.

Counts: Number of passes in each area. Practical for
           determining which function is called most often.

Both: Time and number of passes.

Per Call: Average time spent in each area.

Longest: Longest time spent in an area.

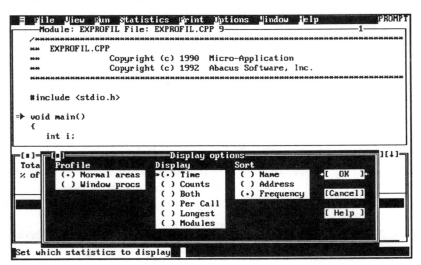

Σ

Lesson Summary

- Analysis session:
  - Copy the executable and source programs in the Turbo Profiler directory
  - Type : tprof <Name of the program>

- Start an analysis: [F10] [R] then Run

- Modify areas: [F3] [Alt]+[F10] then Add area or Remove area

- Modify the statistics type: [F6] [Alt]+[F10] then Display ...

Exercise:

❶ Get statistics on the program SEQUENCE.CPP, which is provided on your companion diskette. Which is the faster of the two functions: recursive or non-recursive?

Appendices

Primary Keywords Of C++

List Of Operators

Hierarchy Of The Operations

Answers For The Exercises

Glossary

ASCII Table

Introduction To Number Systems

The Companion Diskette

Index

Appendices

Appendix A: Primary Keywords Of C++

auto   Allocation class; between two calls of the function the value of the variable is lost. This is the class by default.

break   Instruction to terminate a loop or a switch block case. Used to introduce the different clauses of a switch block.

char   Data type, 1 byte long.

const   Makes a variable value unmodifiable (constant).

continue   Interrupts the execution of a loop by jumping to the test of the loop condition.

default   Introduces the last clause of a switch block.

do   First keyword of a do-while loop.

double   Data type, floating decimal number in double precision.

else   Introduces the alternative of an *if* directive.

enum   Data type with enumeration of the possible values.

extern   Class of memory allocation, used to declare external variables.

float   Data type, floating decimal number in single precision.

for   Introduces a counting loop.

goto   Unconditional jump.

if   Conditional jump statement.

int   Data type, whole number, range of definition depends on the implementation; for Turbo C, Turbo C++: -32768 to +32767.

long	Data type, whole number, -2147483648 to +2147483648.
register	Memory allocation class, asks the compiler to use, if possible, a register to memorize the variable affected.
return	Returns the value of a function.
short	Data type, whole number, -32768 to +32767.
signed	Modifies the data type, the opposite of unsigned.
sizeof	Operator allowing you to evaluate how much memory is needed for a data type.
static	Memory allocation class. For global variables, access reserved to the .C file affected. For local variables, conserves the value between two calls of the function.
struct	Data type for structures.
switch	Introduces a differentiation of several cases.
typedef	Type defined by the user.
union	Data type similar to struct.
unsigned	Modifier restricting a data type to positive values.
void	Data type for functions that do not return any value.
volatile	Modifier of the data type allowing a variable to be modified by external causes (interruptions).
while	Instruction for executing a loop.

Appendix B: List Of Operators

Symbol	Function
()	Parentheses for arithmetic expressions
[]	Square brackets for indexing tables
->	Points to a structure element
.	References a structure element
!	Logical not
~	Inversion bit by bit of a whole operand
++	Increment operator
--	Decrement operator
-	Change sign
(<Type>)	Type conversion
*	Access by pointer
&	Extract the address
sizeof()	Evaluate the memory place
*,/,%	Multiplication, division, remainder from the division
+,-	Addition, subtraction
<<,>>	Shift bit by bit towards the left or the right of an integer
<,>	Comparison: less than or greater than
<=,>=	Comparison: less than or equal to, greater than or equal to
==,!=	Comparison: equal to, not equal to
&,|	Logical AND / OR, bit by bit on an integer
^	Exclusive OR, bit by bit on an integer
&&,||	Logical AND / OR
?:	<Expression> ? <Value if verified> : <Value if false>
=	Assignment
+=,-=,..	Compound assignment operators
,	Separate parameters

Appendix C: Hierarchy Of The Operations

Operator	Priority	Direction of evaluation
() [] -> .	High	---->
! ~ ++ -- (<Type>) sizeof * &	.	<----
* / %	.	---->
+ -	.	---->
<< >>	.	---->
< > <= >=	.	---->
==!=	.	---->
&	.	---->
^	.	---->
|	.	---->
& &	.	---->
||	.	---->
?:	.	<----
= += -= *= /= ...	.	<----
,	Low	---->

Appendix D: Answers For The Exercises

The following section contains suggested solutions to some of the more difficult exercises contained in this book.

3.2.2

```
int address;      %d
char initial;     %c
char letter;      %d
float const;      %g
int age;          %d
```

3.2.3

scanf() command	Select	Type
scanf("%d",&totalfortheday);	3596	int
scanf("%d;%c",&n,&letter);	24;e	int,char
scanf("(%d,%d,%d)",&vect0,&vect1,&vect2);	(2,7,4)	int
scanf("=%g",&expo);	= 2.41	float

3.2.4

Program: LETTER.CPP

```
/**********************************************************
**     LETTER.CPP                                        **
**             Copyright (c) 1990 Micro Application      **
**             Copyright (c) 1992 Abacus Software        **
**********************************************************/
#include <stdio.h>

void main()
{

   char letter1, letter2, letter3;

   printf("Enter three letters:");
   scanf("%c%c%c",&letter1, &letter2, &letter3);
   printf("The corresponding ASCII values of the three
letters are:\n");
   printf("%c--->%d\n%c--->%d\n%c--->%d",letter1, letter1,
letter2, letter2, letter3, letter3);
}
```

3.3.1

```
memory+=1; or ++memory;
move-=nbyte;
word*=8;
coin-=1; or --coin;
A%=B;
part/=nber_persons;
```

3.3.2   Program: AREA.CPP

```
/*********************************************************
**    SURFACE.CPP                                      **
**            Copyright (c) 1990 Micro Application     **
**            Copyright (c) 1992 Abacus Software, Inc. **
*********************************************************/
#include <STDIO.H>

void main()
{
  float radius, area;         /* Define variables */
  printf("Enter the radius of the circle: ");
  scanf("%g", &radius);
  area = radius * radius * 3.14;      /* Calculate area */
  printf("The area of the circle = %g\n", area);
}
```

Program: OCTAL.CPP

3.3.3

```
/*********************************************************
**        OCTAL.CPP                                    **
**            Copyright (c) 1990 Micro Application     **
**            Copyright (c) 1992 Abacus Software, Inc. **
*********************************************************/

#include <stdio.h>

void main()
{
int decimal, octal1,octal2;         /* Define variables */
printf("Enter a decimal number: ");/* Prompt for input */
scanf("%d",&decimal);
octal1=decimal % 8;
octal2 = decimal /8;
printf("The Octal value for the decimal number %d is:
%d%d\n",decimal,octal2,octal1);
}
```

Correct instructions:

4.1.1

```
* if (number<1) ++number;
* if (supply>demand)
      price*=0.95;
  else
      price*=1.07;
* if (frequency==red)
    {
    frequency=green;
    printf("green\n");
    }
```

4.1.2   Program: LOWUPPER.CPP

```
/**********************************************************
**           LOWUPPER.CPP                               **
**                 Copyright (c) 1990 Micro Application  **
**                 Copyright (c) 1992 Abacus Software, Inc. **
**********************************************************/

#include <stdio.h>

void main()

    {
        char letter;                        /* Define Variables */

        printf("Enter a letter: "); /* Get input from user */
        scanf("%c",&letter);

        if (letter >= 65)   /* Is this an uppercase letter? */
        {
                if (letter<= 90) printf("This is an uppercase
                                        character.");

        }
        if (letter >= 97)    /* Is this a lowercase letter? */
        {
                if (letter <= 122) printf("This is a
                                lowercase character.");

        }
        else
        printf("You entered a non-alphabetic character.");

    }
```

          Program: COMPAR3.CPP

4.1.3

```
/**********************************************************
**          COMPAR3.CPP                                 **
**                 Copyright (c) 1990 Micro Application  **
**                 Copyright (c) 1992 Abacus Software, Inc. **
**********************************************************/

#include <stdio.h>

void main()
    {
        int a, b, c, x;                      /* Define variables */

        printf("Enter three whole numbers for a, b and c:");
        scanf("%d,%d,%d",&a, &b, &c);

        if (a > b)                            /* Do first comparison */
        {
                x = a;
                a = b;
                b = x;
        }
        if (b > c)                            /* Second comparison */
        {
```

```
                            x = b;
                            b = c;
                            c = x;
                    }
                    if  (a > b)                    /* Third comparison */
                    {
                            x = a;
                            a = b;
                            b = x;
                    }

            printf("Here are the numbers you entered printed in
    ascending order:\n");
            printf("%d\n%d\n%d\n",a,b,c);
    }
```

4.2.1

Results of running the program:

```
        value  1
        value  2
        value  4
        value  8
        value 16
        value 32
```

The program counts to the first multiple of eight.

```
    Display: 0 1 2 3 4 5 6 7

    while (n==0);          causes an endless cycle (the loop does
                           not end) if n is equal to 0.

    for (x=0; x<1000; ++x);     count to x=1000. The variable x
                                takes the values of 0 to 999
                                (excluding 1000).

    for (money=100; money<10000; money*=1.5)
            printf("Fortune= %g\n",money);     multiply money by
                                               1.5 as long as
                                               money remains
                                               less than 10000.
```

4.2.2

```
    for (number=0;  number<1000; ++number);   number=1000
    for (number=1;  number<1000; number*=2);  number=1024
    for (number=24; number>6;   number/=3);  number=2, if
    number is declared an int
```

4.2.3

Program: SQUARES.CPP

```
/***********************************************************
**      SQUARES.CPP                                       **
**              Copyright (c) 1990 Micro Application       **
**              Copyright (c) 1992 Abacus Software, Inc.   **
***********************************************************/

#include <stdio.h>
```

```
void main()
{
int number;                              /* Define variable */

for (number=1; number *number<500; ++number)
printf("%d squared equals %d\n",number, number*number);
}
```

Program: MULTIPLI.CPP

4.2.4

```
/*************************************************************
**      MULTIPLI.CPP                                       **
**              Copyright (c) 1990 Micro Application       **
**              Copyright (c) 1992 Abacus Software, Inc.   **
*************************************************************/

#include <stdio.h>

void main()
{
    int selection, counter;          /* Define Variables */

    do                               /* Do-While Loop */
    {
            printf("Enter a number: ");
            scanf("%d", &selection);        /* Get input */
            if (selection <0)
                    selection = -selection;
  /* In case of negative value change to positive value. */
    }
    while (selection >10);

    printf("Multiplication Table for %d\n\n",selection);
    for (counter = 1; counter <=10; ++counter)
            printf("%d x %d = %d\n",selection, counter,
selection * counter);
}
```

4.3.1

```
switch (x)
{
case 0:  printf("Error\n");
            break;
default: printf("100/%d=%f\n",x,100./x);
            break;
}
/* Test program for the switch() function*/
void main()
{
    int x;

     printf("Enter a number");
    scanf("%d",&x);
    switch(x)
    {
      case 0 : printf("error \n");
                break;
```

```
        default: printf("100/%d = %f\n",x,100./x);
                break;
    }
}
```

Program: CURRENCY.CPP

4.3.2

```
/***********************************************************
**        CURRENCY.CPP                                    **
**              Copyright (c) 1990 Micro Application      **
**              Copyright (c) 1992 Abacus Software, Inc.  **
***********************************************************/

#include <stdio.h>

void main()
{
char currency;
float amount,exchange;                 /* Define Variables */

printf("Convert:\n1. German Mark\n2. Swiss Franc\n");
printf("3. Japanese Yen\n4. British Pound\n5. Canadian
Dollar\n");
printf("\nEnter the number for type of currency conversion
and\n");
printf("the amount to convert in U.S. Dollars: ");
scanf(" %c %g",&currency, &amount);

switch(currency)
    {
    case '1' : exchange = amount / 1.6035 ;
                                    /* Convert German Mark */
        printf("$%g is equal to %g DM",amount,exchange);
        break;

    case '2' : exchange = amount / 1.47 ;
                                    /* Convert Swiss Franc */
        printf("$%g is equal to %g FF",amount,exchange);
        break;

    case '3' : exchange = amount / 127.35 ;
                                    /* Convert Japanese Yen */
        printf("$%g is equal to %g Yen",amount,exchange);
        break;

    case '4' : exchange = amount / 1.8185 ;
                                    /* Convert British Pound */
        printf("$%g is equal to %g Pounds",amount,exchange);
        break;

    case '5' : exchange = amount / .8328 ;
                                    /* Convert Canadian Dollar */
        printf("$%g is equal to %g Canadian
Dollars",amount,exchange);
        break;

        default: printf("Incorrect entry.\n");
```

```
        }
    }
```

4.3.3
```
    scanf ("%d", &limit);
    for (n=0;n<20;++n)
    {
      if (n>=limit) break;
      printf("Iteration %d\n",n);
    }
```

The loop causes the variable *n* to increase to a specified limit.

If *limit* is assigned a value of 4, the loop displays the following:

```
Iteration 0
Iteration 1
Iteration 2
Iteration 3
```

Program: TABOR.CPP

4.4.1
```
/*********************************************************
**      TABOR.CPP                                       **
**            Copyright (c) 1990 Micro Application      **
**            Copyright (c) 1992 Abacus Software, Inc.  **
*********************************************************/

#include <stdio.h>

void main ()
{
    int a, b, c;                          /* Define Variables */

    printf("    A    |    B     | A  OR B\n");
                                          /* Truth Table */
    printf("---------+---------+-----------\n");
    for (a = 0; a < 2; ++a)
    for (b = 0; b < 2; ++b)
    {
      c = (a || b);                       /* OR Operator */
      if (a) printf("  true   | "); else printf("  false
 | ");
      if (b) printf(" true   | "); else printf(" false  |
");
      if (c) printf(" true \n"); else printf(" false
\n");
    }
}
```

4.4.2
```
a = a && 1;
```
a is an integer. The Boolean value of *a* (equal to or not 0) is combined with a Boolean AND at 1 (true):

Input value	Output value	Explanation
0	0	0 AND 1 are 0
1	1	1 AND 1 are 1
any other	1	any other AND 1 are 1

You can say that a remains "logically" unchanged. Warning! Don't confuse this with the operator && which is a Boolean operator and results in 0 or 1.

The operator & is a binary logical operator executing a true operation bit by bit.

> a = a && (x != y);
> If x is equal to y, (x != y) returns the value "false" which means that a equals 0.
> If x is different from y, (x != y) returns "true" and the value of a remains "logically" unchanged:
> a = 0 gives a = 0
> a other than 0 results in a = 1

4.4.3   The loop turns endlessly since it has no interruption test.

5.1.1   All the results are of type int:

```
3.5*6=21      (int)85.35*2=170
243*-83=-20169    'w'-2024=-1905
(int)(20.35*24)=488  23/9=2
```

5.1.2
```
var=12+'g'; char          var+=2.5; float
var=(1<3); char           var=255+1; int
var=13-274.3; float       var=2/7.; float
```

5.2.1
```
3*(4+2)=18 1&&0||1=1
3*(4>4)+2.5=2.5           3+(n>n-1)=4
(4==5.1)/2+1=1            !1&&0||!0=1
```

5.2.2
```
x=2;                      x=2
x=3+(3>x);                x=4
x+=x-=2;                  x=4
x=(++x-6)*3;              x=-3
x*=(5>x)*(3+23);          x=-78
```

5.2.3
```
a=x*w+3;                  m=k>(b||1);
f*=15-(3+f);              h=n+=12;
g=(g++ +g)*3;             b*=20+3;
```

6.1.1
```
Wrong definitions                    Corrections
unsigned int matrix[3,3];    unsigned int matrix[3][3];
char computer[]='IBM PC';    char computer[]="IBM PC";
char name[8]="Isabelle";     char name[9]="Isabelle";
                             or char name[]="Isabelle";
```

6.1.2
```
char month[12][10]
```

6.1.3
```
int matrix[2][3]={{2,0,3},
                  {4,2,8}
                 };
```

6.1.4
```
/************************************************************
**      BUBBLES.CPP                                      **
**            Copyright (c) 1990 Micro Application        **
**            Copyright (c) 1992 Abacus Software, Inc.    **
************************************************************/

#include <stdio.h>

void sort(int *table,int nelem) /* Bubble Sort function */
{
  int m, n, temp;                      /* Define variables */
  while (--nelem > 0)                  /* Comparison loops */
  {
     for (n = 0; n < nelem; ++n)
     {
        if (table[n] > table[n+1]) /* Compare 2 elements */
        {
            temp = table[n];
                        /* If necessary, swap positions */
                              table[n] = table[n+1];
            table[n+1] = temp;
        }
     }
  }
}
void main()
{
  int val[100],nelem,n;               /* Define variables */
  printf("Number of elements : ");
  scanf("%d",&nelem);
  printf("\n");
  for (n = 0 ; n < nelem ; ++n)           /* Select values */
  {
     printf("Value %d: ", n+1);
     scanf("%d", &val[n]);
  }
  sort(val,nelem);                    /* Call Sort function */
  printf("\nValues after sorting....\n\n");  /* Display */
  for (n = 0; n < nelem; ++n)
     printf("Number %d: %d\n", n+1, val[n]);
}
```

6.2.1
```
Sequence 1: a=4, b=9, c=9
Sequence 2: a=5, b=3, c=6 (ascii code %d)
```

6.2.2
The word *field* represents the address at the beginning of the array. It is also the address of the first element.

The 1st element in the array is *field[0]*.

The address of the first element in the array is *&field[0]* or *field*.

ptr = field indicates that *ptr* points to the first element *field[0]*.

6.2.3

1st program: You cannot assign a new address to a variable designating a table. The instructions *x=y* and *y=ptr* violate this principle. Only pointers can be reassigned.

2nd program: In the lines *ptr = 25* and *number2 = ptr+6*, the operator * has been forgotten.

6.3.1

All the instructions reference the index element 1. The last one modifies *ptr*.

6.3.2

Program: FINDCHAR.CPP

```
/************************************************************
**      FINDCHAR.CPP                                      **
**          Copyright (c) 1990 Micro Application          **
**          Copyright (c) 1992 Abacus Software, Inc.      **
************************************************************/

#include <stdio.h>

void main()
{
  char string[21], *ptr, chara;   /* Define the variable */
  int counter = 1;
  ptr= string;                     /* Initialize the pointer */

  printf("Type a word (Maximum: 20 characters): ");
                                    /* Prompt for input */
  scanf("%s", string);
  printf("Enter the character to search for: ");
  scanf(" %c", &chara);
  while (*ptr != chara && *ptr != '\0')
                                    /* Comparison loop */
  {
     ++counter;
     ++ptr;
  }
  if (*ptr=='\0')                   /* End of test */
   printf("The character %c was not found.\n",chara);
  else
   printf("The character %c was found at the %d
positon.\n", chara, counter);
}
```

6.3.3

The loop must go from *n=0* to *n=20*. But the variable *n* is decremented in each iteration. The array is examined in descending order and the loop runs much longer than expected. The instruction *ptr++=2;* is particularly dangerous. It doesn't just assign a value to the 20 elements of the array, but starts writing in the memory not reserved for the array. If sensitive data is stored there, the system could crash.

6.4.1

```
struct file             /* Definition of the structure */
    {
    char title[20], editor[30];
    int numtedit;
    float price;
    };
                        /* Definition of several variables */
struct file poe, twain, steinway;
```

Information in the struct family:

6.4.2

```
family name, first name and age of father, mother, son,
daughter Age of the father = fam1.father.age;
```

Program: FUNCSTRU.CPP

6.4.3

```
/**************************************************************
**      FUNCSTRU.CPP                                         **
**          Copyright (c) 1990 Micro Application             **
**          Copyright (c) 1992 Abacus Software, Inc.         **
**************************************************************/

#include <stdio.h>

void main ()
{
    struct function                 /* Define structure */
    {
        char  *name;
        float  xval[41], yval[41];
    }strt, par;    /* Note alternative method of defining
                                        the variables. */

    static char *name1 = "Straight", *name2 = "Parabola";
    int    n;
    float  x = -10;

    strt.name = name1;              /* Assign names */
    par.name = name2;

    for (n=0; n<41; ++n)            /* Calculate values */
    {
        strt.xval[n] = x;
        strt.yval[n] = x;
        par.xval[n] = x;
        par.yval[n] = x * x;
        x += 0.5;
    }

    for (n = 0; n < 41; ++n)         /* Display results*/
    {
        printf("%s : x = %g \ty = %g\n", strt.name,
    strt.xval[n], strt.yval[n]);
        printf("\n");
```

```
            }
            for (n = 0; n<41; ++n)
            {
                    printf("%s : x %g \ty =
%g\n",par.name,par.xval[n],par.yval[n]);
            }
        }
```

6.5.1
```
        typedef float *fmatrix[20];
        typedef struct person
        {
            char name[80];
            char address[80];
            int age;
        } Person;
```

6.5.2
```
        typedef struct
        {
            char *name, *tel, *local;
            long int zipcode;
        } ReperTel[50];
```

6.5.3 If you increment a pointer of integers, its address increases by two bytes. On the other hand, a pointer to a array of integers increases by the memory size taken by the array as a whole.

7.1.1
```
        Wrong headers:
        int lis();
        double maximum(double x,y,z)
        void nothing(void)
```

7.1.2
```
        double power(double base, int expo)
        {
            double p=1;
            while (expo-- >0) p*=base;
            return(p);
        }
```

Here is an example of how you can test this function:

```
        /*************************************************************
        **        EXPO2.CPP                                         **
        **             Copyright (c) 1990 Micro Application         **
        **             Copyright (c) 1992 Abacus Software, Inc.     **
        *************************************************************/

        #include <stdio.h>

        double power(double base, int expo)
        {
        double p=1;
        while (expo-- > 0) p*=base;
        return(p);
        }

        void main()
```

```
{double number;
int exponent;
printf("Enter the number, followed by the power of
ten:\n");
scanf("%lg %d",&number,&exponent);
printf(" %lg to the %d power =
%lg\n",number,exponent,power(number,exponent));
}
```

Program: FALL.CPP

7.1.3

```
/*************************************************************
**      FALL.CPP                                          **
**          Copyright (c) 1990 Micro Application          **
**          Copyright (c) 1992 Abacus Software, Inc.      **
*************************************************************/

#include <stdio.h>

/* Function calculating duration of the fall */
double t(double v)
{
  double ft = v / 64;
  return(ft);
}
/* Function calculating the height of the fall */
double h(double t)
{
  double fh = 32 * t * t;
  return(fh);
}
void display(double t, double h)
{
  printf("Duration of fall = %g sec\nHeight = %g feet\n",
t, h);
}
void main()
{
  double V, T, H;                 /* Define the variables */
  printf("Speed [feet/sec]: ");
  scanf("%lg", &V);
  T = t(V);                       /* Call the functions */
  H = h(T);
  display(T, H);
}
```

7.2.1

```
char *find(char text[], char letter)
look for a letter in an array.
int index(char *text, char letter)
look for a letter in an array, return an integer as the
ASCII Code.
void output(double *value)
display a table of values of type double.
struct file look for( struct file *list, char *person)
look for a person in a list.
float *measure(int channel_input)
reads the measurements on an input channel.
```

7.2.2

```
int look for(char *word, char letter)
{
    int n=1;
    while (*word!=letter && *word!='\0')
    {
      ++word;
      ++n
    }
    return(n);
}
```

Program: CODE1.CPP

7.2.3

```
/*************************************************************
**        CODE1.CPP                                        **
**              Copyright (c) 1990 Micro Application       **
**              Copyright (c) 1992 Abacus Software, Inc.   **
*************************************************************/

#include <stdio.h>


void code(char *string)                    /* Coding function */
{
  while (*string != '\0')
  {
     ++(*string);
     ++string;
  }
}
void decode(char *string)                  /* Decode Function */
{
  while (*string != '\0')
  {
     --(*string);
     ++string;
  }
}
void main()
{
  char STRING[21];                       /* Define variable */
  printf("Enter a word [20 characters max] : ");
                                         /* Prompt for input */
  scanf("%s", STRING);
  code(STRING);                          /* Call Code function */
  printf("Here is the coded word : %s\n", STRING);
  decode(STRING);                        /* Call Decode function */
  printf("..and here is the decoded word : %s\n", STRING);
}


argv[1][3] ,  argv[2][0]  , argv[1][9] or argv[2][7]
```

7.3.1

7.3.2   Program: FINDLET.CPP

```
/***********************************************************
**      FINDLET.CPP                                      **
**              Copyright (c) 1990 Micro Application     **
**              Copyright (c) 1992 Abacus Software, Inc. **
***********************************************************/

#include <stdio.h>
#include <stdlib.h>

void exit(int status);
void main(int argc, char *argv[])
{
  char *ptr, letter;          /* Definition of variables */
  int counter = 0, status;
  if (argc != 3) /* Verify correct number of parameters */
  {
     printf("Incorrect number of parameters\n");
     exit(status - '0');
  }
  ptr = argv[1];              /* Initialization of pointer */
  while (*ptr != '\0')                  /* Counting loop */
  {
     if (*ptr == argv[2][0]) ++counter;
    ++ptr;
  }
  printf("The letter %c appears %d times.\n", argv[2][0],
counter);
}
```

7.3.3   Call the Options/Args menu and type the arguments
NOTBEAUT.CPP PRETTY.CPP from the command line (without
putting the name of the program).

7.4.1   Incorrect initializations:

```
int number[8]={12, 14, 25, -13, 2}; There have to be 8
values.
double value [4]={3.2, 2, 5.3, 2.7, 35.2}; There should
only be 4 values
int mat[4][2]={2,3},{4,1},{8,4},{2,6}; A left bracket and
a right bracket are missing.
```

7.4.2   When you initialize arrays without specifying the maximum size,
it is automatically adjusted according to the number of values
indicated. (In our example the number of strings of characters will
determine the size.)

7.4.3   Program: NUMWORD.CPP

```
/*************************************************************
**      NUMWORD.CPP                                        **
**              Copyright (c) 1990 Micro Application       **
**              Copyright (c) 1992 Abacus Software, Inc.   **
*************************************************************/

#include <stdio.h>
#include <stdlib.h>

void exit(int status);

/* Initializations */
char *one_to_19[]  = { "zero" , "one" , "two" , "three" ,
                "four" , "five", "six" , "seven" , "eight" ,
                "nine" , "ten" , "eleven" , "twelve",
                "thirteen" , "fourteen" , "fifteen" ,
                "sixteen" , "seventeen" , "eighteen" ,
                "nineteen"};
char *tens[]= {"twenty","thirty","forty","fifty","sixty",
                "seventy","eighty","ninety"};
void main()
{
int number, n1, n10, status;     /* Define the variables */
printf("Enter a number less than 100: ");
scanf("%d",&number);                       /* Get a number */
n1=number %10;                               /* Unit digit */
n10=number /10;                             /* Tens digit */
/* Make sure number is less than 100 */
if (number>=100)
     {
     printf("Error - Number too large.\n");
     exit(status - '0');
     }
switch (n10)
     {
     case 0:               /* Is the number less than 10 */
     printf("%s\n",one_to_19[number]);
     exit(status - '0');

     case 1:                  /* Is the first digit a '1'? */
     printf("%s\n",one_to_19[number]);
     exit(status - '0');
     break;

     default:     /* If tens digit is something else... */
     printf("%s-%s\n",tens[n10-2],one_to_19[n1]);
     exit(status - '0');

     }
}
```

Non-recursive function:

7.5.1

```
void  fact(int n) {     h=u=1;     do{h*=u++;}     while(u<=n),
printf("factorial %d=%d", n, h);
```

Recursive function:

int fact(int n) { if(n>1) return (fact(n-1)*n); else return (1) }

call:

printf("factorial %d=%d", factor, fact,(factor));

8.1.1

The separate compilation lets you have the use of universal .OBJ modules that you can reuse in all kinds of programs. Therefore, if you want to integrate them in a project, you must link each module.

C compilers are often called "2 pass compilers".

8.1.2

There isn't any difference of principle between functions predefined in the standard library and functions freely created by the user.

8.2.1

Correct declarations:

```
char *find(char *string);
extern int number;
float measure(float x, float y, floatz);
```

The declarations that are incorrect are because of a semicolon (function) or the *extern* keyword (variable) have been omitted.

8.2.2

#include is a non-executable directive. It has no influence on the progress of the program. It only addresses itself to the compiler.

8.2.3

Header CLASS.H, programs CLASS.CPP and AVERAGE.CPP

```
/***********************************************************
**      CLASS.H                                          **
**            Copyright (c) 1990 Micro Application        **
**            Copyright (c) 1992 Abacus Software, Inc.    **
***********************************************************/

typedef int Grade[6];                 /* Define a type */
extern Grade grade;               /* Declare a variable */
float Average();                  /* Declare a function */


/***********************************************************
**      CLASS.CPP                                         **
**         Copyright (c) 1990 Micro Application          **
**         Copyright (c) 1992 Abacus Software, Inc.      **
***********************************************************/

#include <stdio.h>
#include "class.h"                 /* Include the header file */

typedef GRADE grade;

void main()
```

```
    {
      int n;                                  /* Define variable */
      for (n = 0; n < 6; ++n)                          /* Select */
      {
          printf("Grade %d: ", n+1);
          scanf("%d", &grade[n]);
      }
      printf("Average = %g\n", Average());
                /* Call Average function and display results */
    }


    /******************************************************
    **     AVERAGE.CPP                                    **
    **        Copyright (c) 1990 Micro Application        **
    **        Copyright (c) 1992 Abacus Software, Inc.    **
    ******************************************************/

    #include <stdio.h>
    #include "class.h"                     /* Include the header */
    float Average()
    {
      int n, sum = 0;                    /* Define the variables */
      for (n = 0; n < 6; ++n)                        /* Addition */
      {
          sum += grade[n] ;
      }
      return((float)sum / n);            /* Return the Average */
    }
```

8.3.1

```
    strcpy()   <string.h>          sin()      <math.h>
    ceil()     <math.h>            atof()     <math.h>, stdlib.h>
    putch()    <conio.h>           fprintf()  <stdio.h>
```

Program: LENGVECT.CPP

8.3.2

```
    /******************************************************
    **     LENGVECT.CPP                                   **
    **        Copyright (c) 1990 Micro Application        **
    **        Copyright (c) 1992 Abacus Software, Inc.    **
    ******************************************************/
    #include <stdio.h>
    #include <math.h>                  /* Include the math header */

    void main()
    {
      float x, y, z, l;              /* Define the variables */
      printf("l=sqrt(x*x+y*y+z*z)\n");  /* Prompt for input */
      printf("Enter values for Vector Components x, y, z : ");
      scanf("%g , %g , %g", &x, &y, &z);
      l = sqrt(x * x + y * y + z * z);           /* Calculate */
      printf("Vector Length = %g\n", l);           /* Display */
    }
```

8.3.3   Program: REACT.CPP

```
/***********************************************************
**      REACT.CPP                                         **
**          Copyright (c) 1990 Micro Application          **
**          Copyright (c) 1992 Abacus Software, Inc.      **
***********************************************************/

#include <conio.h>          /* Include keyboard-screen I/O */
#include <stdio.h>

void main()
{
  unsigned long n = 999999;          /* Define variable */
                      /* Note: This variable determines the
                      amount of time spent in the Wait loop.
                      It may need to be adjusted for faster or
                                      slower computers. */

  printf("Press any key as soon as you hear the
Beep.\n\n");

  while (--n > 0);                          /* Wait loop */
  printf("\a");
  while (!kbhit()) n++;     /* Loop and wait for reaction */
  getch();
  printf("Reaction time = %ld cycles.\n", n);
                                          /* Display */
}
```

8.4.1   Global extern variables have a global impact and local extern variables have a local impact.

8.4.2   The functions of the static class are only accessible from within their module.

8.4.3
```
int how many()
{
    static int n=1;
    return(n++);
}
```

8.5.1   The parentheses aren't necessary in the macro cls().

8.5.2   #ifndef asks the compiler to compile the sequence that follows only in the event that the variable indicated is not defined.

8.5.3
```
#define NEWLINE        printf("\n")
#define BEEP           printf("\a")
#define STOP           exit(0)
#define PROD(x,y)      (x*y)
```

9.1.1   By using sizeof(DIRECTORY)

9.1.2   Program: GENHELLO.CPP

```
/*************************************************************
**   GENHELLO.CPP                                          **
**          Copyright (c) 1990 Micro Application           **
**          Copyright (c) 1992 Abacus Software, Inc.        **
*************************************************************/

#include <stdio.h>

void main()
{
  FILE *fp;
  fp = fopen("HELLO1.CPP", "wt");
  fprintf(fp,"#include <stdio.h>\n\n");
  fprintf(fp, "void main()\n");
  fprintf(fp, "{\nprintf(\"Hello\");\n}\n");
  fclose(fp);
}
```

9.1.3   Principle: In the function *fwrite()* you give as parameter *<Size>* the size of a single element in the table, and for *<Num>* you put exactly the number of elements necessary.

9.2.1   %d=46, %e=7.363325e-312, %X=2E, %o=56, %u=46, %3x= 2e,
                   %4u= 46 %f=13.520000, %e=1.352000e+01, %g=13.52,
                   %6.2f= 13.52, %8.1E= 1.4E+01, %5.2G= 14

9.2.2   *puts()* is faster.

                   Program: ASCII.CPP

9.2.3
```
/*************************************************************
**      ASCII.CPP                                          **
**          Copyright (c) 1990 Micro Application           **
**          Copyright (c) 1992 Abacus Software, Inc.        **
*************************************************************/

#include <stdio.h>
#include <stdlib.h>

void main()
{
    unsigned char n = 32;
    do
    {
            printf("%3d %02x %c  ",n, n, n);
    }
    while (n++ <255);
}
```

9.3.1   Since the parameter of the function *sqrt()* is not a double type, you must convert it. But this conversion is only automatic if the function has been appropriately declared. That isn't the case here because we forgot to include the header file <math.h>.

Program: INVEST.CPP

9.3.2

```
/************************************************************
**    INVEST.CPP                                          **
**·        Copyright (c) 1990 Micro Application           **
**         Copyright (c) 1992 Abacus Software, Inc.        **
************************************************************/

#include <stdio.h>
#include <math.h>

void main()
{
    double stacap, rate, t;        /* Define variables */
    printf("Starting Investment :");
    scanf("%lg",&stacap);
    printf("Interest rate (in %) :");
    scanf("%lg",&rate);
    printf("Length of time :");
    scanf("%lg",&t);
    rate = 1 + rate / 100;    /* Calculate and display */
    printf("Value earned: %lg",stacap * pow(rate,t));
}
```

The memory area adjacent to *<Destination>* is deleted.

9.4.1

Program: FINDWORD.CPP

9.4.2

```
/************************************************************
**      FINDWORD.CPP                                      **
**         Copyright (c) 1990 Micro Application           **
**         Copyright (c) 1992 Abacus Software, Inc.        **
************************************************************/

#include <stdio.h>            /* Include necessary headers */
#include <string.h>
#include <stdlib.h>

void main()
{
  FILE *fp;                         /* Define variables */
  char file[20], read_word[80], word[80];
  printf("Enter filename to search: ");    /* Get input */
  scanf("%s", file);
  printf("Word to search for: ");
  scanf("%s", word);
  fp = fopen(file, "rt");            /* Open the file */
  if (fp == 0)
  {
      printf("Error: Cannot open file\n");
      exit(0);
```

```
      }
      while (!feof(fp))                           /* Search loop */
      {
         fscanf(fp, "%s", read_word);
         if (strcmp(read_word, word) == 0) break;
      }
      if (feof(fp))                               /* Display */
         printf("The word \"%s\" was not found in this
   file.\n",word);
        else
           printf("The word \"%s\" was found in this file.\n",
   word);
        fclose(fp);
      }
```

9.5.1 In anticipation of the worst case, ordinary arrays have to be given dimensions for a maximum number of elements. Generally the number of elements will be less than this maximum, which means that you waste memory.

9.5.2
```
   ptr=malloc(sizeof(TABLE));
   ptr=malloc(sizeof(INTPTR));
   ptr=malloc(sizeof(STRING));
   ptr=malloc(sizeof(VECTOR));
```

Program: TEXTDISK.CPP

9.5.3
```
   /***********************************************************
   **       TEXTDISK.CPP                                    **
   **          Copyright (c) 1990 Micro Application          **
   **          Copyright (c) 1992 Abacus Software, Inc.      **
   ***********************************************************/

   #include <stdio.h>              /* Include necessary headers */
   #include <conio.h>
   #include <stdlib.h>

   void main()
   {
     FILE *fp;                             /* Declare variables */
     char file[20];
     char **text;                          /* Pointer to table */
     int n_lines, n;
     printf("Number of lines:");                   /* Get input */
     scanf("%d", &n_lines);
     printf("Enter Filename : ");
     scanf("%s\n", file);
         text = (char **)malloc(n_lines * 2);
                                           /* Allocate memory   */

     for (n = 0; n < n_lines; ++n)
     {
        text[n] = (char *)malloc(81);
                               /* Allocate memory for text */
        gets(text[n]);
     }
```

```
                              fp = fopen(file, "wt");    /* Write file to disk */
                              for (n = 0; n < n_lines; ++n)
                                  fprintf(fp, "%s\n", text[n]);
                              fclose(fp);
                          }
```

You just have to rewrite the class like this:

10.1.1

```
class {       struct Position
        {int line, column; } pos;
        public : posscreen (int l=1, int c=1)
                {pos.line=l
                 pos.line=c
                 }
        void place (int l, int c)
            {pos.line=l;pos.line=c}
        void place (int dl=0, int dc=0)
            {pos.line=dl;pos.column==dc} };
```

For example:

10.1.2

```
class vector
{
        Typedef struct vector
        {int x, y, z;};
        public :       vector prod-V (vector V1, vector V2)
{
                vector product;
                product.x =....
                ...
                return (product);
        }
};
```

10.2.1   The member function has to be rewritten for each sub class of the base class, thus making the programmer rewrite as many times as necessary a portion of identical code, making the executable code that much longer.

10.3.1   Add printf statements similar to the addition and multiplication operations, using division and subtraction operators.

Appendix E: Glossary

8086, 8088, 80186, 80286, 80386

Microprocessors manufactured by the Intel Corporation. They are upwardly compatible, which means that the 80836 can execute any program developed for an 8086, 8088, 80186 or 80286 microprocessor. However, the 8088 can't always execute an application developed for one of the later microprocessors. The processors of this family act as main processors for different types of PCs.

Address

The Intel-80xx family of microprocessors form an address from one of the four segment registers, with another register or a constant. The contents of the segment register becomes the segment address, and the other register or constant becomes the offset address. Both addresses are logical addresses that are related to a physical address (the actual number of a memory location). This physical address can be determined by multiplying the segment register by 16 and adding the offset address.

Address area

The number of memory locations addressable by a microprocessor.

Address bus

A line connecting the CPU with memory (RAM and ROM). If the CPU wants to address a memory location, it must first place its address on the address bus in order to set the "switches" for access to this memory location.

Arena header

The data structure which precedes the memory area of the TPA assigned to a program. DOS uses this area to store the memory area's size and other information.

ASCII

Abbreviation for **American Standard Code for Information Interchange**. ASCII is a standardized assignment of numbers from 0 to 255 that represents characters (e.g., letters, numbers). The ASCII codes from 0 to 127 comprise the *standard ASCII character set*, while the codes from 128 to 255 comprise the *extended ASCII character set*.

Assembly language

A few simple instructions that the processor can understand. Every higher level language program is finally translated into these instructions for processing by the CPU.

Asynchronous data transfer

Also known as *serial transfer*. Bytes are transmitted and/or received bit by bit according to a predetermined transfer protocol.

AT

Abbreviation for **Advanced Technology**. AT computers have an 80286 processor.

Attribute

A byte following each character that defines the character's color and appearance for display on the screen.

AUTOEXEC.BAT

Filename for the automatically executing batch file for which DOS searches during the booting process. After DOS is loaded and started, it searches the root directory of the device from which it booted for a file named AUTOEXEC.BAT. During the booting process, this *batch file* executes programs and parameters through the command processor.

Batch files

Text files saved with the file extension .BAT. These files contain DOS commands or command sequences. Batch file execution treats these commands as if the user had entered the commands from the keyboard.

Baud

A measurement of data transfer speed. One baud roughly equals one data bit per second.

BCD

Abbreviation for **Binary Coded Decimal**. This number represents a two-digit decimal number encoded in one byte. The upper four bits represent the most significant digit and the lower four bits represent the least significant digit.

Binary system

The number system understandable by a computer at its lowest level. Binary notation counts from 0 to 1. The first position of a binary number has the value 1, the second has the value 2, the third has the value 4, the fourth has the value 8, etc.

BIOS

Abbreviation for **Basic Input/Output System**. It contains the device drivers which perform access to the peripheral devices such as the keyboard, monitor, disk drives, etc. The BIOS is located in addresses F000:E000—F000:FFFF.

BIOS interrupts

Interrupts 10H to 17H and interrupt 1AH, through which the many functions of the ROM-BIOS can be called.

BIOS version

Release date of the BIOS as stored in the eight bytes starting at memory location F000:FFF5. This version appears in the form Month/Day/Year.

Block driver

The *device drivers* which control access to devices that process data in data blocks (disk drives and hard disks). Block drivers are addressed through a letter (drive specifier) which enables one block driver to control several devices with different letters. The disk driver has the drive specifiers A: and B:, while the hard disk driver can be addressed with the specifier C:.

Boot sector

Contained on every mass storage medium from which DOS can be booted. Sector 0 contains certain information and a short program which loads a DOS boot routine, then initializes DOS.

Booting

The process that starts after the user has switched on the computer. BIOS tests and initializes the various circuit chips in the system, then loads the operating system.

BPB

Abbreviation for **BIOS Parameter Block**. The BPB defines the format and design of a mass storage device (disk drive and hard disk) for DOS. It is available in the boot sector of every mass storage device, but must be passed to DOS by the initialization routine of a block device driver.

CALL

Assembly language instruction that triggers the execution of a subroutine. After the routine ends, a RET instruction executes, which is followed by the instruction following the initial CALL.

Carry flag

Bit 0 in the processor's flag register. Many operating system functions use it to tell the calling program whether the called function executed correctly, or if an error occurred. In the latter case, the carry flag is set (1) after the function call.

Character driver

A device driver which controls access to devices that process characters as bytes. The screen, keyboard and printer are device drivers. Character drivers have their own names, such as CON, PRN and AUX.

Child program

A program which is called by another program. For example, if the FORMAT command is called from the DOS level, the parent program is the command processor.

CLI

Clear interrupts instruction. This instruction instructs the CPU to ignore all subsequent interrupt requests until the STI (STart Interrupts) instruction re-enables interrupt response (the NMI [Non-Maskable Interrupt] is exempt from this instruction).

Clock driver

A character device responsible for getting the time and date from DOS, incrementing the time and date and passing the incremented amounts back to DOS.

Clock generator

Produces several million pulses per second and synchronizes various components of the system with each other.

Cluster

Multiple sectors of a mass storage device. Files and subdirectories can be stored in different clusters. The number of sectors per cluster varies from one device to another.

COM files

Executable programs which must be stored within a 64K memory segment. COM files combine program code, data and stack in this 64K area.

COMMAND.COM

The file containing the MS-DOS command processor.

Command line

A line from which program or batch file calls can be entered into the command processor.

Command parameters

The name for all characters passed in the *command line*, following the program or batch file calls. The EXEC function copies these parameters into the PSP of the loaded program.

Command processor

Also called *shell*. The command processor is a part of the operating system which accepts and processes user input. Its main function is to load and start application programs and batch files.

CON

Abbreviation for **CONsole driver**, the two device drivers which control the keyboard and the screen.

CONFIG.SYS

The DOS configuration file. It contains certain commands for configuring DOS, as well as additional device drivers. CONFIG.SYS loads and executes only once (during the booting process).

Control characters

ASCII characters which represent certain non-alphanumeric characters. This applies to all ASCII codes less than 32. The PC only uses ASCII codes 0, 7, 8, 9, 10, 11, 12 and 13 as control characters.

Cooked mode

Character mode that checks for certain unusual characters, which are either converted to other characters or completely filtered out. Character drivers operate either in *raw mode* or *cooked mode*.

CP/M-80

Early operating system, the predecessor of MS-DOS. CP/M is used by computers that are based upon Z-80 microprocessors.

CPU

Abbreviation for **Central Processing Unit**. The microprocessor which forms the "brain" of a computer.

CRC

Abbreviation for **Cyclical Redundancy Check**. The CRC tests for errors during data transfer to and from a disk.

CRT

Abbreviation for **Cathode Ray Tube**. A CRT generates a screen display with the help of an electron beam which sends electrical impulses to a glass screen at the end of the CRT.

DASD

Abbreviation for **Direct Access Storage Device**. In DOS and BIOS terminology this concept is used for disk drives and hard disks.

Data bus

A data line which connects the CPU with memory (RAM and ROM). Data can be transmitted between the CPU and memory over this line.

Device driver

Driver systems which interface DOS and hardware by making basic functions available for communicating with the hardware. Device driver functions can be called by the higher level DOS functions. DOS differentiates between character drivers and block drivers.

Disks

Flat plastic materials containing magnetic media for storing data. Formatted disks are partitioned into tracks and sectors.

Disk controller

Regulates the activities of the disk drive.

Disk status

Lists the status of the last disk operation. It indicates if and when an error occurred during this disk access.

Disk formats

The PC market supports several disk formats. PC and XT disk drives use 5-1/4" disks that are formatted on one or two sides. Each side contains 40 tracks with eight or nine sectors per track (each sector stores 512 bytes). The capacity of these disks is between 160K (single-sided) and 360K (double-sided). The AT uses 5-1/4" disks with two formatted sides, each side containing 80 tracks with 15 sectors per track (each sector stores 512 bytes). The total capacity of these disks is 1.2 megabytes.

The newest disk formats on the market allow the use of 3-1/2" micro floppy disks.

Display page

Also called *screen page* and *video page*. Some video cards can control one or more display pages. Only one of these pages can be displayed on the screen at one time.

DMA

Abbreviation for **Direct Memory Access**. Transmits data from the circuit chips of a peripheral device directly into memory, without making a detour through the CPU.

DMA controller

A chip capable of transferring large amounts of data directly into memory without passing through the CPU. A good example is the access to a disk drive or hard disk drive.

DOS

Abbreviation for **Disk Operating System**. DOS sets up basic file handling tasks for communicating between computer and disk drive(s).

DTA

Abbreviation for **Disk Transfer Area**. File and directory accesses use the DTA for disk data transmission. Its size depends upon the current operation, where the calling program must ensure that enough memory exists to accept the transmitted data. After the start of a program, DOS places the beginning of the DTA into memory location 128 of the PSP, which makes 128 bytes available.

ECC

Abbreviation for **Error Correction Code**. ECC is used when data is stored on a hard disk. Unlike the CRC, the ECC permits the recognition of errors as well as their correction within certain parameters.

EGA

Abbreviation for **Enhanced Graphic Adapter**. This is a special, high resolution variation on the Color/Graphics Adapter (CGA).

EMM

Abbreviation for Expanded Memory Manager. Allows access to EMS memory.

EMS

Abbreviation for Expanded Memory System. This section of RAM goes beyond the 1 megabyte limit set by PCs and XTs. EMS is only accessible through the EMM.

End character

Also called *return code*. The end character is ASCII code 0, which is sometimes assigned the name NUL. It usually indicates the last character in a character string.

Environment block

Every program has an assigned environment block whose address is stored in the PSP of the current program. The environment block itself consists of a series of ASCII strings which contain certain information, such as the search path for files (PATH).

EOI

Abbreviation for **End Of Interrupt**. This instruction indicates the completion of a hardware triggered interrupt to the interrupt handler.

Extended key code

Keys and key combinations that can be entered with a PC keyboard but have no direct relation to the ASCII character set. They are often entered by pressing and holding the [Alt] key, then entering a three-digit number on the numeric keypad.

EXE files

Executable programs which can be of any length and can store their code, data and stack in different memory segments (see also *COM files*).

EXEC

DOS function for loading and executing programs. The command processor also uses this function to execute applications programs and batch files.

FAR instructions

Machine language instructions that contain an address of a variable or a subroutine with a segment address and an offset address. They can address variables or subroutines located in another memory segment (farther away than 64K).

FAT

Abbreviation for **File Allocation Table**. This is a table located on every external storage medium (disk and hard disk). It informs DOS which areas of a storage medium are available, which areas are already occupied with data, and which areas are useless because of defects. The FAT also links together the different parts of a file.

FCB

Abbreviation for **File Control Block**. DOS controls file access to RAM using FCBs.

Fixed disk

Another term for *hard disk*.

Filter

A program that reads characters from the standard input device, manipulates them in some desired way, and then displays them on the standard output device.

Flag register

A 16-bit register in which several of these bits indicate certain aspects of the processor's status.

Function

A routine that can be called with a DOS or BIOS interrupt.

Garbage collection

A routine that removes variables which are no longer required from the variable memory of a BASIC program. Every BASIC interpreter has garbage collection.

GDT

Abbreviation for **Global Descriptor Table**. The GDT describes the individual memory segments when the processor is in protected mode.

General registers

The processors of the Intel-80xx family have the following general registers: AX, BX, CX, DX, DI, SI and BP. They are all 16 bits wide. The AX, BX, CX and DX registers can be separated into two 8-bit registers. These two half registers are designated as AH, AL, BH, BL, CH, CL, DH and DL.

Handle

A numerical value that acts as a key for access to files and devices. It is passed by DOS to a program which calls one of the functions for opening or creating a file or device.

Hard disk

A mass storage unit consisting of several magnetic media stacked on top of one another. Unlike disks, hard disks are divided into cylinders and sectors. Each of these disks can store data on both their top and bottom sides.

Hard disk format

The PC hard disk format consists of 17 sectors per cylinder and 512 bytes per sector. The number of disks and the number of cylinders per disk may vary.

Hardware interrupt

An interrupt or interrupt request, called by PC hardware, to attract the attention of the CPU to a device (e.g., the keyboard). Certain devices only call certain interrupts.

Hexadecimal system

A number system distantly related to the binary system. The basic numbering of this system goes from 0 to 15, instead of from 0 to 9 (the numbers 10 to 15 are represented by the letters A, B, C, D, E and F). The first position of a hexadecimal number has the value 1, the second 16, the third 256, the fourth 4,096, etc.

IN

Assembly language instruction to read data from a port into the CPU.

Internal commands

All commands whose code is stored in the transient portion of the command processor, and, therefore, don't have to be loaded from a storage medium (e.g., DIR, COPY and VER).

Interrupt

An interruption of a program through an interrupt call, the execution of an interrupt routine and, finally, the resumption of the interrupted program. The processors of the Intel-80xx family can process 256 different interrupts which are divided into hardware and software interrupts.

Interrupt controller

Monitors the various interrupt requests within the system and decides which interrupts to process first.

Interrupt routine

The program called during the appearance of an interrupt. Each interrupt has its own interrupt routine, whose address is stored in the interrupt vector table. The interrupt routine must be terminated with a machine language IRET instruction.

Interrupt vector table

A table containing the addresses of the interrupt routines, which are called when a particular interrupt appears. Each entry in this table consists of two words. The first word contains the offset address and the following word contains the segment address of the interrupt routine. The table starts at memory location 0000:0000, where the address of the interrupt routine for interrupt 0 is stored. The four following memory locations contain the address of the interrupt routine for interrupt 1, etc.

IRET

The Interrupt RETurn assembly language instruction. IRET terminates the execution of an interrupt routine and then continues the execution of the program at the location following the interruption of the program.

Keyboard status

Indicates whether the user has pressed the [Shift], [Ctrl] or [Alt] keys, and whether the [Ins], [Caps Lock], [Num Lock] or [Scroll Lock] modes are active.

Kilobyte

Abbreviated as **K**. Equals 2^{10} or 1,024 bytes.

Math coprocessor

Relieves the CPU of the processing of complicated floating-point mathematical formulas. It also accelerates the processing of worksheets within a spreadsheet program.

Megabyte

Often abbreviated as **meg**. Equal to 2^{10} kilobytes or 1,048,576 bytes.

Media descriptor byte

A byte within the File Allocation Table (FAT), which identifies the mass storage device's current format. DOS can manipulate the various formats of the mass storage which it supports and also checks the media descriptor byte for the current format.

Memory allocation

In all PCs the lower 640K is assigned to RAM. The video RAM follows, and then the ROM, which extends to the 1 megabyte memory limit. ATs may have up to 15 megabytes of additional RAM.

Microprocessor

The brain of a computer. Its main task is to execute assembly language instructions.

Model identification

The type of PC used, as coded into address F000:FFFE. FCH stands for AT, FEH often stands for XT and FFH often stands for PC.

MS-DOS

Abbreviation for **MicroSoft Disk Operating System**. MS-DOS is the primary PC operating system.

Multiprocessing

The simultaneous execution of several programs (not supported by DOS at the time of this writing).

NEAR instructions

Assembly language instructions that contain the offset address of only a variable or a subroutine (no segment address). These instructions can address variables or subroutines located only within the current 64K memory segment.

Nibble

Also spelled *nybble*. Bytes can be subdivided into two nibbles. The low nibble occupies bits 0 to 3 of a byte, while the high nibble occupies bits 4 to 7 of a byte.

NMI

Abbreviation for **Non-Maskable Interrupt**. The NMI remains constantly active. It is the only interrupt not affected by the CLI assembly language instruction.

OUT

An assembly language instruction which sends data to a port.

Overlay

A program loaded into memory allocated for it by another program. The calling program calls certain routines within this overlay as needed.

Paragraph

A group of 16 bytes in the 8088 which starts at a memory location divisible by 16 (e.g., 0, 16, 32, 48, etc.).

Parent program

A program that can execute another program (see *child program*) and continue its own processing after the child program's execution. For example, if a FORMAT command is called from DOS level, the command processor is the parent program.

Parity

A process used to detect errors during serial data transmission. Either even or odd parity can be used.

PC

Abbreviation for **Personal Computer** (i.e., all computers equipped with a 8088 or 8086 processor).

Peripheral interface

Connects the CPU to various peripheral devices (e.g., speaker).

Ports

The connections between the CPU and various other circuit chips within the system. Each chip has one or more assigned ports, which have a specific address. The CPU addresses the individual chips by writing values into the proper port or by reading values from the proper port.

Printer status byte

Describes the current status of the printer. It can indicate whether the printer is out of paper, is switched ONLINE or has not responded (time-out).

PRN

The device designation of the printer.

Program counter

Also called IP (Instruction Pointer). The program counter and the CS segment register combined form the memory address from which the processor will read the next command to be executed.

Protected mode

Allows multiprocessing, more than 1 megabyte of memory and control over virtual memory on computers possessing the 80286 and 80386 processors.

PSP

Abbreviation for **Program Segment Prefix**. The PSP is a 256 byte long data structure, which is placed in front of every program to be executed but not stored with the file on disk or hard disk. The program itself or program data start after this data structure.

RAM

Abbreviation for **Random Access Memory**. This is the memory that the user can read from and write to.

Raw mode

Character mode that transmits all characters from a device to the calling program without any changes (see *cooked mode*).

Real mode

Forces 80286 and 80386 processors to emulate dual high-speed 8088 processors incapable of multiprocessing or control of more than 1 megabyte of memory.

Register

Memory locations inside the processor that provide faster access than memory locations in RAM.

Reset

A resetting and reboot of the system. You can trigger a reset by pressing the Alt Ctrl Del key combination.

Resident

Programs that remain in memory after execution without being overwritten by other programs or data. Resident programs can be recalled later.

ROM

Abbreviation for **Read Only Memory**. ROM can only be read, not written.

ROM BASIC

A small BASIC interpreter, placed in the ROMs of older PCs starting at address F000:6000. ROM BASIC is called by the system when BIOS fails to load the operating system.

RS-232

An interface that permits the computer to communicate with other devices over only one line. The individual data is transmitted serially (i.e., bit by bit).

RTC

Abbreviation for **RealTime Clock**. The battery backed clock on the AT.

Scan code

A code passed to the CPU by the keyboard processor when a key is pressed or released. It indicates the number assigned to the key within the keyboard. For this reason, the scan codes of the various PC keyboards differ from each other.

Sector

The smallest data division of a disk or hard disk. A sector contains 512 bytes.

Segment descriptor

Describes the location and size of the segment in addition to other information. It is used in protected mode on the 80286 and 80386 processors. All segment descriptors are gathered in the global descriptor table (GDT).

Segment register

The processors of the Intel-80xx family have four 16-bit segments that define the beginning of a 64K memory segment. They are named DS, ES, CS and SS.

Software interrupts

An interrupt or interrupt request called by a program using the INT instruction. Each of the 256 existing interrupts can be called using this instruction.

Standard input device

The keyboard. The standard input can be redirected to another device or a file using the < character.

Standard output device

The monitor screen. The standard output can be redirected to another device or a file using the > character.

STI

The **STart Interrupts** assembly language instruction. This instruction disables any previous CLI command and re-enables all inactive interrupts.

Time-out

Occurs during communication between the CPU and a device when the CPU sends data to the device and, after a certain amount of time, the device offers no response.

Timer

Similar to the clock. The timer generates a cyclical signal used to measure time.

TPA

Abbreviation for **Transient Program Area**. This is the part of RAM below the 1 megabyte limit not occupied by DOS that is used for storing programs and data.

UART

Abbreviation for **Universal Asynchronous Receiver Transmitter**. A chip that acts as the controller for the serial interface.

Video controller

Displays a picture on the screen by sending the proper signals to the monitor.

Video RAM

RAM, which is used for storing characters or graphics for display on the screen, made available by a video card. It can be addressed like normal RAM.

Virtual memory

Permits program access to memory, which it assumes to be RAM but is actually a mass storage device. Virtual memory must first be loaded into RAM for access.

Volume

Part of a mass storage device that has files, its own FAT, its own root directory and its own subdirectories. Each volume can have its own volume name. While disks can store only one volume under DOS, hard disks can be divided into several volumes to accommodate several operating systems.

Appendix F: ASCII Table

Dec	Hex	Char	Dec	Hex	Char	Dec	Hex	Char	Dec	Hex	Char
0	00		32	20		64	40	@	96	60	`
1	01	☺	33	21	!	65	41	A	97	61	a
2	02	●	34	22	"	66	42	B	98	62	b
3	03	♥	35	23	#	67	43	C	99	63	c
4	04	♦	36	24	$	68	44	D	100	64	d
5	05	♣	37	25	%	69	45	E	101	65	e
6	06	♠	38	26	&	70	46	F	102	66	f
7	07	•	39	27	'	71	47	G	103	67	g
8	08	◘	40	28	(	72	48	H	104	68	h
9	09	o	41	29	)	73	49	I	105	69	i
10	0A	j	42	2A	*	74	4A	J	106	6A	j
11	0B	k	43	2B	+	75	4B	K	107	6B	k
12	0C	l	44	2C	,	76	4C	L	108	6C	l
13	0D	m	45	2D	-	77	4D	M	109	6D	m
14	0E	♫	46	2E	.	78	4E	N	110	6E	n
15	0F	☼	47	2F	/	79	4F	O	111	6F	o
16	10	►	48	30	0	80	50	P	112	70	p
17	11	◄	49	31	1	81	51	Q	113	71	q
18	12	↕	50	32	2	82	52	R	114	72	r
19	13	‼	51	33	3	83	53	S	115	73	s
20	14	¶	52	34	4	84	54	T	116	74	t
21	15	§	53	35	5	85	55	U	117	75	u
22	16	▬	54	36	6	86	56	V	118	76	v
23	17	↨	55	37	7	87	57	W	119	77	w
24	18	↑	56	38	8	88	58	X	120	78	x
25	19	↓	57	39	9	89	59	Y	121	79	y
26	1A	→	58	3A	:	90	5A	Z	122	7A	z
27	1B	←	59	3B	;	91	5B	[	123	7B	{
28	1C	∟	60	3C	<	92	5C	\	124	7C		
29	1D	↔	61	3D	=	93	5D	]	125	7D	}
30	1E	O	62	3E	>	94	5E	^	126	7E	~
31	1F	P	63	3F	?	95	5F	_	127	7F	Δ

Dec	Hex	Char	Dec	Hex	Char	Dec	Hex	Char	Dec	Hex	Char
128	80	Ç	160	A0	á	192	C0	└	224	E0	α
129	81	ü	161	A1	í	193	C1	┴	225	E1	β
130	82	é	162	A2	ó	194	C2	┬	226	E2	Γ
131	83	â	163	A3	ú	195	C3	├	227	E3	π
132	84	ä	164	A4	ñ	196	C4	─	228	E4	Σ
133	85	à	165	A5	Ñ	197	C5	┼	229	E5	σ
134	86	å	166	A6	ª	198	C6	╞	230	E6	μ
135	87	ç	167	A7	º	199	C7	╟	231	E7	τ
136	88	ê	168	A8	¿	200	C8	╚	232	E8	Φ
137	89	ë	169	A9	⌐	201	C9	╔	233	E9	Θ
138	8A	è	170	AA	¬	202	CA	╩	234	EA	Ω
139	8B	ï	171	AB	½	203	CB	╦	235	EB	δ
140	8C	î	172	AC	¼	204	CC	╠	236	EC	∞
141	8D	ì	173	AD	¡	205	CD	═	237	ED	Ø
142	8E	Ä	174	AE	«	206	CE	╬	238	EE	∈
143	8F	Å	175	AF	»	207	CF	╧	239	EF	∩
144	90	É	176	B0	░	208	D0	╨	240	F0	≡
145	91	æ	177	B1	▒	209	D1	╤	241	F1	±
146	92	Æ	178	B2	▓	210	D2	╥	242	F2	≥
147	93	ô	179	B3	│	211	D3	╙	243	F3	≤
148	94	ö	180	B4	┤	212	D4	╘	244	F4	⌠
149	95	ò	181	B5	╡	213	D5	╒	245	F5	⌡
150	96	û	182	B6	╢	214	D6	╓	246	F6	÷
151	97	ù	183	B7	╖	215	D7	╫	247	F7	≈
152	98	ÿ	184	B8	╕	216	D8	╪	248	F8	°
153	99	Ö	185	B9	╣	217	D9	┘	249	F9	•
154	9A	Ü	186	BA	║	218	DA	┌	250	FA	·
155	9B	¢	187	BB	╗	219	DB	█	251	FB	√
156	9C	£	188	BC	╝	220	DC	▄	252	FC	ⁿ
157	9D	¥	189	BD	╜	221	DD	▌	253	FD	²
158	9E	₧	190	BE	╛	222	DE	▐	254	FE	▪
159	9F	ƒ	191	BF	┐	223	DF	▀	255	FF	

Appendix G: Introduction To Number Systems

Throughout this book we talked about numbers notated in the *binary* and *hexadecimal systems* instead of the normal decimal system. This Appendix presents a brief introduction to these number systems.

Decimal system

Before explaining the new number systems, you should know the basic concepts of the decimal system. The decimal number 1989 can also be written as 1*1000+9*100+8*10+9*1. This shows that if you number the digits from right to left, the first number represents a column of ones, the second number represents a column of tens, the third number represents a column of hundreds and the fourth number represents a column of thousands. The numbers increase from right to left in powers of 10.

The first digit of any number system has the value 1. The factor by which the value increases from one column to the next differs among the number systems. This factor corresponds to the numbers with which the number system works. The factor is 10 with the decimal system because ten different numbers are available for each digit (0 to 9).

This principle of powers for each column also applies to the binary and hexadecimal systems.

Binary system

Since a computer recognizes the numbers 0 and 1 on its lowest functional level, the binary system is essential to computing. The value of the numbers double from column to column because the binary system only uses powers of two for each column (i.e., the numbers 0 and 1 instead of the numbers 0 to 9).

Now let's count the binary places starting from right to left as we did in the decimal example previously described. The first (right hand) position counts as one, the second as two, the third as four and the fourth as eight. The places then follow as 16, 32, 64, 128, etc.

For example, 11001 binary converts to 25 decimal, or the equation 1*16+1*8+0*4+0*2+1*1.

Hexadecimal system

Unlike the binary system, the hexadecimal system operates with more basic numbers than the decimal system. This system counts single digits from 0 to F. Since only the ten numbers of the decimal system are able to represent a number, the numbers from 10 to 15 in hexadecimal use the letters A to F in addition to the numbers 0 to 9. AH represents 10, BH for 11, CH for 12, DH for 13, EH for 14 and FH for 15.

By using 16 numbers or letters for each position, the value by which each position increments is 16.

The first position has the value 1, the second 16, the third 256 and the fourth 4,096.

For example, the hexadecimal number FB3H converts into 4,019 decimal, or 15*256+11*16+3*1.

Hex and binary

The hexadecimal system and the binary system are easily converted back and forth. For example, one four-digit binary number converts to a single-digit hexadecimal number. Because of this, the hexadecimal system is an important part of assembly language programming. It's much simpler to convey a byte (an eight-bit number) using two hexadecimal digits than it is for the developer to compute a 16-bit binary equivalent.

This book denotes all binary numbers by the letter b, and all hexadecimal numbers by the letter H.

The following illustrations should help explain number systems more clearly.

Places	5	4	3	2	1
Decimal:	10000	1000	100	10	1
Binary:	16	8	4	2	1
Hexadecimal:	65536	4096	256	16	1

Number positions in each number system

Comparing selected numbers

Decimal	Binary	Hexadecimal
0	0 (b)	0H
1	1 (b)	1H
2	10 (b)	2H
3	11 (b)	3H
4	100 (b)	4H
5	101 (b)	5H
6	110 (b)	6H
7	111 (b)	7H
8	1000 (b)	8H
9	1001 (b)	9H
10	1010 (b)	AH
11	1011 (b)	BH
12	1100 (b)	CH
128	10000000 (b)	80H
129	10000001 (b)	81H
256	100000000 (b)	100H
1024	10000000000 (b)	400H
4096	1000000000000 (b)	1000H
65535	1111111111111111 (b)	FFFFH

Comparing selected numbers in each number system

Appendix H: The Companion Diskette

Instructions for installing the files on the companion diskette can be found in Section 1.2.

1.   Example files (Directory EXAMPLE)

File	Section	Use
LOADSAVE.TXT	2.1	File used for demonstrating the selections Load and Save.
HELLO.CPP	2.3	Displays the word "Hello" on the screen.
ERROR.CPP	2.5	Non executable program showing how errors are managed in Turbo C++.
HITHERE.CPP	2.5	Program containing errors and useful for solving an exercise.
DEFVAR.CPP	3.1	Non executable program for presenting definitions of variables.
INOUT.CPP	3.2	Input-outputs of initials and a birth date.
SPHERE.CPP	3.3	Calculates the surface and volume of a sphere.
CHARA.CPP	3.3	Program showing the relationship between char and int types.
DIVI13.CPP	4.1	Tests whether a number is divisible by 13.
EQUALIN.CPP	4.1	Solves linear equations with two unknowns.
SUM.CPP	4.2	Calculates the sum of the whole numbers from 1 to N.
ADDITION.CPP	4.2	Finds the sum of two numbers with a floating decimal.
POWER2.CPP	4.2	Calculates the powers of two of numbers less than a given number.
OPERAT.CPP	4.3	Conducts arthimetical operations on two numbers.
TANDF.CPP	4.4	True-False table of the AND operator.
TYPES.CPP	5.1	Operations on various types of data.
ARITH.CPP	5.2	Program showing the hierarchy of the operators.
PARABOLA.CPP	6.1	Graphic representation of a parabola.
POINTER.CPP	6.2	Application examples of pointers.

PTRPAR.CPP	6.3	Draws a parabola using pointers.
STOCK.CPP	6.4	Small inventory control program limited to nuts and bolts.
CHESS.CPP	6.5	Draws a chess board.
EXCHANGE.CPP	6.5	Converts foreign currency into $.
ROUND.CPP	7.1	Rounds off floating point numbers.
BUBBLES.CPP	7.2	Program of sorting by adjacent permutations (Bubble Sort).
VECTOR.CPP	7.2	Calculates the product of two vectors.
CODE.CPP	7.3	Program for encoding a string of characters.
HEX.CPP	7.4	Conversion from the decimal system to hexadecimal.
DAY.CPP	7.4	Calculates the day of the week corresponding to a given date.
SEQUENCE.CPP	7.5	Recursive and non-recursive calculations of the terms of a sequence.
SEQ_ERR.CPP	7.5	Shows errors you shouldn't make when you write recursive functions.
SORT.CPP	8.1	Sorting program called by MAINSORT.CPP.
MAINSORT.CPP	8.1	This is the main program and calls SORT.CPP.
DEGRE2.CPP	8.2	Solves a second-degree linear equation.
DEGRE2.H	8.2	Header file for DEGRE2.PRJ
ROOT.CPP	8.2	File use as part of DEGRE2.PRJ.
ERR.CPP	8.2	File use as part of DEGRE2.PRJ.
ERRMSG.CPP	8.2	File use as part of DEGRE2.PRJ.
RAND.CPP	8.3	Generates random numbers.
RANDOM.CPP	8.3	Generates random numbers.
INTEREST.CPP	8.3	Calculates the interest (Length of time of a savings).
FUEL.CPP	8.4	Calculates fuel consumption.
CONSUME.CPP	8.4	Sets up the statistics for FUEL.CPP.
CHARCNT.CPP	9.1	Looks for a character in a file.
TELDISK.CPP	9.1	Create a small telephone directory.
SCALE.CPP	9.3	Calculates the frequency of the notes of a musical scale.
GAUSS.CPP	9.3	Draws a Gauss curve.
POEM.CPP	9.4	Writes a poem.
SORTSTRI.CPP	9.4	Bubble sort applied to strings of characters.
ENCODE.CPP	9.5	Lets you encrypt a file.
CLASSPOS.CPP	10.1	Program defining the poscreen class.

CLASCHAR.CPP	10.2	C++ program defining the poscreen and poschar classes.
CLPERERR.CPP	10.2	Correction of the preceding program.
CLASSPER.CPP	10.2	Correction of the preceding program.
FRACTION.CPP	10.3	Example of data abstraction.
EXDEBUG.CPP	11.1	Example of how to use the integrated debugger.

Some of these programs are in an executable form in the PROGRAMS directory. Files with the extension .PRJ are data files that are used to compile programs composed of several modules.

The project files for Turbo C++ include an underline (sometimes followed by a "P") in their name. .DSK files are the backup of the Turbo C++ office.

II.   Programs giving possible solutions for the exercises (Directory ANSWERS)

File	Section	Use
LETTER.CPP	3.2	Creates three letters.
AREA.CPP	3.3	Calculates the area of a circle.
OCTAL.CPP	3.3	Converts a decimal number into an octal number.
LOWUPPER.CPP	4.1	Recognizes a lower or uppercase letter.
COMPAR3.CPP	4.1	Compares 3 numbers.
SQUARES.CPP	4.2	List of the squares less than 500.
MULTIPLI.CPP	4.2	Displays a multiplication table.
CURRENCY.CPP	4.3	Converts currency into dollars.
TABOR.CPP	4.4	True-false table for the OR operator.
BUBBLES.CPP	6.1	Sort by adjacent permutations (Bubble Sort).
FINDCHAR.CPP	6.3	Looks for a character in a word.
FUNCSTRU.CPP	6.4	Calculates the coordinates of a straight line and a parabola.
EXPO2.CPP	7.1	Calculates the whole powers of a number x.
FALL.CPP	7.1	Determines the height of a fall.
CODE1.CPP	7.2	Encodes and decodes a word.
FINDLET.CPP	7.3	Looks for a character in a word.
NUMWORD.CPP	7.4	Converts a number into a real word.
CLASS.H	8.2	Header file for CLASS.CPP and AVERAGE.CPP.
CLASS.CPP	8.2	Calculates the average of 6 grades.
AVERAGE.CPP	8.2	Average function.
LENGVECT.CPP	8.3	Determines the length of a vector.

REACT.CPP	8.3	Measures reaction time.
GENHELLO.CPP	9.1	Generates the source code for HELLO.CPP
ASCII.CPP	9.2	Displays a list of ASCII characters.
INVEST.CPP	9.3	Calculates the interest.
FINDWORD.CPP	9.4	Looks for a word in a file.
TEXTDISK.CPP	9.4	Records a text on disk(ette).

The PROGRAM directory contains executable versions of these programs.

III.   Utility Programs (directory UTIL)

GENMAKE.CPP   Helps to generate a MAKE file. This type of program is not generally useful due to the power included with Borland's IDE. We recommend using the Project menu for establishing links. This method is much easier to define and to debug. This file is included for users of C++ from other publishers who may have need of such utilities.

Note: If you may need to modify and recompile this program for use with your version of C++.

```
/*************************************************************
**    GENMAKE.CPP                                         **
**            Copyright (c) 1990 Micro Application        **
**            Copyright (c) 1992 Abacus Software, Inc.    **
*************************************************************/

#include <stdio.h>                        /* Include headers */
#include <stdlib.h>

void main()
{
  char file[50][20], *ptr, fexe[50];
  int nmax = 0, n;
  FILE *fp;
  printf("\n\nMAKEFILE Generator\n(c) 1990 Micro
Application\n(c) Abacus Software, Inc.\n\n");
  printf("Name for .EXE file : ");
                /* Prompt for name of the executable file */
  scanf(" %s", fexe);
  ptr = fexe;   /* Remove .EXE extension (if necessary) */
  while (*ptr != '.' && *ptr != '\0') ptr++;
  if (*ptr == '.') *ptr = '\0';
  printf("\n\n\nNames of source code (.CPP) files to link
(End by entering #) :\n\n");
  do                           /* Get the .CPP file names */
  {
    printf("File #%d : ", nmax+1);                /* Loop */
    scanf(" %s", file[nmax]);
```

```
      ptr = file[nmax];  /* Remove extensions (if needed) */
      while (*ptr != '.' && *ptr != '\0') ptr++;
      if (*ptr == '.') *ptr = '\0';
   }
   while (file[nmax++][0] != '#');
                              /* Exit loop if '#' is entered */
   --nmax;
   fp = fopen("MAKEFILE","w");
                                  /* Open MAKEFILE for writing */
   fprintf(fp,"#  Make file for %s.exe\n\n", fexe);
/**********************************************************/
/*            Call the Compiler                          */
   fprintf(fp,".c.obj:\n\tcl -AS -c $*.c\n\n");
/*                      cl -AS -c $*.c                   */
/**********************************************************/
   for (n = 0; n < nmax; ++n)
      fprintf(fp,"%s.obj : %s.c\n\n", file[n], file[n]);
   fprintf(fp,"\n%s.exe :\\\n", fexe);
   if (nmax > 0) fprintf(fp," %s.obj", file[0]);
   for (n = 1; n < nmax; ++n)
      fprintf(fp,"\\\n %s.obj", file[n]);
   fprintf(fp,"\n");
   fprintf(fp,"\tdel %s.LNK\n", fexe);
                                      /* Delete old .LNK files */
   for (n = 0; n < nmax; ++n)   /* Create a new .LNK file */
   {
      fprintf(fp,"\techo %s.obj", file[n]);
      if (n+1 < nmax) fprintf(fp,"+");
      fprintf(fp," >> %s.LNK\n", fexe);
   }
   fprintf(fp,"\techo %s.exe >> %s.LNK\n", fexe, fexe);
   fprintf(fp,"\techo NUL >> %s.LNK\n", fexe);
/**********************************************************/
/*                 Call the Linker                       */
   fprintf(fp,"\tlink @%s.LNK /NOI;\n", fexe);
/*              link @%s.LNK /NOI                         */
/**********************************************************/
   fclose(fp);                              /* Close MAKEFILE */
}
```

HEADER.MAK
This file creates a macro for the Interactive Development Environment (the Turbo C++ Editor) which places a header at the beginning of a text file which has been loaded.

The Turbo Editor Macro Language is a powerful utility that can be used to change the Turbo C++ editor. In order to create a new macro, you must first create a macro script, similar to the one below for creating a header, and then compile it using the Turbo Editor Macro Compiler (TEMC).

Although adding macros to the IDE provides a means of customizing your programming environment, you won't find much information about writing Turbo C++ editor macros in the printed documentation. For information about macros, open the DOC directory, located at the root of your Turbo C directory and print the UTIL.DOC file.

This file contains information about using TEMC and other utility programs supplied with Turbo C++.

```
/**********************************************************
**      HEADER.MAK                                      **
**              Copyright (c) 1992 Abacus Software, Inc. **
**                                                      **
**      This file inserts a standard Header into any file.**
**      Compile this macro by copying this file into the **
**      same directory as TC.EXE                        **
**      (for Turbo C++) or BC.EXE (Borland C++). From the**
**      DOS command line, enter:                        **
**              TEMC HEADER.MAK TCCONFIG.TC             **
**      This macro may be executed from the IDE by       **
**      pressing ALT-H.                                  **
**********************************************************/

macro MakeHeader
        HomeCursor;              /* Move cursor to start of file */
        SetInsertMODE;
                                 /* Make sure Insert Mode is on */
        InsertText("/*********************************\n");
        InsertText("**    PROGRAM.CPP    **\n");
        InsertText("**          Written by <Your Name>  **\n");
        InsertText("*********************************/\n");
        InsertText("\n");
end;

ALT-H           :MakeHeader;
```

HEADER.CPP   This program places a standard header in a text file. The header must have been created and saved in a file named HEADER.TXT. IF HEADER.TXT includes the characters "#########", the name of the file is inserted into the header.

```
/**********************************************************
**      HEADER.CPP                                      **
**              Copyright (c) 1990 Micro Application     **
**              Copyright (c) 1992 Abacus Software, Inc. **
**********************************************************/

// This program places a standard header in a text file.
// The header must have been created and saved in a file
named HEADER.TXT
```

```
// IF HEADER.TXT includes the characters "#########" the
name of the
// file is inserted into the header.

//                   SYNTAX: HEADER <filename>

#include <stdio.h>              /* Include necessary headers */
#include <stdlib.h>

// Link latest version of READ.CPP   */

char *read(char *);                          /* Declaration */
void error(char *message)      /* In case of an error.... */
{
  printf("ERROR: %s\n", message);        /* Error message */
  exit(0);
}
void main(int argc, char *argv[])
                  /* Get parameters from DOS command line */
{
  FILE *file;                          /* Define variables */
  char *text0, *text1, *ptr0, *ptr1, *ptr;
  int len, n = 1;
                                      /* Check the parameters */
  if (argc != 2) error("Correct Syntax: HEADER
<filename>");
  ptr0 = text0 = read("HEADER.TXT");
  if (text0 == 0) error("HEADER.TXT not found");
  ptr1 = text1 = read(argv[1]);
  if (text1 == 0) error("Cannot read file");
  file = fopen(argv[1],"wt");         /* Open for writing */
  if (file == 0) error("Cannot open file for writing");
  while (*ptr0 != '#' && *ptr0 != '\0') ++ptr0;
                                          /* Look for '#' */
  for (ptr = text0; ptr < ptr0; ++ptr) fputc(*ptr, file);
  if (*ptr0 == '#')       /* Enter the name of the file */
  {
    while (*++ptr0 == '#') ++n;
    fprintf(file, "%-*s", n, argv[1]);
  }
  while (*ptr0 != '\0') fputc(*ptr0++, file);
                                          /* Write the rest */
  while (*ptr1 != '\0') fputc(*ptr1++, file);
                                          /* of the file */
  free(text0);                          /* Free memory */
  free(text1);
  fclose(file);                          /* Close the file */
}
```

ARGS.CPP   Is a model program for taking arguments from the command line. It is designed with the idea that you will take and convert it according to your needs.

```
/**********************************************************
**      ARGS.CPP                                         **
**             Copyright (c) 1990 Micro Application      **
**             Copyright (c) 1992 Abacus Software, Inc.  **
**                                                       **
** This program provides a template for taking           **
** arguments from the DOS command line and passing them  **
** to a C++ program. It is designed to be modified and   **
** used with your programs. Correct arguments for argc   **
** must be inserted below for program to compile.        **
**********************************************************/

#include <stdio.h>                     /* Include header files */
#include <stdlib.h>

void error(char *message)              /* In case of an error */
{
  printf("Error: %s\n", message);
                                  /* Display Error message */
  exit(0);
}

void main(int argc, char *argv[])
        /* Get the arguments from the DOS Command line. */
{                               * Check for correct syntax */
  if (argc != ...)              /* Replace ... in this line and
                                the following statement with the
                                correct syntax for your
                                application. */
    error("SYNTAX ERROR: Correct Syntax:.... ");
}
```

READTEXT.CPP   Loads a text file into a string of characters. Module ready for you to take and develop.

```
/**********************************************************
**      READTEXT.CPP                                     **
**             Copyright (c) 1990 Micro Application      **
**             Copyright (c) 1992 Abacus Software, Inc.  **
**********************************************************/

//   This program provides a function, readtext(), which
//   allows reading text into memory. This function can be
//   incorporated into any program by inserting its name
//   into the list of files of a Project as discussed  in
//   Chapter 8 of "Turbo C++ Step by Step".  Before this
//   module can be called, it must be declared by using the
//
//   char *readtext(char *);   Declaration for read();
//
//   This function returns a pointer to the newly allocated
```

```
//  block. In case of an error, a null (zero) is returned.

#include <stdio.h>
#include <io.h>
#include <alloc.h>   /* For QuickC or MSC use <malloc.h> */
#include <stdlib.h>

char *readtext(char *file)          /* Read the text file */
{
  FILE *fp;                          /* Define variables */
  int finish;
  char *text;
  fp = fopen(file, "rt");                    /* Open the file */
  if (fp == 0) return(0);
  finish = filelength(fileno(fp));
                                  /* Convert to a string */
  text = malloc(finish+1);
                                      /* Reserve memory */
  if (text == 0) return(0);
  finish = fread(text, 1, finish, fp);
  text[finish] = '\0';
  fclose(fp);                              /* Close the file */
  return(text);         /* Return the pointer to the text */
}
```

WRITTEXT.CPP   Records a string of characters on the hard
                drive or diskette. Module designed for you to
                develop.

```
/********************************************************
**      WRITTEXT.CPP                                   **
**            Copyright (c) 1990 Micro Application     **
**            Copyright (c) 1992 Abacus Software, Inc. **
********************************************************/

/* The writtext() function allows recording any string  of
characters on a hard drive or diskette. This function can
be included with any program  by including it as part of
the file list in a project. Before this function can be
called from other modules, it must be declared:

                char *writtext(char *);

  The function returns a Boolean value indicating whether
the text has been saved correctly. The allocated memory
block is also released.

*/

#include <stdio.h>
#include <io.h>
#include <alloc.h>   /* For Quick-C or MSC use <malloc.h>
*/
#include <stdlib.h>

int writtext(char *file, char *text)
                            /* Save 'text into a file */
```

```
                {
                  FILE *fp;                           /* Define variables */
                  char *ptr = text;
                  fp = fopen(file, "wt");              /* Open the file */
                  if (fp == 0) return(0);
                  while (*ptr != '\0') putchar(*ptr++);
                                                       /* Write the file */
                  free(text);
                  fclose(fp);                          /* Close the file */
                  return(1);
                }
```

ANSI.H   This is a header file containing screen
                   command macros. It is designed to be included
                   in your programs by using #include.

```
    /**********************************************************
    **    ANSI.H                                            **
    **            Copyright (c) 1990 Micro Application      **
    **            Copyright (c) 1992 Abacus Software, Inc.  **
    **********************************************************
    ** This header contains macros for managing the screen **
    ** display.                                             **
    **                                                      **
    ** In order for these functions to be accessible, you   **
    ** must install the ANSI.SYS device drive by adding the **
    ** following line to your CONFIG.SYS file:              **
    **                                                      **
    **                 DEVICE=ANSI.SYS                      **
    **********************************************************/

    #define C_GOTO(x,y) printf("\x1B[%d;%dH", y, x)
                                            /* x from 1 to 80 */
                                            /* y from 1 to 25 */
    #define C_TOP            printf("\x1B[1A")
                                 /* Move the cursor up one line */
    #define C_BOTTOM         printf("\x1B[1B")
                               /* Move the cursor down one line */
    #define C_RIGHT          printf("\x1B[1C")
                                        /* Move cursor right */
    #define C_LEFT           printf("\x1B[1d")
                                         /* Move cursor left */
    #define C_SAVE           printf("\x1B[s")
                                      /* Save cursor position */
    #define C_RESTORE        printf("\x1B[u")
                                   /* Restore cursor position */
    #define CLS              printf("\x1B[2J")
                                         /* Clear the screen */
    #define DLN              printf("\x1B[K")
                                           /* Delete a line */
                                   /* Modes for text display */
    #define NORM      printf("\x1B[0m")    /* Normal Mode */
    #define HILITE    printf("\x1B[1m")  /* Highlight Mode */
    #define BLNK      printf("\x1B[5m")      /* Blink Mode */
    #define INVERSE   printf("\x1B[7m")  /* Inverse Video */
    #define UNDERLINE printf("\x1B[4m")     /* Underline */
                                   /* (for monochrome systems) */
```

ANSI.CPP   This is a sample program demonstrating how
                      to use the ANSI.H header file.

```
/***********************************************************
**    ANSI.CPP                                          **
**            Copyright (c) 1990 Micro Application      **
**            Copyright (c) 1992 Abacus Software, Inc.  **
***********************************************************/

#include <stdio.h>                        /* Include Headers */
#include <conio.h>
/* Include special header for ANSI definitions */
#include "ansi.h"

void main()
{
  CLS;                                   /* Clear the screen */
  NORM;                                  /* Set Normal Mode */
  printf("This text is in Normal Mode.\n");
  HILITE;
  printf("This text is displayed in Highlight Mode.\n");
  NORM;
  BLNK;
  printf("This text is displayed in Blink Mode.\n");
  NORM;
  INVERSE;
  printf("Finally, this line is displayed in Inverse
Mode.\n");
  NORM;
}
```

Index

% (modulo) operators 54
%c 38
%d 37, 38
%ld 78
%u 78
& operator 96, 110
(n>limit) 68
\n 23
(value!=0) 68
+ and * operators 207
++ increment operator
.... 101, 191
++number 80
80186 252
80286 252
80386 252
8086 252
8088 252

A

abnormal program behavior
.... 213
abs() 175
<Access> 166
Add Watch 214
ADDITION.CPP 61
Address 252
Address area 252
Address bus 252
addressing operator 92
All Routines 219
allocate 183
allocated memory 184
Alternate 8
Alternate command set 16
anc_mi 158
AND logical operator 69
appointments 108
Arena header 252
argc 126, 128
argc variables 127
arguments 115
argv 128
argv table 128
argv variables 127
ARITH.CPP 81
Arithmetic expressions
.... 75-83
arithmetic operations 42

Arrays 87, 106
    Array index 88
    String arrays 88
ASCII 252
Assembly language 253
assignments 42
associate class 201
Asynchronous data transfer
.... 253
AT 253
Attribute 253
auto 158
auto classes 158
auto variable 156, 158
AUTOEXEC.BAT 6, 253

B

backup copies 3
<Base> 175
base class 201
Base-list 191
Basic accessing 165
Basic Input/Output System
(BIOS) 254
batch file 253
Baud 253
BCD 253
Binary Coded Decimal
(BCD) 253
binary file 166
binary mode 166
Binary system 254, 271
BIOS 254
BIOS interrupts 254
BIOS Parameter Block ... 255
BIOS version 254
blank characters 173
<Block> 58
Block driver 254
block structure 51
BOOLEAN 68
BOOLEAN type 108
Boolean variables 69
Boot sector 254
Booting 254
Borland IDE 8
Borland's Turbo C++ 3
Both 220
BPB 255

break statement...............65
breakpoints....................213
Bubble Sort.........92, 122, 181
BUBBLES.CPP........122, 182
buttons 14
by reference.............121, 178
by value.........................121

C

CALL..............................255
Call stack 215
Carry flag.....................255
case...............................64
cday()............................133
changename()..................201
*char *gets(char *<String>)
................................173
char type 38
char type variable 40, 43
char variables.............35, 47
CHARA.CPP...................46
<Character>....................179
character array..............88
Character driver............255
character pointer............122
CHARCNT.CPP..............167
Char_Pos........................196
check boxes.....................14
CHESS.CPP 108
Child program................255
CLASCHAR.CPP 195
Class..............................191
        Char_Pos class........197
        Data abstraction 205
        Screen_pos class 192
class type.......................191
class-key.......................191
class-name 191
CLASSPOS.CPP......191, 194
CLI 255
Clock driver...................255
Clock generator 255
Close Project menu item...142
closed blocks....................51
CLPERERR.CPP 199
Cluster...........................256
cnumber variable............119
code() function...............186
CODE.CPP.............127, 185
coding argument.............122
coding method...............128
col...............................192
column().........................192
COM files 256
combine() function...........181
Command line 256

Command parameters.....256
Command processor 256
Command Set window 8
COMMAND.COM 256
Comments 21
Common User Interface
(CUI)............................16
Communication 119
companion diskette 8
Comparison operators..53-57
Compile..........................144
compiler 24
compiling directives.......159
compound operators.....46, 79
computer program............21
CON..............................256
conditional jumps 51
CONFIG.SYS..............6, 256
<conio.h>......................153
conio.h............................152
constant 38
constant expression...........43
construct types................106
constructor.............. 193, 197
CONSUM.CPP...............156
consume()........................157
consume() functio............158
CONSUME.CPP.............157
contents of a variable 42
control character.............23
Control characters.....23, 256
conventional operators 89
conversion errors..............76
convert().........................132
convert() function 131
Cooked mode..................257
cos().............................175
Counts...........................220
CP/M-80........................257
.CPP 22
.CPP extension..................22
.CPP file........................141
CPU.............................257
crash 88
CRC.............................257
CRT 257
CTABLE 110
cur variable 110
Current routine...............219

D

DASD..............................257
data abstraction...... 191, 205
Data bus 257
data fields......................98
data output.....................37

DAY.CPP......................132
Debug..................213, 214
Debug menu 214
debugging session............213
decimal point.................45
decimal system..............271
declaration 33, 145-151
declaring variables 33
decrement.....................44
decrementation...............79
default active button 14
default active field.........14
default configuration........9
default statement............66
DEGRE2.CPP.................147
DEGRE2.H....................147
DEGRE2.PRJ 147, 149
Delete watch 215
Derived classes 191
<Destination> string......178
Device driver.................257
Directories menu item........9
Disk controller 258
Disk formats 258
Disk status....................258
Disks 257
displace()......................192
displace() function..........193
display().......................201
Display 219
Display page 258
display() function....119, 201
displaying on the screen... 36
displaying text and variable
parameters......................37
DIVI13.CPP 54
DMA.............................258
DMA controller 258
do-while..................58, 61
do-while loop .. 101, 105, 128
do-while statement..........59
Done 144
DOS..............................258
DOS command line 24
double assignment............82
double bordered button.....14
double type 75, 77
double value....................78
double variables...............78
DTA..............................259
duration of variables......155
dweek...........................133
d_km variables..............158

E

ECC.............................259
edit commands 16
Edit menu.......................17
Editor.......................16, 20
    Block commands.........17
    Cursor movements..16, 17
    Edit window 16
    Replace commands 18
    Search commands ..17-18
EGA.............................259
else statement.............54, 70
EMM.............................259
EMS.............................259
Emulation option..............45
ENCODE.CPP...............185
End character.................259
Environment block..........259
Environment menu item......8
EOF (End of File) 166
EOI.............................259
EQUALIN.CPP 55
ERR.CPP............. 147, 149
ERRMSG.CPP 147, 149
Error messages..........26-29
    Types..........................26
error()..................... 147, 148
Errors...........................26
Evaluate/modify...........214
Every line in module.......219
EXCHANGE.CPP...........109
EXDEBUG.CPP.............215
EXE files......................260
EXEC...........................260
executable instruction.......89
executable program 24
execution errors 213
Execution Profile window
....219
exit() function 128
exit(status-'0')...............128
exp().............................175
<Exponent> 175
exponential mode.............45
<Expression>........42, 51, 58
<Expression> parameter ..68
EXPROFIL.CPP.............217
EXPROFIL.EXE..............217
Extended key code..........260
extern 146, 155, 156, 158
External.................. 146, 156
External function
declarations...................146
external library programs
....24

F

FAR instructions 260
FAT 260
fatal errors.................... 26
FCB 260
feof() function..............168
FFDC 98
FFDE 98
fflush(stdin) 39
fgetc()........................170
field array...................... 99
file access mode.............168
File Allocation Table (FAT)
...................................263
File menu 14
file selector dialog box..... 14
file structure...................34
file type........................ 14
file type filter................. 14
FILE type pointer 165
filelength().....................186
fileno()........................186
Filter..........................260
Find menu item............... 17
first C program.............. 20
Fixed disk.....................260
Flag register...................261
float 75
float type................. 33, 45
Float type constants........ 45
fopen() function 165
for................................ 58
for loop 60, 96, 101
for statement............. 59, 60
Formal variables............115
format specification .. 37, 40,
172
<Format string>............. 37
format string 38
<ForPtr>........................184
fp file pointer................170
fraction class...........207, 208
fread().............................170
free function 184
free()..........................186
friend function..............208
FUEL.CPP....................156
FUEL.EXE....................156
FUEL.PRJ....................156
function..................115, 261
function declaration........145
function keys 13
Function libraries
        File access.................
        File pointer.............165

Keyboard management
..........................171-174
Screen management
..........................171-174
Functions...........21, 115-120,
..............................126-129
    column()...................192
    fflush(stdin)..............39
    fopen().....................165
    fprintf()..............171-174
    free..........................184
    line()........................192
    main()...........21, 126-129
    Mathematical functions
   174-177
    Memory management
   183-187
    place()......................193
    printf()...........37, 55, 115
    scanf()......38, 66, 93, 115,
   171-174
    sprintf()....................179
    sscanf()....................179
fwrite() 170

G

Garbage collection...........261
Gauss distribution function
...................................177
Gauss function 176
GAUSS.CPP....................176
GDT............................261
General registers............261
global................146, 156, 158
global definition............129
Global variables............129,
........................130-134, 156
Go to Cursor............. 213, 215

H

Handle...........................261
Hard disk.......................261
Hard disk format............261
Hardware interrupt 262
Header files 145, 152
        Standard library header
        files..................151-155
HELLO.CPP....................22
HEX.CPP.......................130
hexadecimal conversion
table.............................132
Hexadecimal system.....262,
..............................271, 272
hex_number 131, 132

High level languages 92

I

IDE 13
if statement 51, 56, 161
if-else statement 66
IN 262
INCLUDE 152
increment 44
<Increment-exp> expressions
.... 60
increment operator 46
incrementation 79
index of the statistic()
function 158
index variable 60
<Init-exp> expression 60
initialized 43
initializing structures 130
inline functions 198
INOUT.C 46
INOUT.CPP 39
Input 36
input-output instruction .. 165
input/output statement ... 173
insert mode 17
INSTALL.EXE 3
Installation 3, 10
    Borland Turbo C++ 3, 8
    Companion diskette ... 8,
    10
installation process 9
Instructions
    do-while 58-64
    for 58-64
    printf() 21
    switch 64-68
    while 58-64
int 75
*int getch() 173
*int getche() 173
*int kbhit() 173
*int putch(int <Character>)
.... 173
*int puts(char *<String>)
.... 173
int type 33
int type variables 38
int variable 33, 40
Integrated debugger . 213-216
Integrated Development
Environment 13
    Cursor keys 13
    Dialog boxes 13
    Help function 14
    Hotkeys 13

Intel Corporation 252
INTEREST 153
INTEREST.CPP 154
INTERET1.CPP 154
interface 165
internal characteristics of
the hardware 165
Internal commands 262
internal if statement 56
Interrupt 262
Interrupt controller 262
Interrupt routine 262
Interrupt vector table 262
iptr pointer 96
IRET 263
isolated statement 53

K

kbhit() function 152
keyboard combinations 13
Keyboard status 263
Keywords 225-226
Kilobyte 263

L

language translator 24
libraries 151
line() 192
linefeed character 23
Lines in routine 219
link editor 24
linker 24, 141
<List of symbols> 160
<List of the parameters>
.... 115
ln 192
load() 170
local menu 218
local range 129
log() function 154
logical expression 53
Logical operators 68-71
Logical variables 68-71
long 75
long type 78
long variable 78
Longest 220
<LongMax> characters ... 178

M

macro.................................160
main function..................21
main program...................21
main().................................21
main() function........115, 126
MAINSORT.CPP....143, 144,
....145
MAKE.............. 142, 144, 149
malloc()..........................184
Manipulations of strings ..89
Math coprocessor............263
<math.h>.................154, 174
math.h..............................151
Mathematical functions
.... 174-177
mathematical operators..75
Media descriptor byte.....263
Megabyte.......................263
member functions 192
Member-list 191
members..........................103
Memory............................33
Memory allocation 263
Memory management
functions.................. 183-187
Microprocessor...............263
minor errors.................... 26
mm....................................38
Model identification 264
module window 218
Modules 141-162
Modules with source 219
modulus operator............. 43
Month...............................133
move() function...............197
moving a block.................. 19
MS-DOS 264
multi-dimensional array . 90
multi-pass compilers 159
multiple inheritances.....197
Multiprocessing..............264

N

n index structure..............110
<Name>............................160
<Name of the type>.......107
<Nbyte>..........................184
NEAR instructions..........264
nested comments 22
neutral stock mark..........105
Newton's method 149
Nibble 264
Nmax..............................158

NMI 264
non-recursive equivalent of
the function...................134
nonstandard types..........122
null character 88
null pointer.....................166
number.................61, 80, 121
Number crunching..........174
Number systems 271-273
    Binary system..........271
    Decimal system........271
    Hex and binary 272
    Hexadecimal system
....272
number variable..............61
number++..........................80

O

.OBJ (= Object code).........24
Object Oriented
Programming........... 191, 198
offset address..................252
on-line Help 151
on-line Help files............18
Open menu 14
Open Project File..........144
Open Project menu item...142
OPERAT.CPP...................65
operation variable..........66
Operators 68-71, 227
Options menu 8, 9
Option I Preferences 16
orig_number...................118
OUT 264
output...............................36
Output Directory.............. 9
<Output string>.............179
overlapped brackets.......133
overlapping loops 70
Overlay...........................264
Overwrite mode..............17

P

parabola...........................89
PARABOLA.CPP......89, 100
parabolic values 89
Paragraph.......................264
Parameters 120-126
parent class.....................191
Parent program 265
Parentheses 117
Parity............................265
par[21]...........................89
par[] array......................89

passing parameters.........120
PC....................................265
Per Call........................220
Peripheral interface.......265
person............................201
person class....................201
pfich file pointer............168
physical modes of the
recording process............165
pi.....................................45
place() function..............193
place()...........................192
POEM.CPP.....................179
point of origin.................88
<Pointer>.......................184
pointer- and array-based
operations.......................95
POINTER.CPP................95
Pointers...87, 92-102, 106, 111
        Pointer arithmetic
       97-102
        Pointer variables.......92
Ports...............................265
pos variable....................193
position...........................119
pow() function.................176
POWER2.CPP...................62
Preferences........................8
Preprocessor directives
..............................159-162
prep_phrase....................181
primary edit commands...18
Primary keywords...225-226
Printer status byte..........265
printf()..21-22, 36-38, 40, 61,
..................115, 153, 179, 186
printf() function..............109
PRN...............................265
Processing strings of
characters......................178
Program counter..............265
program portions.............51
project............................142
        SORT_P...................144
Project menu....................142
Protected mode................265
prototyping.....................145
PSP.................................266
PTRPAR.CPP....................100
*ptr variable....................121
public.............................193
putc()............................170
pv()...............................125

R

RAM...............................266
rand() function................181
RAND.CPP.......................152
random()........................137
randomize()....................137
rate of interest................154
Raw mode.......................266
README file.......................7
real letter........................40
Real mode.......................266
realloc().........................184
recursive function............134
recurs_seq......................135
Register..........................266
Replace menu item..........18
Reset..............................266
Resident.........................266
result..............................80
return values.......21, 120-126
return() statement..........118
ROM...............................266
ROM BASIC.....................266
ROM-BIOS.....................254
root().................147, 148
ROOT.CPP.............147, 148
ROUND.CPP.................117
round_decimal() function
....................................119
round_whole_number()
function...................118, 119
Routines in module.........219
RS-232...........................267
RTC................................267
Run................................213
run bar...........................213
Run menu.................213, 217
Run option......................217

S

S......................................45
Save As menu item..........15
Save menu item................15
save()............................170
SCALE.CPP.....................176
Scan code.......................267
scanf()..........38, 40, 115, 148
scanf() function........125, 173
screen page......................258
Screen_pos()...................192
Search menu.....................17
Sector.............................267
segment address.............252
Segment descriptor.........267

Segment register.............267
select a block...................17
select menu options..........13
selection area...................14
separator.........................22
SEQUENCE.CPP.............134
serial transfer.................253
SET INCLUDE................152
shell..............................256
short...............................75
sin().............................175
single pass compiler........159
Software interrupts.........267
sort() function... 122, 145, 182
SORT.CPP.................143, 144
source code.......................24
source code files................22
Source Directories..............9
<Source> string..............178
space variable...............101
space[]............................89
special messages..............26
specific input parameter..51
SPHERE.CPP....................44
sprintf().........................179
sscanf().........................179
Standard input device....267
Standard library header
files...........................151-155
Standard output device...267
standard types................106
stat array......................158
<Statement>....................51
Statements.......................51
        break.........................65
        if............................51-57
        if...else......................52
static.................88, 156, 158
static class......................156
static tables...................156
Static variables......156, 158
statistic() function..........158
statistics()....................157
<stdio.h>.................153, 165
stdio.h...........................152
<STDIO.H> file.............151
stdlib.h..........................151
Step Over......................213
STI................................268
STOCK.CPP....................103
stopping points...............213
storage classes................155
store data......................165
strcat()..........................181
strcpy() function......181, 182
STRING..........................107
string array......................88
<string.h>.....................178

string.h..........................151
<String of characters>...160
string tables...................181
Strings
        Manipulating.....178-183
struct article type...........105
struct type......................191
Structures....87, 102-106, 111,
....191
sub-programs...................21
subject...........................181
subject string.................181
sum variable.....................61
SUM.CPP..........................60
switch block.....................66
switch statement..............64
symbolic stack...............215
syntactical errors...........213
syntax errors.................213
system failure..................88

T

TABLE................... 109, 123
table()............................132
table() function..............131
Tables.......................87-111
tan()..............................175
TANDF.CPP.....................69
TCPP................................9
TEL.DAT data file.........170
TELDISK.CPP................169
test the search command...19
<Text>............................21
text files........................166
text mode.......................166
This line........................219
Time..............................220
time()............................154
Time-out........................268
Timer.............................268
Toggle Breakpoint..........214
TPA......................252, 268
Trace Into..............213, 215
transfer various parameters
....36
translation.......................24
Turbo C IDE.....................9
Turbo C++......................191
Turbo C++ Help system...145
Turbo C++ programming
environment...................198
Turbo Profiler..........216-221
<Type>...........................115
<Type A/S>....................130
type conversion..............118
typedef................... 107, 109

Types.....................119
    Void 117
TYPES.CPP 77

U

UART 268
undefined symbol............215
unions.....................191
unsigned.....................75
unsigned int type 78
unsigned int type variable
........................78
upwardly compatible 252
Utilities 213-221
    Integrated debugger
   213-216
    Turbo Profiler....216-221

V

V 45
val.............................123
valid ranges....................75
<Value>........................175
<Var> 42, 80
variable...................42, 119
variable definition..........34
variable parameter........37
Variable types.............75-83
    char........................75
    double.....................75
    float 75
    int.........................75
    long.......................75
    short......................75
    unsigned char 75
    unsigned int...............75
    unsigned long.............75
    unsigned short 75
Variables...............33-48, 75
    Arithmetic operations
   42-48
    Assignments 42-48
    charchar..................33
    External...................156
    float 33
    Global variables
   129-134
    Input/output..........36-42
    Local variables 156
    Operations............42-48
    Predefined types 33
    Static......................156
    Storage classes ..155-159
vect type.....................125

VECTOR.CPP 124, 130
verb..........................181
video cards 258
Video controller.............268
video page....................258
Video RAM....................268
virtual..........................204
Virtual memory 268
void............................117
Void functions..............117
void() type 119
volume.....................45, 268

W-Z

Warnings........................26
Watch window 214
Watches.......................214
while 58
while block......................61
while loop..60, 119, 152, 168,
....215
while statement..............59
whole type 70
yy..................................38

Abacus

pc catalog

Order Toll Free 1-800-451-4319

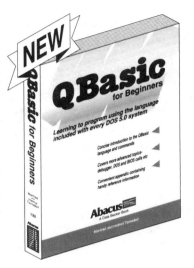

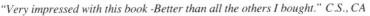

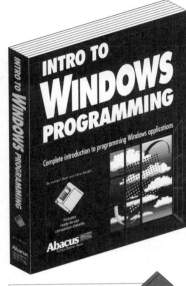

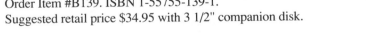

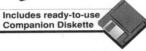

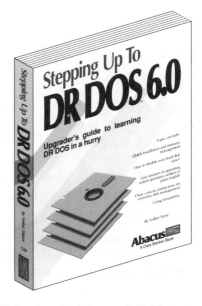

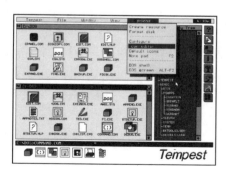